most loved recipe collection most loved recipe collection most loved recipe collection

# most loved

# Slow Cooker

# Creations

**Pictured on divider:**
Pot Roast, page 46

We gratefully acknowledge the following
suppliers for their generous support of our
Test and Photography Kitchens:

Broil King Barbecues
Corelle®
Hamilton Beach® Canada
Lagostina®
Proctor Silex® Canada
Tupperware®

Our special thanks to the following businesses
for providing props for photography:

Casa Bugatti
Cherison Enterprises Inc.
Chintz & Company
Creations By Design
Danesco Inc.
Emile Henry
Hamilton Beach® Canada
Le Gnome
Linens 'N Things
Mikasa Home Store
Out of the Fire Studio
Pier 1 Imports
Pfaltzgraff Canada
Pyrex®
Scona Clayworks
Stokes
The Basket House
The Bay
Totally Bamboo
Treasure Barrel
Winners Stores
Zenari's

Pictured from left: Slow Cooker Dolmades, page 34; Chicken And Dumpling Soup, page 30; Cajun Chicken, page 76; Hot Tea Wassail, page 8.

## table of contents

# the Company's Coming story

*"never share a recipe you wouldn't use yourself"*

Jean Paré (pronounced "jeen PAIR-ee") grew up understanding that the combination of family, friends and home cooking is the best recipe for a good life. From her mother, she learned to appreciate good cooking, while her father praised even her earliest attempts in the kitchen. When Jean left home, she took with her a love of cooking, many family recipes and an intriguing desire to read cookbooks as if they were novels!

When her four children had all reached school age, Jean volunteered to cater the 50th anniversary celebration of the Vermilion School of Agriculture, now Lakeland College, in Alberta, Canada. Working out of her home, Jean prepared a dinner for more than 1,000 people, launching a flourishing catering operation that continued for over 18 years. During that time, she had countless opportunities to test new ideas with immediate feedback—resulting in empty plates and contented customers! Whether preparing cocktail sandwiches for a house party or serving a hot meal for 1,500 people, Jean Paré earned a reputation for great food, courteous service and reasonable prices.

As requests for her recipes increased, Jean was often asked the question, "Why don't you write a cookbook?" Jean responded by teaming up with her son, Grant Lovig, in the fall of 1980 to form Company's Coming Publishing Limited. The publication of *150 Delicious Squares* on April 14, 1981 marked the debut of what would soon become one of the world's most popular cookbook series.

The company has grown since those early days when Jean worked from a spare bedroom in her home. Nowadays every Company's Coming recipe is *kitchen-tested* before it is approved for publication.

Company's Coming cookbooks are distributed in Canada, the United States, Australia and other world markets. Bestsellers many times over in English, Company's Coming cookbooks have also been published in French and Spanish.

Familiar and trusted in home kitchens around the world, Company's Coming cookbooks are offered in a variety of formats. Highly regarded as kitchen workbooks, the softcover Original Series, with its lay-flat plastic comb binding, is still a favourite among readers.

Jean Paré's approach to cooking has always called for *quick and easy recipes* using *everyday ingredients*. That view has served her well. The recipient of many awards, including the Queen Elizabeth Golden Jubilee Medal, Jean was appointed Member of the Order of Canada, her country's highest lifetime achievement honour.

Jean continues to share what she calls The Golden Rule of Cooking: *Never share a recipe you wouldn't use yourself.* It's an approach that has worked—*millions of times over!*

# foreword

For a while in the '70s and '80s, it seemed that almost every bride had to write a thank-you note for a slow cooker. Often she used it once or twice, and then relegated it to the back of a kitchen cupboard with her husband's college drinking mugs. In the 1990s, the slow cooker would show up again, but at flea markets or garage sales.

So why is there such a slow cooker revival in the new millennium? To begin with, manufacturers have updated the rather dowdy look of the original models, creating sleek, stainless steel versions that look fabulous on any counter.

More importantly, we're all beginning to realize that a fast food diet isn't doing us, or our families, much good. But how can we get a healthy, homemade meal on the table when our busy lives have us spending time everywhere but in our kitchens? A slow cooker can gently simmer away all day, and the only thing you have to do is get home in time to enjoy it. You control the fat, the salt and every other ingredient in your family's meal.

With *Most Loved Slow Cooker Creations*, a treasury of favourite recipes published over the years at Company's Coming, we show you how to serve up great-tasting entrées such as Coq Au Vin, Corned Beef Brisket and Barbecued Shredded Pork Sandwiches. Our Slow Cooker Dolmades are always a hit (and a great potluck dish), while our wonderful party beverages let you take part in the fun without having to fuss over drinks. And if all you want is a steaming bowl of something filling when you come in on a winter evening, check out our Tex-Mex Taco Soup or our hot-and-sour Chinese Mushroom Soup.

All you need to do is pop the ingredients into your slow cooker before you go out the door. If mornings are too hectic, do your slicing and dicing the night before (preferably while the rest of the family is doing the dishes!). Fill the slow cooker, pop the liner in the fridge and stick it into your slow cooker before you leave for the day. You can spend the day anticipating the delicious meal you'll enjoy when you get home that night!

*Jean Paré*

## nutrition information

Each recipe is analyzed using the most current version of the Canadian Nutrient File from Health Canada, which is based on the United States Department of Agriculture (USDA) Nutrient Database.

- If more than one ingredient is listed (such as "butter or hard margarine"), or if a range is given (1 – 2 tsp., 5 – 10 mL), only the first ingredient or first amount is analyzed.

- For meat, poultry and fish, the serving size per person is based on the recommended 4 oz. (113 g) uncooked weight (without bone), which is 2 – 3 oz. (57 – 85 g) cooked weight (without bone)—approximately the size of a deck of playing cards.

- Milk used is 1% M.F. (milk fat), unless otherwise stated.

- Cooking oil used is canola oil, unless otherwise stated.

- Ingredients indicating "sprinkle," "optional," or "for garnish" are not included in the nutrition information.

- The fat in recipes and combination foods can vary greatly depending on the sources and types of fats used in each specific ingredient. For these reasons, the amount of saturated, monounsaturated and polyunsaturated fats may not add up to the total fat content.

Vera C. Mazurak, Ph.D.
Nutritionist

*The spicy apple aroma of this hot toddy will fill your house with a festive scent. Garnish each mug with a fresh cinnamon stick for a little added flair. Cut out the brandy to make it kid-friendly.*

# Cranberry Apple Warmer

| | | |
|---|---|---|
| Apple juice | 4 cups | 1 L |
| Cranberry cocktail | 4 cups | 1 L |
| Water | 2 cups | 500 mL |
| Brown sugar, packed | 1/4 cup | 60 mL |
| Cinnamon sticks (4 inches, 10 cm, each) | 3 | 3 |
| Ground nutmeg | 1/4 tsp. | 1 mL |
| Brandy (optional) | 1/2 cup | 125 mL |

Combine first 6 ingredients in 3 1/2 to 4 quart (3.5 to 4 L) slow cooker. Cook, covered, on Low for 6 to 7 hours or on High for 3 to 3 1/2 hours. Discard cinnamon sticks. Makes about 10 cups (2.5 L).

Divide brandy into 8 mugs. Add cranberry mixture. Stir. Serves 8.

*1 serving: 153 Calories; 0.2 g Total Fat (trace Mono, 0.1 g Poly, trace Sat); 0 mg Cholesterol; 39 g Carbohydrate; 0 g Fibre; 0 g Protein; 10 mg Sodium*

Pictured at right.

*Life is short—eat dessert first! Dress up this rich and creamy treat with a dash of your favourite nut-flavoured liqueur.*

# Caramel Hot Chocolate

| | | |
|---|---|---|
| Water | 6 cups | 1.5 L |
| Skim milk powder | 2 cups | 500 mL |
| Can of sweetened condensed milk | 11 oz. | 300 mL |
| Cocoa, sifted if lumpy | 3/4 cup | 175 mL |
| Caramel flavouring syrup | 1/2 cup | 125 mL |
| Miniature multi-coloured marshmallows, for garnish | | |

Combine first 4 ingredients in 3 1/2 to 4 quart (3.5 to 4 L) slow cooker. Cook, covered, on Low for about 6 hours or on High for about 3 hours until boiling.

Add syrup. Stir until smooth.

Garnish individual servings with marshmallows. Makes about 8 cups (2 L).

*1 cup (250 mL): 301 Calories; 4.7 g Total Fat (0.4 g Mono, 0.2 g Poly, 2.9 g Sat); 19 mg Cholesterol; 53 g Carbohydrate; 2 g Fibre; 16 g Protein; 264 mg Sodium*

Pictured at right.

1. Cranberry Apple Warmer, page 6
2. Caramel Hot Chocolate, page 6
3. Hot Buttered Cranberry, page 10

*With the warming qualities of tea, mulled wine and apple cider, wassail (pronounced WAHS-uhl) is the ultimate winter warmer-upper. Brew up this bevvie whenever the mercury heads south.*

### about slow cooker sizes

Slow cookers come in a variety of sizes from the very wee, used to make dips and fondues, to the quite mammoth, used to feed larger numbers. Generally, the most popular sizes range from 3.5 to 5 quarts (3.5 to 5 L). When choosing a slow cooker, don't just opt for a larger size and assume it will work well with small quantities. In order to cook evenly and in the time stated in the recipe, a slow cooker must be filled at least half full—unless stated otherwise. So always use the size suggested in the recipe.

# Hot Tea Wassail

| | | |
|---|---|---|
| Boiling water | 6 cups | 1.5 L |
| Orange pekoe tea bags | 4 | 4 |
| Dry (or alcohol-free) red wine | 3 cups | 750 mL |
| Large lemon, cut into | 1 | 1 |
|    1/2 inch (12 mm) thick slices | | |
| Liquid honey | 1/2 cup | 125 mL |
| Cinnamon sticks (4 inches, 10 cm, each) | 2 | 2 |
| Small unpeeled cooking apples | 3 | 3 |
|    (such as McIntosh), cored | | |
| Whole allspice | 12 | 12 |
| Whole cloves | 12 | 12 |

Pour boiling water over tea bags in 3 1/2 to 4 quart (3.5 to 4 L) slow cooker. Let steep, covered, for 10 minutes. Squeeze and discard tea bags.

Add next 4 ingredients. Stir.

Pierce skin on apples several times with tip of paring knife. Push allspice and cloves into slits in apples. Add to wine mixture. Cook, covered, on Low for 2 hours. Strain and discard solids. Makes about 10 cups (2.5 L).

*1 cup (250 mL): 115 Calories; 0 g Total Fat (0 g Mono, 0 g Poly, 0 g Sat); 0 mg Cholesterol; 15 g Carbohydrate; 0 g Fibre; trace Protein; 3 mg Sodium*

Pictured at right.

*The relatively small amount of butter in this spiced cranberry drink adds a richness and body you don't traditionally find in mulled drinks. Excellent!*

**hot spiced cranberry**

You can lighten up a bit and omit the butter—it still makes a great sweet treat.

# Hot Buttered Cranberry

| | | |
|---|---|---|
| Pineapple juice | 4 cups | 1 L |
| Cans of jellied cranberry sauce (14 oz., 398 mL, each) | 2 | 2 |
| Water | 3 cups | 750 mL |
| Brown sugar, packed | 1/2 cup | 125 mL |
| Ground cinnamon | 1/2 tsp. | 2 mL |
| Ground cloves | 1/2 tsp. | 2 mL |
| Ground allspice | 1/4 tsp. | 1 mL |
| Ground nutmeg | 1/4 tsp. | 1 mL |
| Salt | 1/8 tsp. | 0.5 mL |
| Butter | 1/4 cup | 60 mL |
| Dark (navy) rum (optional) | 1 cup | 250 mL |

Combine first 9 ingredients in 3 1/2 to 4 quart (3.5 to 4 L) slow cooker. Cook, covered, on Low for 4 hours.

Add butter and rum. Stir until butter is melted. Makes about 12 cups (3 L).

*1 cup (250 mL): 212 Calories; 3.9 g Total Fat (1.0 g Mono, 0.2 g Poly, 2.4 g Sat); 10 mg Cholesterol; 46 g Carbohydrate; 1 g Fibre; trace Protein; 76 mg Sodium*

Pictured on page 7.

*Dress up your regular red wine in grand style by adding citrus juice and spices—the result will be a sweet departure from the everyday. Garnish with fresh orange slices.*

**cranberry mulled wine**

For a more tart treat, use the same amount of cranberry cocktail instead of orange juice.

# Mulled Wine

| | | |
|---|---|---|
| Dry (or alcohol-free) red wine | 8 cups | 2 L |
| Orange juice | 2 cups | 500 mL |
| Corn syrup | 2/3 cup | 150 mL |
| Medium unpeeled orange, sliced | 1 | 1 |
| Lemon juice | 1 tsp. | 5 mL |
| Cinnamon sticks (4 inches, 10 cm, each), broken up and crushed | 3 | 3 |
| Whole allspice | 1 tsp. | 5 mL |
| Whole cloves | 1 tsp. | 5 mL |

Combine first 5 ingredients in 3 1/2 to 4 quart (3.5 to 4 L) slow cooker.

*(continued on next page)*

Place next 3 ingredients on 10 inch (25 cm) square of double-layered cheesecloth. Draw up corners and tie with string. Submerge in liquid in slow cooker. Cook, covered, on Low for 3 hours. Remove and discard spice bag. Discard orange slices. Makes about 9 cups (2.25 L).

*1 cup (250 mL): 271 Calories; 0.2 g Total Fat (trace Mono, trace Poly, trace Sat); 0 mg Cholesterol; 30 g Carbohydrate; 0 g Fibre; 1 g Protein; 46 mg Sodium*

Pictured below.

Mulled Wine, page 10

*For those who think the spice is right, this hot-and-sour soup full of crunchy bamboo and water chestnuts is sure to heat things up—and the addition of chewy Chinese mushrooms makes this brothy best a filling meal.*

### variation

Have some leftovers in your fridge? Use the same amount of diced cooked beef, chicken, shrimp or tofu instead of pork.

# Chinese Mushroom Soup

| | | |
|---|---|---|
| Chinese dried mushrooms | 15 | 15 |
| Boiling water | 2 cups | 500 mL |
| Prepared chicken broth | 6 cups | 1.5 L |
| Can of shoestring-style bamboo shoots, drained | 8 oz. | 227 mL |
| Can of sliced water chestnuts, drained | 8 oz. | 227 mL |
| Rice vinegar | 1/3 cup | 75 mL |
| Soy sauce | 1/4 cup | 60 mL |
| Dried crushed chilies | 1 tsp. | 5 mL |
| Diced cooked pork | 1 cup | 250 mL |
| Sliced green onion | 2 tbsp. | 30 mL |

Put mushrooms into small heatproof bowl. Add boiling water. Stir. Let stand for about 20 minutes until softened. Drain. Remove and discard stems. Slice thinly. Transfer to 3 1/2 to 4 quart (3.5 to 4 L) slow cooker.

Add next 6 ingredients. Stir. Cook, covered, on Low for 8 to 10 hours or on High for 4 to 5 hours.

Add pork and green onion. Stir well. Cook, covered, on High for 10 to 15 minutes until heated through. Makes about 8 1/2 cups (2.1 L).

*1 cup (250 mL): 117 Calories; 4.7 g Total Fat (2.0 g Mono, 0.6 g Poly, 1.6 g Sat); 14 mg Cholesterol; 10 g Carbohydrate; 3 g Fibre; 9 g Protein; 936 mg Sodium*

Pictured at right.

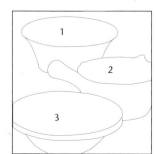

1. Scotch Broth, page 15
2. French Onion Soup, page 14
3. Chinese Mushroom Soup, above

*This rich and hearty, chock-full-of-goodness soup is packed to the brim with beef and veggies. It makes the perfect wintry evening supper when served with garlic bread or crusty rolls.*

# Beef Vegetable Soup

| | | |
|---|---|---|
| Cooking oil | 2 tsp. | 10 mL |
| Lean ground beef | 1 lb. | 454 g |
| Water | 3 cups | 750 mL |
| Can of diced tomatoes (with juice) | 14 oz. | 398 mL |
| Diced peeled potato | 1 1/2 cups | 375 mL |
| Frozen mixed vegetables | 1 1/2 cups | 375 mL |
| Can of condensed tomato soup | 10 oz. | 284 mL |
| Chopped onion | 1 cup | 250 mL |
| Thinly sliced carrot | 1 cup | 250 mL |
| Diced celery | 1/2 cup | 125 mL |
| Granulated sugar | 1 tsp. | 5 mL |
| Salt | 1/2 tsp. | 2 mL |
| Pepper | 1/4 tsp. | 1 mL |
| Liquid gravy browner (optional) | 1 tsp. | 5 mL |

Heat cooking oil in large frying pan on medium. Add beef. Scramble-fry for about 10 minutes until no longer pink. Drain. Transfer to 4 to 5 quart (4 to 5 L) slow cooker.

Add remaining 12 ingredients. Stir. Cook, covered, on Low for 9 to 10 hours or on High for 4 1/2 to 5 hours. Makes about 11 cups (2.75 L).

*1 cup (250 mL): 147 Calories; 4.6 g Total Fat (1.9 g Mono, 0.7 g Poly, 1.5 g Sat); 23 mg Cholesterol; 17 g Carbohydrate; 3 g Fibre; 11 g Protein; 403 mg Sodium*

*You can get just as fancy as you please with your slow cooker—and this decadent soup is case in point. Topped with the traditional cheese-laden croûte (toasted bread slice), this recipe is proof that fine dining is just a slow cooker away.*

# French Onion Soup

| | | |
|---|---|---|
| Thinly sliced onion | 4 cups | 1 L |
| Water | 4 cups | 1 L |
| Beef bouillon powder | 4 tsp. | 20 mL |
| French bread slices (1/4 inch, 6 mm, thick) | 8 | 8 |
| Grated mozzarella cheese | 1 cup | 250 mL |
| Grated Parmesan cheese, sprinkle | | |

Combine first 3 ingredients in 3 1/2 to 4 quart (3.5 to 4 L) slow cooker. Cook, covered, on Low for 8 to 10 hours or on High for 4 to 5 hours. Makes about 5 1/2 cups (1.4 L).

*(continued on next page)*

Ladle soup into 4 ovenproof bowls. Place on baking sheet with sides. Place 2 bread slices over soup in each bowl. Sprinkle 1/4 cup (60 mL) mozzarella cheese over each. Sprinkle with Parmesan cheese. Broil on centre rack in oven until cheese is bubbly and golden. Serves 4.

*1 serving: 257 Calories; 8.0 g Total Fat (2.6 g Mono, 0.6 g Poly, 4.3 g Sat); 24 mg Cholesterol; 36 g Carbohydrate; 3 g Fibre; 11 g Protein; 1134 mg Sodium*

Pictured on page 13.

## Scotch Broth

| | | |
|---|---|---|
| Cooking oil | 1 tbsp. | 15 mL |
| Stewing lamb (or beef), trimmed of fat and cut into 1/2 inch (12 mm) pieces | 1 1/2 lbs. | 680 g |
| Prepared beef broth | 8 cups | 2 L |
| Chopped onion | 2 cups | 500 mL |
| Chopped carrot | 1 1/2 cups | 375 mL |
| Chopped yellow turnip | 1 cup | 250 mL |
| Pearl barley | 2/3 cup | 150 mL |
| Chopped celery | 1/2 cup | 125 mL |
| Salt | 1/8 tsp. | 0.5 mL |
| Pepper | 1/4 tsp. | 1 mL |
| Frozen peas | 1/2 cup | 125 mL |
| Chopped fresh parsley (or 1 tbsp., 15 mL, flakes) | 1/4 cup | 60 mL |

*Kick up yer kilts! This unique soup made with lamb and barley is sure to put some hop in your Scotch.*

Heat cooking oil in large frying pan on medium-high. Add lamb. Cook for 8 to 10 minutes, stirring occasionally, until browned. Transfer to 4 to 5 quart (4 to 5 L) slow cooker.

Add next 8 ingredients. Stir. Cook, covered, on Low for 8 to 10 hours or on High for 4 to 5 hours.

Add peas and parsley. Stir. Cook, covered, on High for about 5 minutes until peas are tender. Makes about 12 cups (3 L).

*1 cup (250 mL): 174 Calories; 4.7 g Total Fat (1.9 g Mono, 0.7 g Poly, 1.2 g Sat); 37 mg Cholesterol; 19 g Carbohydrate; 3 g Fibre; 14 g Protein; 405 mg Sodium*

Pictured on page 13.

*Don't tie yourself to the stove—this Thai delight is made in your slow cooker. Creamy carrots, peanut undertones and a gentle spicy heat make this soup vibrant and velvety.*

## tip

When toasting nuts, seeds or coconut, cooking times will vary for each type of nut—so never toast them together. For small amounts, place ingredient in an ungreased shallow frying pan. Heat on medium for 3 to 5 minutes, stirring often, until golden. For larger amounts, spread ingredient evenly in an ungreased shallow pan. Bake in a 350°F (175°C) oven for 5 to 10 minutes, stirring or shaking often, until golden.

# Carrot Satay Soup

| Prepared chicken broth | 3 cups | 750 mL |
|---|---|---|
| Sliced carrot | 3 cups | 750 mL |
| Chopped onion | 1 cup | 250 mL |
| Chopped celery | 1/2 cup | 125 mL |
| Brown sugar, packed | 2 tbsp. | 30 mL |
| Finely grated gingerroot | 2 tsp. | 10 mL |
| (or 1/2 tsp., 2 mL, ground ginger) | | |
| Garlic cloves, minced | 2 | 2 |
| (or 1/2 tsp., 2 mL, powder) | | |
| Salt | 1/4 tsp. | 1 mL |
| Cayenne pepper | 1/8 tsp. | 0.5 mL |
| Cream cheese, softened | 1/4 cup | 60 mL |
| Smooth peanut butter | 3 tbsp. | 50 mL |
| Soy sauce | 1 tbsp. | 15 mL |

Sesame seeds, toasted (see Tip),
    for garnish

Combine first 9 ingredients in 3 1/2 to 4 quart (3.5 to 4 L) slow cooker. Cook, covered, on Low for 5 to 6 hours or on High for 2 1/2 to 3 hours.

Add next 3 ingredients. Stir. Carefully process with hand blender or in blender until smooth (see Safety Tip).

Garnish individual servings with sesame seeds. Makes about 6 cups (1.5 L).

*1 cup (250 mL): 152 Calories; 8.2 g Total Fat (2.2 g Mono, 1.4 g Poly, 3.3 g Sat); 10 mg Cholesterol; 17 g Carbohydrate; 3 g Fibre; 5 g Protein; 1060 mg Sodium*

Pictured at right.

**Safety Tip:** Follow manufacturer's instructions for processing hot liquids.

Left: Curried Cauliflower Soup, page 21
Right: Carrot Satay Soup, above

*No need to man the helm—your slow cooker will take over in our version of this traditional tomato-based clam chowder. Serve with buns or crusty bread for dunking.*

So what's in a name? A chowder by any other name would taste as sweet? Hardly! When it comes to chowder, it's all about the name. Clam chowders are probably the most well-known—New England-style chowder has a cream base, whereas Manhattan-style has a tomato base. Then there are the chowders that don't have seafood at all, like corn chowder. So what is it that all these chowders have in common? They're hearty—you won't ever come across a delicate or light-tasting chowder.

# Manhattan Clam Chowder

| | | |
|---|---|---|
| Cans of whole baby clams (5 oz., 142 g, each) | 2 | 2 |
| Water | 6 cups | 1.5 L |
| Cans of diced tomatoes (with juice), 14 oz. (398 mL) each | 2 | 2 |
| Chopped onion | 2 cups | 500 mL |
| Chopped unpeeled red potato | 2 cups | 500 mL |
| Diced celery | 1 cup | 250 mL |
| Can of tomato paste | 5 1/2 oz. | 156 mL |
| Diced carrot | 1/2 cup | 125 mL |
| Bacon slices, cooked crisp and crumbled | 5 | 5 |
| Dried thyme | 1 tsp. | 5 mL |
| Cayenne pepper | 1/4 tsp. | 1 mL |

Drain liquid from clams into 5 to 7 quart (5 to 7 L) slow cooker. Transfer clams to small bowl. Chill, covered.

Add next 10 ingredients to slow cooker. Stir. Cook, covered, on Low for 8 to 10 hours or on High for 4 to 5 hours. Add clams. Stir. Cook, covered, on High for about 10 minutes until heated through. Makes about 14 cups (3.5 L).

*1 cup (250 mL): 88 Calories; 1.7 g Total Fat (0.4 g Mono, 0.2 g Poly, 0.5 g Sat); 19 mg Cholesterol; 14 g Carbohydrate; 2 g Fibre; 6 g Protein; 335 mg Sodium*

Pictured at right.

Top: Manhattan Clam Chowder, above
Bottom: Chunky Zucchini Soup, page 20

*Loaded with veggies and the fine flavours of smoky ham and dill, this unique soup is the perfect fare to bring to your next potluck—and your slow cooker is the perfect carrying case!*

## food fun

Dill has been a household staple for years—since 400 B.C., some historians assert. And although we know and love dill as a food additive, it seems our ancestors used it for almost everything but. Dill seeds were burned in the home as an all-natural air freshener. Dill tea was given to people who had trouble sleeping, and medicinally it was used to settle all sorts of tummy troubles. But perhaps the most paradoxical use of dill concerned witches. Dill was suggested to repel witches, yet witches were also reported to favour it in their potion-making.

# Chunky Zucchini Soup

| | | |
|---|---|---|
| Chopped zucchini (with peel) | 4 cups | 1 L |
| Chopped peeled potato | 3 cups | 750 mL |
| All-purpose flour | 1/4 cup | 60 mL |
| Prepared chicken broth | 6 cups | 1.5 L |
| Sliced leek (white part only) | 3 cups | 750 mL |
| Chopped fresh dill (or 2 1/4 tsp., 11 mL, dried) | 3 tbsp. | 50 mL |
| Chopped cooked ham | 3 cups | 750 mL |
| Can of evaporated milk | 6 oz. | 170 mL |
| Chopped fresh dill (or 1 1/4 tsp., 6 mL, dried) | 1 1/2 tbsp. | 25 mL |

Put zucchini and potato into 4 to 5 quart (4 to 5 L) slow cooker. Add flour. Toss gently until vegetables are coated.

Add next 3 ingredients. Stir. Cook, covered, on Low for 8 to 9 hours or on High for 4 to 4 1/2 hours. Cool slightly. Transfer about 3 cups (750 mL) vegetable mixture to blender or food processor using slotted spoon. Process until smooth (see Safety Tip). Return to slow cooker.

Add remaining 3 ingredients. Stir. Cook, covered, on High for about 15 minutes until heated through. Makes about 12 cups (3 L).

*1 cup (250 mL): 181 Calories; 7.0 g Total Fat (2.9 g Mono, 0.9 g Poly, 2.5 g Sat); 33 mg Cholesterol; 17 g Carbohydrate; 2 g Fibre; 13 g Protein; 789 mg Sodium*

Pictured on page 19.

**Safety Tip:** Follow manufacturer's instructions for processing hot liquids.

# Curried Cauliflower Soup

| | | |
|---|---|---|
| Cooking oil | 1 tbsp. | 15 mL |
| Chopped onion | 1 1/2 cups | 375 mL |
| Chopped carrot | 1 cup | 250 mL |
| Chopped celery | 1 cup | 250 mL |
| Curry paste (or 1 tbsp., 15 mL, powder) | 2 tbsp. | 30 mL |
| Garlic cloves, minced (or 1/2 tsp., 2 mL, powder) | 2 | 2 |
| Prepared vegetable broth | 5 cups | 1.25 L |
| Medium peeled potatoes, cubed | 2 | 2 |
| Salt | 1/4 tsp. | 1 mL |
| Chopped cauliflower | 2 1/2 cups | 625 mL |
| Plain yogurt | 1/2 cup | 125 mL |
| Chopped fresh cilantro or parsley | 2 tbsp. | 30 mL |

Heat cooking oil in large frying pan on medium. Add next 3 ingredients. Cook for 5 to 10 minutes, stirring often, until onion is softened.

Add curry paste and garlic. Heat and stir for about 1 minute until fragrant. Transfer to 3 1/2 to 4 quart (3.5 to 4 L) slow cooker.

Add next 3 ingredients. Stir. Cook, covered, on Low for 8 to 10 hours or on High for 4 to 5 hours. Carefully process with hand blender or in blender until smooth (see Safety Tip).

Add cauliflower and yogurt. Stir. Cook, covered, on High for about 45 minutes until cauliflower is tender-crisp.

Add cilantro. Stir. Makes about 8 cups (2 L).

*1 cup (250 mL): 126 Calories; 3.8 g Total Fat (1.3 g Mono, 0.6 g Poly, 1.0 g Sat); 3 mg Cholesterol; 20 g Carbohydrate; 3 g Fibre; 3 g Protein; 537 mg Sodium*

Pictured on page 17.

**Safety Tip:** Follow manufacturer's instructions for processing hot liquids.

*Dare to make something deliciously different for dinner! The quaint combination of cauliflower and curry makes for a colourful and spicy soup.*

## about overcooking

Just because food can cook safely for hours in a slow cooker doesn't mean you can leave your recipe cooking for a couple extra hours with no dire effects. If you're cooking on the low setting, you can usually get away with an extra hour or possibly two—maximum! But going over the allotted time when cooking on the high setting will definitely overcook and possibly dry out your food. Most of our recipes have both a low and high-temperature cooking option, so if you think you're going to be running late, opt for the low setting.

*You'll have more time to dance around the sombrero while this little fiesta of flavour is heating things up in your slow cooker. Serve with nacho chips.*

# Tex-Mex Taco Soup

| | | |
|---|---|---|
| Cooking oil | 2 tsp. | 10 mL |
| Lean ground beef | 1 lb. | 454 g |
| Prepared beef broth | 6 cups | 1.5 L |
| Can of kidney beans, rinsed and drained | 19 oz. | 540 mL |
| Chopped red onion | 2 cups | 500 mL |
| Can of diced tomatoes (with juice) | 14 oz. | 398 mL |
| Chopped celery | 1 1/2 cups | 375 mL |
| Grated carrot | 1 1/2 cups | 375 mL |
| Chopped green pepper | 1 cup | 250 mL |
| Chunky salsa | 1 cup | 250 mL |
| Brown sugar, packed | 1 tsp. | 5 mL |
| Dried basil | 1 tsp. | 5 mL |
| Chopped fresh parsley (or 3/4 tsp., 4 mL, flakes) | 1 tbsp. | 15 mL |
| Sour cream | 1/2 cup | 125 mL |
| Grated Monterey Jack cheese | 1/2 cup | 125 mL |

Heat cooking oil in large frying pan on medium. Add beef. Scramble-fry for about 10 minutes until no longer pink. Drain. Transfer to 5 to 7 quart (5 to 7 L) slow cooker.

Add next 10 ingredients. Stir. Cook, covered, on Low for 8 to 10 hours or on High for 4 to 5 hours.

Add parsley. Stir.

Spoon sour cream and sprinkle cheese on individual servings. Makes about 14 cups (3.5 L).

*1 cup (250 mL): 281 Calories; 7.1 g Total Fat (2.2 g Mono, 1.0 g Poly, 3.0 g Sat); 26 mg Cholesterol; 37 g Carbohydrate; 7 g Fibre; 19 g Protein; 581 mg Sodium*

Pictured at right.

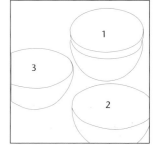

1. Pasta e Fagioli, page 24
2. Tex-Mex Taco Soup, above
3. Squash And Lentil Soup, page 25

# Pasta e Fagioli

*While you're out on the gondola, consider romancing your slow cooker with this Italian favourite.*

| | | |
|---|---|---|
| Bacon slices, diced | 6 | 6 |
| Chopped onion | 1 cup | 250 mL |
| Sliced carrot | 1 cup | 250 mL |
| Sliced celery | 1 cup | 250 mL |
| Garlic cloves, minced (or 1/2 tsp., 2 mL, powder) | 2 | 2 |
| Dried basil | 1 tsp. | 5 mL |
| Dried oregano | 1 tsp. | 5 mL |
| Pepper | 1/2 tsp. | 2 mL |
| Can of white kidney beans, rinsed and drained | 19 oz. | 540 mL |
| Can of diced tomatoes (with juice) | 28 oz. | 796 mL |
| Prepared chicken broth | 3 cups | 750 mL |
| Water | 1 cup | 250 mL |
| Tomato paste (see Tip) | 1/4 cup | 60 mL |
| Bay leaves | 2 | 2 |
| Water | 5 cups | 1.25 L |
| Salt | 1/2 tsp. | 2 mL |
| Tubetti | 1 cup | 250 mL |
| Chopped fresh parsley | 2 tbsp. | 30 mL |
| Grated Parmesan cheese | 1/4 cup | 60 mL |

Cook bacon in medium frying pan on medium until crisp. Transfer to 4 to 5 quart (4 to 5 L) slow cooker using slotted spoon.

Heat 2 tsp. (10 mL) drippings in same frying pan on medium. Add next 7 ingredients. Cook for 5 to 10 minutes, stirring often, until onion is softened. Add to slow cooker.

Measure 1 cup (250 mL) beans onto plate. Mash with fork. Add to slow cooker. Add next 5 ingredients and remaining beans. Stir. Cook, covered, on Low for 7 to 8 hours or on High for 3 1/2 to 4 hours. Discard bay leaves.

Combine water and salt in large saucepan. Bring to a boil. Add tubetti. Boil, uncovered, for 10 to 12 minutes, stirring occasionally, until tender but firm. Drain. Add to slow cooker.

Add parsley. Stir.

*(continued on next page)*

Sprinkle cheese on individual servings. Makes about 12 cups (3 L).

*1 cup (250 mL): 208 Calories; 5.9 g Total Fat (1.9 g Mono, 0.4 g Poly, 2.7 g Sat); 12 mg Cholesterol; 28 g Carbohydrate; 3 g Fibre; 12 g Protein; 854 mg Sodium*

Pictured on page 23.

# Squash And Lentil Soup

| | | |
|---|---|---|
| Cooking oil | 2 tsp. | 10 mL |
| Chopped onion | 2 cups | 500 mL |
| Garlic cloves, minced | 2 | 2 |
| (or 1/2 tsp., 2 mL, powder) | | |
| Finely grated gingerroot | 1 tsp. | 5 mL |
| (or 1/4 tsp., 1 mL, ground ginger) | | |
| Curry powder | 1 tbsp. | 15 mL |
| Prepared chicken broth | 6 cups | 1.5 L |
| Chopped butternut squash | 5 cups | 1.25 L |
| (about 1 1/2 lbs., 680 g), see Tip, page 99 | | |
| Dried red split lentils | 1 1/2 cups | 375 mL |
| Plain yogurt | 1/3 cup | 75 mL |

*This velvety soup is a smooth operator with the mild sweetness of squash, the spiciness of ginger and curry, and the tang of yogurt.*

Heat cooking oil in large frying pan on medium. Add next 3 ingredients. Cook for 5 to 10 minutes, stirring often, until onion is softened.

Add curry powder. Heat and stir for 1 to 2 minutes until fragrant. Transfer to 4 to 5 quart (4 to 5 L) slow cooker.

Add next 3 ingredients. Stir. Cook, covered, on Low for 6 to 8 hours or on High for 3 to 4 hours until lentils and squash are tender. Carefully process with hand blender or in blender until smooth (see Safety Tip).

Add yogurt. Stir. Cook, covered, on High for about 15 minutes until heated through. Makes about 9 1/2 cups (2.4 L).

*1 cup (250 mL): 213 Calories; 3.0 g Total Fat (1.0 g Mono, 0.6 g Poly, 0.6 g Sat); 2 mg Cholesterol; 38 g Carbohydrate; 8 g Fibre; 11 g Protein; 951 mg Sodium*

Pictured on page 23.

**Safety Tip:** Follow manufacturer's instructions for processing hot liquids.

Tender pork and diced vegetables add a great deal of substance to this spicy soup. Although it takes a little time to prepare, the results are worth it! Serve with ciabatta bread or hot cornbread.

## food fun

It's not called "jerk" because an unlikeable guy invented it. Jerk-style cooking actually comes from Jamaica. There are usually two components to jerk cooking—the spices and the cooking method. The spices are generally used as a meat rub, and combine to form a spicy, yet sweet flavour. The cooking style is usually slow barbecuing over an open fire—as evidenced by the outdoor jerk stands that are found scattered throughout busy Jamaican streets.

# Jazzy Jerk Soup

| Ingredient | Imperial | Metric |
|---|---|---|
| Cooking oil | 2 tbsp. | 30 mL |
| Boneless pork loin chops, cut into 1/2 inch (12 mm) thick slices | 1 lb. | 454 g |
| Finely grated gingerroot (or 3/4 tsp., 4 mL, ground ginger) | 1 tbsp. | 15 mL |
| Paprika | 2 tsp. | 10 mL |
| Salt | 1 1/2 tsp. | 7 mL |
| Dried crushed chilies | 3/4 tsp. | 4 mL |
| Dried thyme | 1/2 tsp. | 2 mL |
| Ground cinnamon | 1/4 tsp. | 1 mL |
| Ground allspice | 1/8 tsp. | 0.5 mL |
| Coarsely ground pepper, sprinkle | | |
| Ground cloves, sprinkle | | |
| Chopped onion | 1 cup | 250 mL |
| Garlic clove, minced (or 1/4 tsp., 1 mL, powder) | 1 | 1 |
| Prepared chicken broth | 1 cup | 250 mL |
| Prepared chicken broth | 3 cups | 750 mL |
| Diced peeled potato | 2 cups | 500 mL |
| Diced peeled sweet potato | 2 cups | 500 mL |
| Diced yellow turnip | 2 cups | 500 mL |
| Can of cream-style corn | 14 oz. | 398 mL |
| Can of stewed tomatoes (with juice), coarsely chopped (see Note) | 14 oz. | 398 mL |
| Sliced carrot | 1 cup | 250 mL |
| Coarsely shredded fresh spinach leaves, lightly packed | 2 cups | 500 mL |

Heat cooking oil in large frying pan on medium-high. Add next 10 ingredients. Cook for about 10 minutes, stirring occasionally, until pork is browned.

Add onion and garlic. Cook for 2 minutes, stirring occasionally. Stir in first amount of broth, scraping any brown bits from bottom of pan. Transfer to 4 to 5 quart (4 to 5 L) slow cooker.

Add next 7 ingredients. Stir. Cook, covered, on Low for 7 to 8 hours or on High for 3 1/2 to 4 hours.

*(continued on next page)*

Add spinach. Stir. Cook, covered, on High for about 5 minutes until spinach is wilted. Makes about 12 cups (3 L).

*1 cup (250 mL): 178 Calories; 4.6 g Total Fat (2.3 g Mono, 1.2 g Poly, 0.9 g Sat); 24 mg Cholesterol; 25 g Carbohydrate; 3 g Fibre; 11 g Protein; 1014 mg Sodium*

Pictured below.

**Note:** Cut tomatoes with a paring knife or kitchen shears while still in the can.

Left: Cock-A-Leekie, page 28
Right: Jazzy Jerk Soup, page 26

*You needn't search the Scottish moors for a taste of traditional fare. Sound the bagpipes—this soup comes straight from the Highlands to your slow cooker. And although the name seems a bit nonsensical, it's actually derived from its traditional ingredients: rooster and leeks.*

## Cock-A-Leekie

| | | |
|---|---|---|
| Bacon slices, diced | 4 | 4 |
| Sliced leek (white part only) | 4 cups | 1 L |
| Pearl barley | 1/2 cup | 125 mL |
| Chopped carrot | 1 cup | 250 mL |
| Chopped celery | 1/2 cup | 125 mL |
| Bone-in chicken parts, skin removed (see Note) | 3 1/2 lbs. | 1.6 kg |
| Prepared chicken broth | 7 cups | 1.75 L |
| PEPPER BOUQUET GARNI | | |
| Whole black peppercorns | 8 | 8 |
| Sprigs of fresh parsley | 4 | 4 |
| Sprig of fresh thyme | 1 | 1 |
| Bay leaf | 1 | 1 |
| Can of evaporated milk | 3 3/4 oz. | 110 mL |
| All-purpose flour | 1 tbsp. | 15 mL |

Cook bacon in large frying pan on medium for about 5 minutes until almost crisp.

Add leek. Cook for about 5 minutes, stirring occasionally, until leek starts to soften. Transfer to 5 to 7 quart (5 to 7 L) slow cooker.

Layer next 4 ingredients, in order given, over leek mixture. Pour broth over chicken.

**Pepper Bouquet Garni:** Place first 4 ingredients on 10 inch (25 cm) square piece of cheesecloth. Draw up corners and tie with string. Submerge in liquid in slow cooker. Cook, covered, on Low for 8 to 10 hours or on High for 4 to 5 hours. Remove and discard bouquet garni. Transfer chicken to cutting board using slotted spoon. Remove chicken from bones. Discard bones. Cut chicken into bite-sized pieces. Return to slow cooker.

Whisk evaporated milk into flour in small bowl until smooth. Add to soup. Stir well. Cook, covered, on High for about 5 minutes until boiling and slightly thickened. Makes about 12 cups (3 L).

*1 cup (250 mL): 270 Calories; 8.5 g Total Fat (3.9 g Mono, 2.0 g Poly, 3.3 g Sat); 98 mg Cholesterol; 15 g Carbohydrate; 2 g Fibre; 32 g Protein; 1043 mg Sodium*

Pictured on page 27.

**Note:** Use whichever cuts of chicken you prefer as long as the weight used is equal to that listed.

# Split Pea Soup

| | | |
|---|---|---|
| Water | 5 cups | 1.25 L |
| Green split peas, rinsed and drained | 2 cups | 500 mL |
| Finely chopped onion | 1 cup | 250 mL |
| Can of flaked ham (with liquid), broken up (or 1 cup, 250 mL, diced cooked ham) | 6.5 oz. | 184 g |
| Diced celery | 1/2 cup | 125 mL |
| Medium carrot, thinly sliced | 1 | 1 |
| Chicken bouillon powder | 1 tbsp. | 15 mL |
| Parsley flakes | 1 tsp. | 5 mL |
| Ground thyme | 1/4 tsp. | 1 mL |
| Salt | 1/2 tsp. | 2 mL |
| Pepper | 1/4 tsp. | 1 mL |

Combine all 11 ingredients in 3 1/2 to 4 quart (3.5 to 4 L) slow cooker.
Cook, covered, on Low for 8 to 10 hours or on High for 4 to 5 hours.
Makes about 8 cups (2 L).

*1 cup (250 mL): 207 Calories; 2.9 g Total Fat (0.9 g Mono, 0.2 g Poly, 0.6 g Sat); 11 mg Cholesterol; 28 g Carbohydrate; 5 g Fibre; 16 g Protein; 816 mg Sodium*

*The trick to a good split pea soup is giving it time to properly simmer and blend its flavours—and there's no better way to do that than in a slow cooker.*

*Without our slow cookers we'd certainly swoon! This traditional Southern fave, in soup form, will leave all the beaus and belles feeling satisfied.*

# Chicken And Dumpling Soup

| | | |
|---|---|---|
| Chopped onion | 1/2 cup | 125 mL |
| Chopped peeled potato | 1 cup | 250 mL |
| Chopped carrot | 1 cup | 250 mL |
| Shredded green cabbage, lightly packed | 1 cup | 250 mL |
| Small fresh whole white mushrooms, halved | 1 cup | 250 mL |
| Boneless, skinless chicken thighs,<br>    cut into 1 inch (2.5 cm) pieces | 1 lb. | 454 g |
| Prepared chicken broth | 2 cups | 500 mL |
| Can of condensed cream of mushroom soup | 10 oz. | 284 mL |
| Dried rosemary, crushed | 1/4 tsp. | 1 mL |
| Dried thyme | 1/4 tsp. | 1 mL |
| Paprika | 1/4 tsp. | 1 mL |
| Pepper | 1/4 tsp. | 1 mL |
| Bay leaf | 1 | 1 |

ROSEMARY DUMPLINGS

| | | |
|---|---|---|
| All-purpose flour | 1 cup | 250 mL |
| Grated Parmesan cheese | 2 tbsp. | 30 mL |
| Baking powder | 1 tsp. | 5 mL |
| Dried rosemary, crushed | 1/8 tsp. | 0.5 mL |
| Large egg, fork-beaten | 1 | 1 |
| Buttermilk (or soured milk, see Tip) | 3 tbsp. | 50 mL |
| Cooking oil | 2 tbsp. | 30 mL |

Layer first 6 ingredients, in order given, in 3 1/2 to 4 quart (3.5 to 4 L) slow cooker.

Combine next 6 ingredients in small bowl. Pour over chicken. Add bay leaf. Cook, covered, on Low for 6 hours or on High for 3 hours. Discard bay leaf. Stir. Bring to a boil on High. Makes about 6 cups (1.5 L).

**Rosemary Dumplings:** Measure first 4 ingredients into medium bowl. Stir. Make a well in centre.

*(continued on next page)*

Combine remaining 3 ingredients in small bowl. Add to well. Stir until just moistened. Spoon mounds of batter, using 1 tbsp. (15 mL) for each, in single layer over soup. Cook, covered, on High for about 30 minutes until wooden pick inserted in centre of dumpling comes out clean. Serves 6.

*1 serving: 368 Calories; 17.4 g Total Fat (6.3 g Mono, 3.0 g Poly, 4.8 g Sat); 91 mg Cholesterol; 30 g Carbohydrate; 2 g Fibre; 23 g Protein; 1147 mg Sodium*

Pictured below.

*This richly flavoured side has all the delicious essence and creamy texture of a traditional rice risotto—but it's made with barley.*

## tip

To peel tomatoes, cut an 'X' on the bottom of each tomato, just through the skin. Then place the tomatoes in boiling water for 30 seconds and immediately transfer to a bowl of ice water. Let stand until cool enough to handle, then peel and discard skins.

# Herbed Barley Risotto

| | | |
|---|---|---|
| Cooking oil | 1 tbsp. | 15 mL |
| Finely chopped onion | 1 cup | 250 mL |
| Sliced fresh white mushrooms | 2 cups | 500 mL |
| Garlic cloves, minced (or 1 tsp., 5 mL, powder) | 4 | 4 |
| Prepared vegetable broth | 2 2/3 cups | 650 mL |
| Medium tomatoes, peeled (see Tip), quartered, seeds removed | 3 | 3 |
| Pearl barley | 1 cup | 250 mL |
| Dry (or alcohol-free) white wine | 1/2 cup | 125 mL |
| Dried oregano | 1/2 tsp. | 2 mL |
| Dried rosemary, crushed | 1/2 tsp. | 2 mL |
| Salt | 1/4 tsp. | 1 mL |
| Pepper | 1/4 tsp. | 1 mL |
| Grated Parmesan cheese | 1/3 cup | 75 mL |
| Chopped fresh parsley | 2 tbsp. | 30 mL |

Heat cooking oil in medium frying pan on medium. Add onion. Cook for 5 to 10 minutes, stirring often, until softened.

Add mushrooms and garlic. Cook for 3 to 5 minutes, stirring occasionally, until mushrooms are softened. Transfer to 3 1/2 to 4 quart (3.5 to 4 L) slow cooker.

Add next 8 ingredients. Stir. Cook, covered, on Low for 8 to 9 hours or on High for 4 to 4 1/2 hours.

Add cheese and parsley. Stir. Makes about 4 cups (1 L).

*1 cup (250 mL): 343 Calories; 7.5 g Total Fat (2.1 g Mono, 1.3 g Poly, 1.7 g Sat); 7 mg Cholesterol; 54 g Carbohydrate; 6 g Fibre; 12 g Protein; 634 mg Sodium*

Pictured at right.

Left: Slow Cooker Dolmades, page 34
Top Right: Herbed Barley Risotto, above

*Dolmades (pronounced dohl-MAH-dehs) are the Greek equivalent of the cabbage roll. Grape leaves, available in the import section of your grocery store, are rolled around a flavourful filling of rice, lamb, mint and raisins. Garnish with lemon wedges or a curl of lemon zest and serve with tzatziki or plain yogurt.*

### food fun

Did you know that purple, brown and yellow raisins all come from the same grape? The way a raisin is dried will determine its colour. In North America, most raisins are made from Thompson Seedless grapes. Dark purple/black raisins are sun-dried, light/medium brown raisins have been mechanically dehydrated, and gold/yellow raisins have been mechanically dehydrated and treated with sulphur dioxide. Sulphur dioxide is used on many dried fruits and prevents light-coloured fruits from darkening.

# Slow Cooker Dolmades

| | | |
|---|---|---|
| Water | 2 1/2 cups | 625 mL |
| Salt | 1 tsp. | 5 mL |
| Basmati (or long grain) white rice | 1 3/4 cups | 425 mL |
| Olive (or cooking) oil | 1 tbsp. | 15 mL |
| Diced onion | 1 1/2 cups | 375 mL |
| Lean ground lamb | 1 lb. | 454 g |
| Garlic cloves, minced (or 3/4 tsp., 4 mL, powder) | 3 | 3 |
| Dried mint leaves | 1 tsp. | 5 mL |
| Dried oregano | 1 tsp. | 5 mL |
| Parsley flakes | 1 tsp. | 5 mL |
| Salt | 1 tsp. | 5 mL |
| Pepper | 1/4 tsp. | 1 mL |
| Raisins, chopped (optional) | 1/2 cup | 125 mL |
| Jars of grape leaves (17 oz., 473 mL, each), rinsed and drained, tough stems removed (see Note) | 2 | 2 |
| Boiling water | 4 1/3 cups | 1.1 L |
| Lemon juice | 1/2 cup | 125 mL |
| Olive (or cooking) oil | 3 tbsp. | 50 mL |
| Garlic cloves, halved (or 1/4 tsp., 1 mL, powder) | 4 | 4 |
| Granulated sugar | 1/2 tsp. | 2 mL |

Combine water and salt in medium saucepan. Bring to a boil. Add rice. Stir. Reduce heat to medium-low. Simmer, covered, for about 12 minutes until liquid is absorbed and rice is almost tender. Cool. Fluff with fork.

Heat first amount of olive oil in large frying pan. Add onion. Cook for 5 to 10 minutes, stirring often, until softened.

Add lamb and first amount of garlic. Scramble-fry for about 5 minutes until lamb is no longer pink. Drain. Transfer to large bowl.

Add next 6 ingredients and rice. Stir well.

*(continued on next page)*

Place grape leaves on work surface, vein-side up, stem-side (bottom of leaf) closest to you. Line bottom of 5 quart (5 L) slow cooker with a few small or torn leaves. Place 1 to 2 tbsp. (15 to 30 mL) lamb mixture about 1/2 inch (12 mm) from bottom of leaf. Fold bottom of leaf over lamb mixture. Fold in sides. Roll up from bottom to enclose filling. Do not roll too tightly as rice will expand. Repeat with remaining leaves and lamb mixture. Arrange rolls, seam-side down, close together in layers over leaves in slow cooker. Separate layers with small or torn leaves. Place any remaining leaves over top.

Combine remaining 5 ingredients in medium bowl. Slowly pour over dolmades, allowing all air spaces to fill, until water mixture is just visible on sides. Set aside any remaining water mixture. Cook, covered, on Low for 3 1/2 to 4 hours, checking after 2 1/2 hours and adding more water mixture if necessary. Turn off slow cooker. Let stand, covered, for at least 30 minutes to allow rolls to set. Drain and discard any remaining liquid. Carefully transfer dolmades to large serving platter. Cool. Serve at room temperature. Store any remaining rolls in airtight containers in freezer for up to 1 month. Makes about 75 dolmades.

*1 dolmade: 49 Calories; 2.4 g Total Fat (1.1 g Mono, 0.3 g Poly, 0.8 g Sat); 4 mg Cholesterol; 5 g Carbohydrate; trace Fibre; 2 g Protein; 433 mg Sodium*

Pictured on page 33.

**Note:** Choose the best grape leaves for rolling and save the smaller or torn leaves for separating layers and lining the bottom of the slow cooker.

*Got a big batch of people coming for dinner? Well, this big batch of creamy, tangy potatoes will satisfy everyone's starch cravings—not to mention free up the oven for your entrée.*

# Make-Ahead Potatoes

| | | |
|---|---|---|
| Medium peeled potatoes, quartered | 9 | 9 |
| Block of light cream cheese, softened and cut up | 8 oz. | 250 g |
| Light sour cream | 1 cup | 250 mL |
| Dried chives | 1 tbsp. | 15 mL |
| Parsley flakes | 1 tsp. | 5 mL |
| Onion powder | 1/2 tsp. | 2 mL |
| Garlic powder | 1/4 tsp. | 1 mL |
| Salt | 1 tsp. | 5 mL |
| Pepper | 1/4 tsp. | 1 mL |

Pour water into large saucepan or Dutch oven until about 1 inch (2.5 cm) deep. Add potato. Cover. Bring to a boil. Reduce heat to medium. Boil gently for 12 to 15 minutes until tender. Drain. Mash.

Beat remaining 8 ingredients in medium bowl until combined. Add to potato. Mix well. Transfer to greased 3 1/2 to 4 quart (3.5 to 4 L) slow cooker. Cook, covered, on Low for 6 to 8 hours or on High for 3 to 4 hours, stirring occasionally. Makes about 8 cups (2 L).

*1 cup (250 mL): 264 Calories; 7.1 g Total Fat (0 g Mono, 0.1 g Poly, 4.7 g Sat); 23 mg Cholesterol; 42 g Carbohydrate; 3 g Fibre; 8 g Protein; 455 mg Sodium*

*All dressed up and no place to go? Never! These baby red potatoes, adorned with an irresistibly creamy dressing, are heading straight to your dinner plate.*

### variation

If you want to up the flavour factor of Dressed Red Potatoes, use half an envelope of ranch dressing mix and half an envelope of dill dressing mix instead of just one or the other.

# Dressed Red Potatoes

| | | |
|---|---|---|
| Red baby potatoes, cut in half | 2 1/2 lbs. | 1.1 kg |
| Can of condensed cream of potato soup | 10 oz. | 284 mL |
| Block of light cream cheese, softened and cut up | 8 oz. | 250 g |
| Envelope of buttermilk dill (or ranch) dressing mix | 1 oz. | 28 g |
| Parsley flakes | 1 tsp. | 5 mL |

Put potato into 3 1/2 to 4 quart (3.5 to 4 L) slow cooker.

Beat remaining 4 ingredients in medium bowl until combined. Spoon over potato. Cook, covered, on Low for 6 to 7 hours or on High for 3 to 3 1/2 hours. Makes about 9 1/2 cups (2.4 L).

*1 cup (250 mL): 223 Calories; 4.5 g Total Fat (0.1 g Mono, 0.2 g Poly, 2.9 g Sat); 13 mg Cholesterol; 25 g Carbohydrate; 2 g Fibre; 5 g Protein; 685 mg Sodium*

# Lentil Potato Mash

| | | |
|---|---|---|
| Red baby potatoes, larger ones cut in half | 1 lb. | 454 g |
| Prepared vegetable broth | 1 3/4 cups | 425 mL |
| Can of light coconut milk | 14 oz. | 398 mL |
| Chopped onion | 1 cup | 250 mL |
| Chopped peeled sweet potato | 1 cup | 250 mL |
| Dried red split lentils | 1 cup | 250 mL |
| Smooth peanut butter | 1/4 cup | 60 mL |
| Curry powder | 2 tsp. | 10 mL |
| Soy sauce | 2 tsp. | 10 mL |
| Finely grated gingerroot | 1 tsp. | 5 mL |
| (or 1/4 tsp., 1 mL, ground ginger) | | |
| Garlic clove, minced | 1 | 1 |
| (or 1/4 tsp., 1 mL, powder) | | |
| Chili paste (sambal oelek) | 1/2 tsp. | 2 mL |
| Granulated sugar | 1/2 tsp. | 2 mL |
| Salt | 1/2 tsp. | 2 mL |
| Chopped fresh parsley | 1 tbsp. | 15 mL |

Combine first 14 ingredients in 3 1/2 quart (3.5 L) slow cooker. Cook, covered, on Low for 7 to 8 hours or on High for 3 1/2 to 4 hours. Mash. Transfer to serving bowl.

Sprinkle with parsley. Makes about 5 1/2 cups (1.4 L).

*1 cup (250 mL): 351 Calories; 11.9 g Total Fat (2.9 g Mono, 1.7 g Poly, 4.8 g Sat); 0 mg Cholesterol; 47 g Carbohydrate; 9 g Fibre; 15 g Protein; 498 mg Sodium*

*This delightful curried mash of lentils, potatoes and sweet potatoes is a sure winner. If you don't like potato skins in your mash, make sure to peel the baby potatoes.*

## about coconut milk

Contrary to what one would expect, coconut milk is not the liquid found inside a coconut. The juice inside the coconut is quite watery and wouldn't lend the same rich, creamy texture to Asian, African and Polynesian dishes that coconut milk does. The canned coconut milk you buy at the store comes from squeezing juice out of the actual meat of the coconut.

## Sufferin' Succotash

*There will be no suffering involved when you tuck into this creamy southern staple.*

| | | |
|---|---|---|
| Frozen kernel corn | 2 cups | 500 mL |
| Frozen lima beans | 2 cups | 500 mL |
| Chopped onion | 1 1/2 cups | 375 mL |
| Can of condensed cream of mushroom soup | 10 oz. | 284 mL |
| Sliced celery | 1/2 cup | 125 mL |
| Jar of sliced pimiento, chopped | 2 oz. | 57 mL |
| Dried basil | 1/4 tsp. | 1 mL |
| Garlic powder | 1/4 tsp. | 1 mL |
| Salt | 1/2 tsp. | 2 mL |
| Pepper | 1/8 tsp. | 0.5 mL |
| Grated medium Cheddar cheese | 1/3 cup | 75 mL |

Combine first 10 ingredients in 3 1/2 quart (3.5 L) slow cooker. Cook, covered, on Low for 8 to 10 hours or on High for 4 to 5 hours. Stir. Transfer to serving bowl.

Sprinkle with cheese. Makes about 4 cups (1 L).

*1 cup (250 mL): 296 Calories; 8.0 g Total Fat (0.9 g Mono, 0.3 g Poly, 3.0 g Sat); 13 mg Cholesterol; 46 g Carbohydrate; 7 g Fibre; 12 g Protein; 918 mg Sodium*

Pictured at right.

## Carrot Onion Bake

*A perfect side is as easy as a medley of carrots and onions. The slow cooking allows the natural flavours to really come through. Use a crinkle cutter on the carrots for a showier presentation.*

| | | |
|---|---|---|
| Diagonally sliced carrot | 6 cups | 1.5 L |
| Sliced onion | 1 1/2 cups | 375 mL |
| Water | 1/2 cup | 125 mL |
| Salt | 1/2 tsp. | 2 mL |
| SAUCE | | |
| All-purpose flour | 1 tbsp. | 15 mL |
| Salt, sprinkle | | |
| Pepper, sprinkle | | |
| Milk | 1/2 cup | 125 mL |
| Grated medium (or sharp) Cheddar cheese | 1/2 cup | 125 mL |
| TOPPING | | |
| Butter (or hard margarine) | 1 tbsp. | 15 mL |
| Fine dry bread crumbs | 1/4 cup | 60 mL |

*(continued on next page)*

Combine first 4 ingredients in 3 1/2 to 4 quart (3.5 to 4 L) slow cooker. Cook, covered, on High for 4 to 5 hours. Drain. Transfer to serving bowl. Cover to keep warm.

**Sauce:** Combine first 3 ingredients in small saucepan. Slowly add milk, stirring constantly with whisk, until smooth. Heat and stir on medium until boiling and thickened.

Add cheese. Heat and stir until cheese is melted. Add to vegetable mixture. Stir.

**Topping:** Melt butter in separate small saucepan on medium. Add bread crumbs. Heat and stir until crumbs are browned. Sprinkle over vegetable mixture. Makes about 6 cups (1.5 L).

*1 cup (250 mL): 155 Calories; 5.8 g Total Fat (1.6 g Mono, 0.4 g Poly, 3.4 g Sat); 16 mg Cholesterol; 22 g Carbohydrate; 4 g Fibre; 5 g Protein; 211 mg Sodium*

Pictured below.

Left: Carrot Onion Bake, page 38
Right: Sufferin' Succotash, page 38

*The smoky flavour of the sausage in this dish is contrasted by the unexpected sweet and fruity aftertaste. Serve over couscous for a pretty presentation.*

# Fruity Beans And Sausage

| | | |
|---|---|---|
| Can of chickpeas (garbanzo beans), rinsed and drained | 19 oz. | 540 mL |
| Can of baked beans in molasses | 14 oz. | 398 mL |
| Can of pineapple tidbits, drained and juice reserved | 14 oz. | 398 mL |
| Can of red kidney beans, rinsed and drained | 14 oz. | 398 mL |
| Smoked ham sausage, cut into 1/4 inch (6 mm) slices | 1/2 lb. | 225 g |
| Medium unpeeled cooking apple (such as McIntosh), diced | 1 | 1 |
| Chopped onion | 1/2 cup | 125 mL |
| Apple cider vinegar | 2 tbsp. | 30 mL |
| Fancy (mild) molasses | 2 tbsp. | 30 mL |
| Dry mustard | 1 tsp. | 5 mL |
| Reserved pineapple juice (optional) | 2 tbsp. | 30 mL |
| Cornstarch (optional) | 1 tbsp. | 15 mL |

Combine first 10 ingredients in 3 1/2 to 4 quart (3.5 to 4 L) slow cooker. Cook, covered, on Low for 6 to 7 hours or on High for 3 to 3 1/2 hours.

Stir pineapple juice into cornstarch in small cup. Add to slow cooker. Stir. Cook, covered, on High for about 5 minutes until boiling and slightly thickened. Makes about 7 cups (1.75 L).

*1 cup (250 mL): 317 Calories; 6.1 g Total Fat (0.4 g Mono, 0.6 g Poly, 0.2 g Sat); 2 mg Cholesterol; 50 g Carbohydrate; 11 g Fibre; 16 g Protein; 726 mg Sodium*

Pictured at right.

*This medley of beans gets its uniquely sweet and tangy taste from sweet Spanish onions, brown sugar and cider vinegar. A bean lover's delight!*

# Sweet Bean Pot

| | | |
|---|---|---|
| Bacon slices, diced | 8 | 8 |
| Thinly sliced Spanish onion | 1 1/2 cups | 375 mL |
| Garlic cloves, minced (or 1/2 tsp., 2 mL, powder) | 2 | 2 |
| Brown sugar, packed | 1 cup | 250 mL |
| Apple cider vinegar | 1/2 cup | 125 mL |
| Dry mustard | 1 tsp. | 5 mL |
| Salt | 1/2 tsp. | 2 mL |

*(continued on next page)*

| | | |
|---|---|---|
| Cans of baked beans in tomato sauce (14 oz., 398 mL, each) | 2 | 2 |
| Can of lima beans, rinsed and drained | 19 oz. | 540 mL |
| Can of pinto beans, rinsed and drained | 19 oz. | 540 mL |
| Can of red kidney beans, rinsed and drained | 19 oz. | 540 mL |
| Can of white kidney beans, rinsed and drained | 19 oz. | 540 mL |

Cook bacon in medium frying pan on medium until almost crisp. Drain all but 2 tbsp. (30 mL) drippings.

Add onion. Cook for 5 to 10 minutes, stirring often, until onion is softened and bacon is crisp.

Add garlic. Heat and stir for 1 to 2 minutes until fragrant.

Add next 4 ingredients. Stir. Bring to a boil.

Put remaining 5 ingredients into 4 to 5 quart (4 to 5 L) slow cooker. Add bacon mixture. Stir. Cook, covered, on Low for 6 hours or on High for 3 hours. Makes about 10 cups (2.5 L).

*1 cup (250 mL): 390 Calories; 5.9 g Total Fat (2.2 g Mono, 1.0 g Poly, 1.7 g Sat); 12 mg Cholesterol; 70 g Carbohydrate; 14 g Fibre; 16 g Protein; 1001 mg Sodium*

### about brown sugar

So what's the difference between brown sugar and white sugar? Brown sugar is actually white sugar that has had molasses added to it. The molasses gives it its soft texture, rich colour and characteristic taste. Brown sugar will get hard if it loses its moisture, so to rehydrate, place a small amount in a microwave-safe bowl and set side by side with a bowl of water in the microwave. Microwave on high for approximately one minute until soft.

Fruity Beans And Sausage, page 40

*Served either hot or cold, this homemade sauce puts the canned stuff to shame. Add more sugar if you have a sweet tooth.*

# Applesauce

| | | |
|---|---|---|
| **Medium cooking apples (such as McIntosh), peeled and sliced** | 8 | 8 |
| **Water** | 1/2 cup | 125 mL |
| **Granulated sugar** | 1/2 cup | 125 mL |

Combine apple and water in 3 1/2 quart (3.5 L) slow cooker. Cook, covered, on Low for 4 to 5 hours or on High for 2 to 2 1/2 hours.

Sprinkle sugar over top. Stir. Makes about 4 cups (1 L).

*1/2 cup (125 mL): 108 Calories; 0.2 g Total Fat (trace Mono, 0.1 g Poly, trace Sat); 0 mg Cholesterol; 28 g Carbohydrate; 2 g Fibre; trace Protein; trace Sodium*

Pictured on page 45.

*The tartness of home-cooked cranberry sauce just can't be paralleled by the stuff from the can. Let it cook, undisturbed, in your slow cooker, while the rest of your holiday fare monopolizes your oven and stove.*

# Cranberry Sauce

| | | |
|---|---|---|
| **Granulated sugar** | 2 cups | 500 mL |
| **Boiling water** | 1 cup | 250 mL |
| **Fresh (or frozen) cranberries** | 4 cups | 1 L |

Combine sugar and water in 3 1/2 quart (3.5 L) slow cooker.

Add cranberries. Stir. Cook, covered, on High for about 1 1/2 hours until cranberries are split. Sauce will thicken as it cools. Makes about 3 1/2 cups (875 mL).

*2 tbsp. (30 mL): 60 Calories; 0 g Total Fat (0 g Mono, 0 g Poly, 0 g Sat); 0 mg Cholesterol; 15 g Carbohydrate; 1 g Fibre; 0 g Protein; trace Sodium*

Pictured on page 45.

# Stuffing

| | | |
|---|---|---|
| Hot water | 1 1/2 cups | 375 mL |
| Butter (or hard margarine) | 1/4 cup | 60 mL |
| Chicken bouillon powder | 1 tbsp. | 15 mL |
| Parsley flakes | 1 tbsp. | 15 mL |
| Poultry seasoning | 2 tsp. | 10 mL |
| Salt | 1 tsp. | 5 mL |
| Pepper | 1/4 tsp. | 1 mL |
| Dry white bread cubes | 10 cups | 2.5 L |
| Chopped celery | 1 cup | 250 mL |
| Chopped onion | 1 cup | 250 mL |

*If the oven's already stuffed with turkey, stuff this flavourful dressing into your slow cooker instead.*

Measure first 7 ingredients into extra-large heatproof bowl. Stir until butter is melted.

Add remaining 3 ingredients. Toss until coated. Transfer to greased 3 1/2 to 4 quart (3.5 to 4 L) slow cooker. Cook, covered, on Low for 5 to 6 hours (see Note). Makes about 8 cups (2 L).

*1/2 cup (125 mL): 91 Calories; 3.6 g Total Fat (0.9 g Mono, 0.4 g Poly, 2.0 g Sat); 8 mg Cholesterol; 13 g Carbohydrate; 1 g Fibre; 2 g Protein; 532 mg Sodium*

**Note:** If you prefer a more moist stuffing, add a bit more hot water while cooking. Stir.

*Jalapeño peppers add an unexpected kick to this scrumptious stuffing.*

# Spicy Sausage And Bread Stuffing

| | | |
|---|---|---|
| Package of frozen sausage meat, thawed | 13 oz. | 375 g |
| Herb (or garlic) seasoned croutons | 10 cups | 2.5 L |
| Finely chopped sliced pickled jalapeño peppers (see Tip) | 2 tbsp. | 30 mL |
| Butter (or hard margarine) | 1/2 cup | 125 mL |
| Chopped celery (with leaves) | 2 cups | 500 mL |
| Chopped onion | 2 cups | 500 mL |
| Chopped fresh parsley (or 2 tbsp., 30 mL, flakes) | 1/2 cup | 125 mL |
| Dried sage | 2 tsp. | 10 mL |
| Dried oregano | 1 tsp. | 5 mL |
| Dried thyme | 1 tsp. | 5 mL |
| Pepper, sprinkle | | |
| Can of condensed chicken broth | 10 oz. | 284 mL |
| Hot water, approximately | 1/2 cup | 125 mL |
| Butter (or hard margarine) | 1 tbsp. | 15 mL |

Heat large frying pan on medium-high. Add sausage. Scramble-fry for about 10 minutes until browned. Drain. Transfer to extra-large bowl.

Add croutons and jalapeño pepper. Stir.

Melt first amount of butter in same frying pan on medium. Add celery and onion. Cook for about 10 minutes, stirring often, until softened.

Add next 5 ingredients. Stir. Add to sausage mixture. Stir.

Drizzle with broth and enough hot water until mixture holds together lightly.

Grease 3 1/2 to 4 quart (3.5 to 4 L) slow cooker with second amount of butter. Spoon stuffing into slow cooker. Pack down lightly. Cook, covered, on Low for about 2 hours until heated through. Makes about 8 cups (2 L).

*1/2 cup (125 mL): 263 Calories; 17.9 g Total Fat (7.2 g Mono, 1.7 g Poly, 7.8 g Sat); 35 mg Cholesterol; 20 g Carbohydrate; 2 g Fibre; 6 g Protein; 659 mg Sodium*

Pictured at right.

1. Spicy Sausage And Bread Stuffing, page 44
2. Cranberry Sauce, page 42
3. Applesauce, page 42

*Imagine coming home to the inviting aroma of a hot pot roast dinner, complete with potatoes and vegetables. No scrambling or fuss to make dinner—simply pull out the plates.*

## pot roast gravy

To make a quick thick gravy for your Pot Roast, combine 2 tbsp. (30 mL) of flour, 1/4 tsp. (1 mL) of salt and a pinch of pepper in a small saucepan. On medium heat, slowly whisk in 1 cup (250 mL) of strained liquid from the Pot Roast. Keep stirring until the gravy is boiling and thickened. For a more flavourful gravy, you can add up to 1 tsp. (5 mL) of bouillon powder or a little more salt and pepper. Makes about 1 cup (250 mL).

*Certainly not short on flavour, these short ribs are coated in a tangy barbecue sauce and are fall-off-the-bone tender.*

# Pot Roast

| | | |
|---|---|---|
| Medium peeled potatoes, quartered | 4 | 4 |
| Medium carrots, cut into 4 pieces each | 4 | 4 |
| Medium onions, cut into 8 wedges each | 2 | 2 |
| Boneless beef blade (or cross-rib) roast | 3 lbs. | 1.4 kg |
| Boiling water | 1/2 cup | 125 mL |
| Beef bouillon powder | 1 tsp. | 5 mL |
| Liquid gravy browner (optional) | 1/2 tsp. | 2 mL |
| Fresh (or frozen) whole green beans, halved | 2 cups | 500 mL |

Layer first 3 ingredients, in order given, in 5 to 7 quart (5 to 7 L) slow cooker. Place roast over top.

Combine next 3 ingredients in small bowl. Pour over roast. Cook, covered, on Low for 10 to 12 hours or on High for 5 to 6 hours until roast is tender.

Add green beans. Cook, covered, on High for 15 to 20 minutes until tender-crisp. Transfer roast to cutting board. Cover with foil. Let stand for 10 minutes. Cut roast into thin slices. Transfer vegetables to serving bowl using slotted spoon. Serves 8.

*1 serving: 468 Calories; 28.1 g Total Fat (12.0 g Mono, 1.1 g Poly, 11.1 g Sat); 115 mg Cholesterol; 22 g Carbohydrate; 4 g Fibre; 33 g Protein; 197 mg Sodium*

Pictured on divider and at right.

# Barbecue Beef Ribs

| | | |
|---|---|---|
| Cooking oil | 2 tbsp. | 30 mL |
| Beef short ribs, bone-in, trimmed of fat | 3 lbs. | 1.4 kg |
| Barbecue sauce | 1 cup | 250 mL |
| Fancy (mild) molasses | 2 tbsp. | 30 mL |
| White vinegar | 2 tbsp. | 30 mL |
| Soy sauce | 1 tbsp. | 15 mL |
| Salt | 1 1/2 tsp. | 7 mL |
| Pepper | 1/2 tsp. | 2 mL |
| Chopped onion | 1/2 cup | 125 mL |

*(continued on next page)*

Heat cooking oil in large frying pan on medium. Add ribs. Cook for about 5 minutes, turning occasionally, until browned on all sides. Transfer to 5 to 7 quart (5 to 7 L) slow cooker.

Combine next 6 ingredients in medium bowl.

Add onion. Stir. Pour over ribs. Cook, covered, on Low for 8 to 10 hours or on High for 4 to 5 hours. Serves 4.

*1 serving:* 748 Calories; 42.7 g Total Fat (19.4 g Mono, 3.8 g Poly, 15.4 g Sat); 163 mg Cholesterol; 18 g Carbohydrate; 4 g Fibre; 69 g Protein; 1847 mg Sodium

Pot Roast, page 46

*Full of fresh herbs, this bean and beef stew has a hint of spring in it. Complete with fluffy, melt-in-your-mouth biscuits, this is wholesome cooking at its best.*

### tip

To make soured milk, measure 2 tsp. (10 mL) white vinegar or lemon juice into a 3/4 cup (175 mL) liquid measure, then add enough milk to make 3/4 cup (175 mL). Stir and let stand for 1 minute.

# Beef And Biscuits

| | | |
|---|---|---|
| Stewing beef | 2 lbs. | 900 g |
| Can of diced tomatoes (with juice) | 28 oz. | 796 mL |
| Can of red kidney beans, rinsed and drained | 19 oz. | 540 mL |
| Chopped onion | 1 cup | 250 mL |
| Water | 1/2 cup | 125 mL |
| Chopped fresh oregano (or 1 1/2 tsp., 7 mL, dried) | 2 tbsp. | 30 mL |
| Beef bouillon powder | 4 tsp. | 20 mL |
| Chili powder | 2 tsp. | 10 mL |
| Granulated sugar | 1 tsp. | 5 mL |
| Ground coriander | 3/4 tsp. | 4 mL |
| Ground cumin | 3/4 tsp. | 4 mL |
| Salt | 1/4 tsp. | 1 mL |
| BISCUITS | | |
| All-purpose flour | 1 1/2 cups | 375 mL |
| Yellow cornmeal | 1/2 cup | 125 mL |
| Grated Parmesan cheese | 1/3 cup | 75 mL |
| Chopped fresh cilantro or parsley (or 1 1/2 tsp., 7 mL, dried) | 2 tbsp. | 30 mL |
| Baking powder | 1 tbsp. | 15 mL |
| Baking soda | 1/2 tsp. | 2 mL |
| Salt, just a pinch | | |
| Pepper, just a pinch | | |
| Cold butter (or hard margarine), cut up | 3 tbsp. | 50 mL |
| Buttermilk (or soured milk, see Tip), approximately | 3/4 cup | 175 mL |

Combine first 12 ingredients in 4 to 5 quart (4 to 5 L) slow cooker. Cook, covered, on Low for 8 to 10 hours or on High for 4 to 5 hours. Bring to a boil on High. Makes about 6 1/2 cups (1.6 L).

**Biscuits:** Measure first 8 ingredients into large bowl. Stir. Cut in butter until mixture resembles coarse crumbs. Make a well in centre.

Add buttermilk to well. Stir until soft dough forms. Turn out onto lightly floured surface. Knead 8 times. Roll or pat out to 1/2 inch (12 mm) thickness. Cut out circles with lightly floured 2 inch (5 cm) biscuit cutter. Arrange biscuits, just touching, over beef mixture. Cook, covered, on High for about 30 minutes until wooden pick inserted in centre of biscuit comes out clean. Serves 8.

*1 serving: 703 Calories; 21.5 g Total Fat (7.5 g Mono, 1.2 g Poly, 10.9 g Sat); 91 mg Cholesterol; 75 g Carbohydrate; 11 g Fibre; 53 g Protein; 1437 mg Sodium*

# Dijon Beef Stew

| | | |
|---|---|---|
| Baby carrots | 1 lb. | 454 g |
| Baby potatoes, larger ones cut in half | 1 lb. | 454 g |
| Chopped green pepper | 1 1/4 cups | 300 mL |
| Chopped onion | 1 1/4 cups | 300 mL |
| All-purpose flour | 1/4 cup | 60 mL |
| Paprika | 1/4 tsp. | 1 mL |
| Stewing beef | 1 1/2 lbs. | 680 g |
| Cooking oil | 2 tsp. | 10 mL |
| Prepared beef broth | 1 1/2 cups | 375 mL |
| Dijon mustard | 1/3 cup | 75 mL |
| Worcestershire sauce | 2 tsp. | 10 mL |
| Dried oregano | 1/2 tsp. | 2 mL |
| Chopped red pepper | 3/4 cup | 175 mL |

Put first 4 ingredients into 4 to 5 quart (4 to 5 L) slow cooker.

Combine flour and paprika in large resealable freezer bag. Add beef. Seal bag. Toss until coated.

Heat cooking oil in large frying pan on medium. Add beef. Reserve remaining flour mixture. Cook for 5 to 10 minutes, stirring occasionally, until browned on all sides. Add to slow cooker.

Combine next 4 ingredients and remaining flour mixture in same frying pan. Heat and stir on medium until slightly thickened. Add to slow cooker. Stir. Cook, covered, on Low for 8 to 10 hours or on High for 4 to 5 hours.

Add red pepper. Stir. Cook, covered, on High for about 10 minutes until red pepper is tender-crisp. Makes about 8 cups (2 L).

*1 cup (250 mL): 251 Calories; 8.9 g Total Fat (3.8 g Mono, 0.8 g Poly, 3.2 g Sat); 47 mg Cholesterol; 21 g Carbohydrate; 3 g Fibre; 21 g Protein; 405 mg Sodium*

*A healthy amount of Dijon gives this stew an interestingly piquant edge. Garnish with chopped fresh dill and serve with rolls or salad.*

## about dijon

Dijon mustard is aptly named after the city in France where it was invented. The original Dijon mustard was differentiated from other mustards because it used the juice from unripe grapes instead of the usual vinegar. This substitution resulted in a smoother, less-harsh mustard. Because Dijon has a smoother taste than prepared yellow mustard, it is inadvisable to substitute one for the other in recipes.

*Perhaps one of our most often-requested slow cooker dishes, this beef delight gets rave reviews from people who have never liked corned beef before!*

### about corned beef

So what is corned beef anyway? It is simply beef that has been pickled in brine. The recipe for corned beef dates back many hundreds of years when people would brine their beef as a way of preserving it. The term "corned" actually relates to the coarse "corns" or grains of salt that were used in the brining process.

# Corned Beef Dinner

| | | |
|---|---|---|
| Baby carrots | 1 lb. | 454 g |
| Red baby potatoes, larger ones cut in half | 1 lb. | 454 g |
| Medium yellow turnip, cut into 1 inch (2.5 cm) cubes | 1 | 1 |
| Chopped onion | 2 cups | 500 mL |
| Corned beef brisket | 2 lbs. | 900 g |
| Water | 4 cups | 1 L |
| Bay leaves | 2 | 2 |
| Whole black peppercorns | 1 tbsp. | 15 mL |

Layer first 4 ingredients, in order given, in 5 to 7 quart (5 to 7 L) slow cooker. Place corned beef over onion, fat-side up.

Pour water over corned beef. Add bay leaves and peppercorns. Cook, covered, on Low for 8 to 10 hours or on High for 4 to 5 hours. Discard bay leaves. Transfer corned beef to large serving platter. Cut into thin slices. Transfer vegetables to serving bowl using slotted spoon. Serve with beef. Discard any remaining liquid in slow cooker. Serves 6.

*1 serving: 310 Calories; 11.7 g Total Fat (5.5 g Mono, 0.6 g Poly, 3.8 g Sat); 104 mg Cholesterol; 27 g Carbohydrate; 3 g Fibre; 23 g Protein; 1285 mg Sodium*

Pictured at right.

*Wok? Who needs it? You can serve up some great Asian flavours right in your slow cooker. Serve this fresh-tasting delight over aromatic basmati rice.*

## about snow peas

Some people refer to the snow pea as *mange-tout*—French for "eat-all." We think it's a very fitting name indeed! Though the entire pod is edible, you may wish to remove the tough fiber that runs along the side by snapping off the stem end and pulling it down the side of the pod where the peas are attached.

# Chinese Pepper Steak

| | | |
|---|---|---|
| Large onion, thinly sliced | 1 | 1 |
| Cooking oil | 1 tbsp. | 15 mL |
| Beef inside round steak, cut into strips | 2 lbs. | 900 g |
| Can of diced tomatoes (with juice) | 14 oz. | 398 mL |
| Soy sauce | 1/4 cup | 60 mL |
| Beef bouillon powder | 1 tsp. | 5 mL |
| Garlic clove, minced (or 1/4 tsp., 1 mL, powder) | 1 | 1 |
| Granulated sugar | 1 tsp. | 5 mL |
| Salt | 3/4 tsp. | 4 mL |
| Pepper | 1/8 tsp. | 0.5 mL |
| Fresh bean sprouts | 1 1/2 cups | 375 mL |
| Snow peas, trimmed | 1 1/2 cups | 375 mL |
| Medium green pepper, thinly sliced | 1 | 1 |
| Medium red pepper, thinly sliced | 1 | 1 |
| Water | 3 tbsp. | 50 mL |
| Cornstarch | 2 tbsp. | 30 mL |

Put onion into 3 1/2 to 4 quart (3.5 to 4 L) slow cooker.

Heat large frying pan on medium-high until very hot. Add cooking oil. Add beef. Stir-fry for about 5 minutes until browned. Add to slow cooker.

Combine next 7 ingredients in medium bowl. Pour over beef. Cook, covered, on Low for 6 to 7 hours or on High for 3 to 3 1/2 hours.

Add next 4 ingredients. Stir.

Stir water into cornstarch in small cup. Add to slow cooker. Stir. Cook, covered, on High for about 15 minutes until liquid is slightly thickened and vegetables are tender-crisp. Makes about 9 cups (2.25 L).

*1 cup (250 mL): 223 Calories; 8.7 g Total Fat (3.5 g Mono, 0.9 g Poly, 2.5 g Sat); 59 mg Cholesterol; 12 g Carbohydrate; 2 g Fibre; 24 g Protein; 844 mg Sodium*

Pictured at right.

# Dilly Beef Dinner

| | | |
|---|---|---|
| Diced peeled potato | 4 cups | 1 L |
| Thinly sliced carrot | 3 cups | 750 mL |
| Thinly sliced celery | 3/4 cup | 175 mL |
| Sliced (or chopped) onion | 1 1/2 cups | 375 mL |
| Flank (or brisket) steak, cut into 6 equal pieces | 2 lbs. | 900 g |
| Can of diced tomatoes (with juice) | 14 oz. | 398 mL |
| Dried dillweed | 1 1/2 tsp. | 7 mL |
| Salt | 1 tsp. | 5 mL |
| Pepper | 1/4 tsp. | 1 mL |

*Serve this dill-luxe blend of steak and veggies to your family, then sit back and watch their dill-lighted reactions.*

Layer first 4 ingredients, in order given, in 5 to 7 quart (5 to 7 L) slow cooker.

Arrange steak over onion.

Combine remaining 4 ingredients in small bowl. Pour over steak. Cook, covered, on Low for 8 to 10 hours or on High for 4 to 5 hours. Serves 6.

*1 serving: 415 Calories; 13.7 g Total Fat (5.5 g Mono, 0.6 g Poly, 5.7 g Sat); 64 mg Cholesterol; 33 g Carbohydrate; 5 g Fibre; 38 g Protein; 725 mg Sodium*

Chinese Pepper Steak, page 52

*Don't be fooled by the name. The curry spice in this hotpot is actually quite mild. Sweet, fruity and nice, it's best served over rice.*

## food fun

When you bite into an apricot, whether fresh or dried, consider that apricots were once believed to cause fever. Foolish superstition? Perhaps, but one with a grain of truth to it—or should we say, a seed? If digested the seed inside the apricot releases a type of cyanide that can, indeed, make you sick if eaten in large amounts. But stick to the delicious fruit and you can't go wrong.

# Beef Curry Hotpot

| | | |
|---|---|---|
| Cooking oil | 1 tbsp. | 15 mL |
| Beef inside round (or blade) steak, trimmed of fat and cut into 1 inch (2.5 cm) cubes | 2 lbs. | 900 g |
| Medium cooking apples (such as McIntosh), peeled and chopped | 3 | 3 |
| Medium onions, sliced | 2 | 2 |
| Chopped tomato | 2 cups | 500 mL |
| Curry powder | 2 tsp. | 10 mL |
| Can of condensed beef broth | 10 oz. | 284 mL |
| Water | 1 cup | 250 mL |
| Chopped dried apricot | 1/2 cup | 125 mL |
| Raisins | 1/3 cup | 75 mL |
| All-purpose flour | 1 tbsp. | 15 mL |
| Brown sugar, packed | 1 tbsp. | 15 mL |
| Pepper, sprinkle | | |

Heat cooking oil in large frying pan on medium-high. Add beef. Cook for 5 to 10 minutes, stirring occasionally, until no longer pink. Transfer to 4 to 5 quart (4 to 5 L) slow cooker.

Add apple and onion to same frying pan. Cook on medium for about 5 minutes, stirring often, until softened. Add to slow cooker.

Add tomato and curry powder to same frying pan. Heat and stir for about 2 minutes until heated through. Add to slow cooker.

Add next 4 ingredients. Stir. Cook, covered, on Low for 6 to 8 hours or on High for 3 to 4 hours.

Combine remaining 3 ingredients in small cup. Add to slow cooker. Stir. Cook, covered, on High for 10 to 15 minutes until boiling and slightly thickened. Makes about 8 cups (2 L).

*1 cup (250 mL): 272 Calories; 8.2 g Total Fat (3.3 g Mono, 0.9 g Poly, 2.3 g Sat); 67 mg Cholesterol; 24 g Carbohydrate; 3 g Fibre; 26 g Protein; 343 mg Sodium*

# Hungarian Goulash

| Ingredient | Imperial | Metric |
|---|---|---|
| Chopped onion | 1 1/2 cups | 375 mL |
| All-purpose flour | 2 tbsp. | 30 mL |
| Paprika | 2 tsp. | 10 mL |
| Garlic powder | 1/4 tsp. | 1 mL |
| Salt | 1 tsp. | 5 mL |
| Pepper | 1/4 tsp. | 1 mL |
| Stewing beef, cut into 3/4 inch (2 cm) cubes | 1 1/2 lbs. | 680 g |
| Can of diced tomatoes (with juice) | 14 oz. | 398 mL |
| Beef bouillon powder | 2 tsp. | 10 mL |
| Granulated sugar | 1 tsp. | 5 mL |
| Liquid gravy browner (optional) | 1/2 tsp. | 2 mL |
| Sour cream | 1/2 cup | 125 mL |

This hearty beef and tomato blend gets its distinctive flavour from a healthy portion of paprika and just enough sour cream to give it a touch of tang. Superb!

Put onion into 3 1/2 to 4 quart (3.5 to 4 L) slow cooker.

Combine next 5 ingredients in large resealable freezer bag. Add beef. Seal bag. Toss until coated. Add to slow cooker. Discard any remaining flour mixture.

Combine next 4 ingredients in medium bowl. Add to slow cooker. Stir. Cook, covered, on Low for 8 to 10 hours or on High for 4 to 5 hours.

Add sour cream. Stir. Serves 6.

*1 serving: 273 Calories; 13.4 g Total Fat (5.2 g Mono, 0.6 g Poly, 6.2 g Sat); 71 mg Cholesterol; 11 g Carbohydrate; 1 g Fibre; 27 g Protein; 1004 mg Sodium*

*Comfort food goes exotic. Ginger, garlic, sherry and Asian vegetables turn a humble stew into a Far East feast. Serve over rice noodles.*

### tip

To slice meat easily, place it in the freezer for about 30 minutes until it's just starting to freeze, and then cut. If using from frozen state, partially thaw before cutting.

# Ginger Beef Stew

| | | |
|---|---|---|
| Medium onions, cut into wedges | 2 | 2 |
| Medium carrot, sliced diagonally | 1 | 1 |
| Can of sliced water chestnuts, drained | 8 oz. | 227 mL |
| Roasted red peppers, drained and blotted dry, cut into strips | 1 cup | 250 mL |
| Cooking oil | 1 tbsp. | 15 mL |
| Beef inside round steak, trimmed of fat and cut into 1/2 inch (12 mm) thick slices | 1 1/2 lbs. | 680 g |
| Finely grated gingerroot (or 1 1/2 tsp., 7 mL, ground ginger) | 2 tbsp. | 30 mL |
| Garlic cloves, minced (or 1/2 tsp., 2 mL, powder) | 2 | 2 |
| Water | 2/3 cup | 150 mL |
| Dry sherry (or prepared beef broth) | 1/4 cup | 60 mL |
| Brown sugar, packed | 1 tbsp. | 15 mL |
| Soy sauce | 3 tbsp. | 50 mL |
| Cornstarch | 1 tbsp. | 15 mL |
| Snow peas, trimmed | 1 cup | 250 mL |

Layer first 4 ingredients, in order given, in 3 1/2 quart (3.5 L) slow cooker.

Heat cooking oil in large frying pan on medium. Add beef. Cook for 8 to 10 minutes, stirring occasionally, until browned.

Add ginger and garlic. Heat and stir for about 1 minute until fragrant.

Add next 3 ingredients. Stir. Bring to a boil. Pour over red pepper. Cook, covered, on Low for 8 to 9 hours or on High for 4 to 4 1/2 hours.

Stir soy sauce into cornstarch in small cup. Add to slow cooker. Stir. Add snow peas. Stir. Cook, covered, on High for about 10 minutes until snow peas are tender-crisp and sauce is boiling and thickened. Makes about 5 cups (1.25 L).

*1 cup (250 mL): 335 Calories; 11.6 g Total Fat (4.8 g Mono, 1.3 g Poly, 3.2 g Sat); 80 mg Cholesterol; 23 g Carbohydrate; 5 g Fibre; 32 g Protein; 739 mg Sodium*

Pictured at right.

*Get all your wining and dining done with one fantastic and rather fancy-tasting dish. Great served with noodles or mashed potatoes.*

## about slow cooker safety

Slow cookers heat foods at a relatively low temperature that is still hot enough to safely prevent bacteria from growing—but don't assume there are no safety issues involved with slow cookers. Never let your ingredients warm to room temperature before turning the slow cooker on. If you want to do the preparation the night before, keep the ingredients separate and refrigerated until it is time to turn the slow cooker on. And if you have a slow cooker with a timer, make sure the timer is set for no longer than two hours after you've left the food in it. Finally, never, never use a slow cooker to reheat food.

# Beef In Red Wine

| | | |
|---|---|---|
| All-purpose flour | 3 tbsp. | 50 mL |
| Salt, sprinkle | | |
| Stewing beef, cut into 1 1/2 inch (3.8 cm) cubes | 1 lb. | 454 g |
| Cooking oil | 2 tsp. | 10 mL |
| Thinly sliced onion | 2 cups | 500 mL |
| Thinly sliced carrot | 1 cup | 250 mL |
| Dry (or alcohol-free) red wine | 1 cup | 250 mL |
| Garlic cloves, minced (or 1/2 tsp., 2 mL, powder) | 2 | 2 |
| Pepper | 1/4 tsp. | 1 mL |
| Bay leaves | 2 | 2 |
| Sprig of fresh rosemary (or thyme) | 1 | 1 |

Combine flour and salt in large resealable freezer bag. Add beef. Seal bag. Toss until coated.

Heat cooking oil in large frying pan on medium-high. Add beef. Discard any remaining flour mixture. Cook for about 5 minutes, stirring occasionally, until browned. Transfer to 3 1/2 quart (3.5 L) slow cooker.

Layer onion and carrot, in order given, over beef.

Combine next 3 ingredients in small bowl. Pour over carrot. Add bay leaves and rosemary sprig. Cook, covered, on Low for 6 to 8 hours or on High for 3 to 4 hours. Discard bay leaves and rosemary sprig. Makes about 4 cups (1 L).

*1 cup (250 mL): 429 Calories; 16.2 g Total Fat (7.4 g Mono, 1.5 g Poly, 5.5 g Sat); 84 mg Cholesterol; 20 g Carbohydrate; 3 g Fibre; 35 g Protein; 125 mg Sodium*

Pictured at right.

# Onion Beef Ragout

| | | |
|---|---|---|
| Stewing beef, cut into 3/4 inch (2 cm) cubes | 2 lbs. | 900 g |
| Envelope of green peppercorn sauce mix | 1 1/4 oz. | 38 g |
| Medium onions, cut into 8 wedges each | 3 | 3 |
| Water | 1 cup | 250 mL |
| Dry (or alcohol-free) red wine | 1/2 cup | 125 mL |

Put beef into 4 to 5 quart (4 to 5 L) slow cooker. Sprinkle with sauce mix. Stir until coated. Arrange onion over beef.

Combine water and wine in small bowl. Pour over onion. Cook, covered, on Low for 8 to 9 hours or on High for 4 to 4 1/2 hours. Makes about 8 cups (2 L).

*1 cup (250 mL): 237 Calories; 10.2 g Total Fat (4.2 g Mono, 0.4 g Poly, 4.0 g Sat); 63 mg Cholesterol; 8 g Carbohydrate; 1 g Fibre; 26 g Protein; 349 mg Sodium*

Pictured below.

*Let's call it stew—French-style. So easy and tasty the French would have only one word for it: magnifique! Serve with mashed potatoes and green beans.*

Top: Beef In Red Wine, page 58
Bottom: Onion Beef Ragout, above

*"Steak" out your claim to great taste with this hearty medley of beef and veggies in a tomato sauce.*

# Steak Bake

| | | |
|---|---|---|
| Medium onion, sliced | 1 | 1 |
| Medium peeled potatoes, quartered | 4 | 4 |
| Medium carrots, sliced | 4 | 4 |
| Beef inside round (or blade) steak, cut into 6 equal pieces | 2 lbs. | 900 g |
| Can of diced tomatoes (with juice) | 14 oz. | 398 mL |
| Can of condensed tomato soup | 10 oz. | 284 mL |
| Salt | 1 tsp. | 5 mL |
| Pepper | 1/4 tsp. | 1 mL |
| Garlic powder | 1/4 tsp. | 1 mL |
| Water | 1/4 cup | 60 mL |
| All-purpose flour | 2 tbsp. | 30 mL |
| Can of cut green beans, drained | 14 oz. | 398 mL |
| Chopped green onion, for garnish | | |

Layer first 4 ingredients, in order given, in 5 to 7 quart (5 to 7 L) slow cooker.

Combine next 5 ingredients in medium bowl. Pour over steak. Cook, covered, on Low for 8 to 10 hours or on High for 4 to 5 hours. Transfer steak to plate using slotted spoon. Cover to keep warm.

Stir water into flour in small cup until smooth. Add to slow cooker. Stir. Cook, covered, on High for 15 minutes until boiling and slightly thickened.

Add green beans and steak. Stir until heated through.

Garnish with green onion. Serves 6.

*1 serving: 381 Calories; 11.2 g Total Fat (4.0 g Mono, 0.9 g Poly, 3.6 g Sat); 88 mg Cholesterol; 36 g Carbohydrate; 4 g Fibre; 37 g Protein; 1163 mg Sodium*

Pictured at right.

*Take it slow with this rich and decadent classic. Tender beef in a creamy red wine tomato sauce just shouldn't be rushed. Serve over egg noodles or rice.*

### tip

If a recipe calls for less than an entire can of tomato paste, freeze the unopened can for 30 minutes. Open both ends and push the contents through one end. Slice off only what you need and freeze the remaining paste in a resealable freezer bag or plastic wrap for future use.

# Slow Stroganoff Stew

| | | |
|---|---|---|
| All-purpose flour | 3 tbsp. | 50 mL |
| Stewing beef | 2 lbs. | 900 g |
| Cooking oil | 2 tbsp. | 30 mL |
| Cooking oil | 2 tsp. | 10 mL |
| Sliced fresh white mushrooms | 1 1/2 cups | 375 mL |
| Thinly sliced onion | 1 1/2 cups | 375 mL |
| Paprika | 2 tsp. | 10 mL |
| Can of diced tomatoes (with juice) | 14 oz. | 398 mL |
| Dry (or alcohol-free) red wine | 1/2 cup | 125 mL |
| Prepared beef broth | 1/2 cup | 125 mL |
| Tomato paste (see Tip) | 3 tbsp. | 50 mL |
| Granulated sugar | 1/2 tsp. | 2 mL |
| Salt | 1/4 tsp. | 1 mL |
| Pepper | 1/4 tsp. | 1 mL |
| Sour cream | 1/3 cup | 75 mL |

Measure flour into large resealable freezer bag. Add beef. Seal bag. Toss until coated.

Heat first amount of cooking oil in large frying pan on medium. Add beef. Discard any remaining flour. Cook for 8 to 10 minutes, stirring occasionally, until browned. Transfer to 3 1/2 to 4 quart (3.5 to 4 L) slow cooker.

Heat second amount of cooking oil in same frying pan on medium. Add mushrooms and onion. Cook for 5 to 10 minutes, stirring occasionally and scraping any brown bits from bottom of pan, until onion is softened.

Add paprika. Heat and stir for 1 minute. Add to slow cooker.

Add next 7 ingredients. Stir. Cook, covered, on Low for 9 to 10 hours or on High for 4 1/2 to 5 hours.

Add sour cream. Stir. Makes about 5 1/2 cups (1.4 L).

*1 cup (250 mL): 446 Calories; 23.6 g Total Fat (10.7 g Mono, 2.7 g Poly, 7.8 g Sat); 97 mg Cholesterol; 16 g Carbohydrate; 1 g Fibre; 38 g Protein; 527 mg Sodium*

# Sauerkraut Beef Dinner

| | | |
|---|---|---|
| Chopped onion | 1 cup | 250 mL |
| Jar of sauerkraut, rinsed and well drained | 28 oz. | 796 mL |
| Beef inside round steak, trimmed of fat and cut into 1 inch (2.5 cm) cubes | 2 lbs. | 900 g |
| Can of diced tomatoes (with juice) | 14 oz. | 398 mL |
| Prepared beef broth | 1/4 cup | 60 mL |
| Tomato paste (see Tip, page 62) | 2 tbsp. | 30 mL |
| Caraway seed | 1 tsp. | 5 mL |
| Garlic clove, minced (or 1/4 tsp., 1 mL, powder) | 1 | 1 |
| Granulated sugar | 1 tsp. | 5 mL |
| Salt | 1/4 tsp. | 1 mL |
| Pepper | 1/2 tsp. | 2 mL |
| Red potatoes, halved lengthwise and cut into 1/4 inch (6 mm) slices | 1 lb. | 454 g |

Layer first 3 ingredients, in order given, in 4 to 5 quart (4 to 5 L) slow cooker.

Combine next 8 ingredients in medium bowl. Pour over beef.

Arrange potato over top. Cook, covered, on Low for 8 to 10 hours or on High for 4 to 5 hours. Transfer potato to plate using slotted spoon. Transfer beef and sauerkraut mixture to serving bowl using slotted spoon. Discard any remaining liquid in slow cooker. Serves 8.

*1 serving: 255 Calories; 8.1 g Total Fat (2.9 g Mono, 0.5 g Poly, 2.7 g Sat); 66 mg Cholesterol; 19 g Carbohydrate; 4 g Fibre; 26 g Protein; 971 mg Sodium*

*Aromatic caraway seed adds an unexpected anise-like flavour to tangy sauerkraut, tender beef and juicy tomatoes. Complete with red potatoes, it's a full meal deal.*

## about caraway seeds

Caraway seeds have been recommended as a cure-all for everything from colds to tooth decay, but caraway is most prized for its aromatically delicate licorice taste with its sharp underlying bite. If you're a fan of this savoury seed, lightly toast it and add it to stews, sauerkraut and soups for a nifty new taste sensation.

*Here's another one of our most-requested slow cooker recipes. Readers and staff enjoy these fajitas because of the combination of tender spiced beef and both soft-cooked and crisp vegetables.*

# Slow Cooker Fajitas

| | | |
|---|---|---|
| Beef sirloin tip steak, cut into thin strips, about 3 inches (7.5 cm) long | 1 1/2 lbs. | 680 g |
| Thickly sliced fresh white mushrooms | 2 cups | 500 mL |
| Large onion, cut into 8 wedges | 1 | 1 |
| Medium red pepper, cut into 1/2 inch (12 mm) wide strips | 1 | 1 |
| Medium yellow pepper, cut into 1/2 inch (12 mm) wide strips | 1 | 1 |
| Finely chopped pickled jalapeño pepper (see Tip), optional | 1 tbsp. | 15 mL |
| Water | 1/4 cup | 60 mL |
| Envelope of fajita seasoning mix | 1 oz. | 28 g |
| Flour tortillas (7 1/2 inch, 19 cm, diameter) | 10 | 10 |
| Ripe medium avocado, diced | 1 | 1 |
| Lemon juice | 2 tsp. | 10 mL |
| Shredded lettuce, lightly packed | 1 cup | 250 mL |
| Grated jalapeño Monterey Jack cheese | 2/3 cup | 150 mL |
| Light (or fat-free) sour cream | 2/3 cup | 150 mL |
| Medium tomato, seeds removed and diced | 1 | 1 |

Put first 6 ingredients into 3 1/2 to 4 quart (3.5 to 4 L) slow cooker.

Stir water into seasoning mix in small bowl until smooth. Add to slow cooker. Stir. Cook, covered, on Low for 5 to 6 hours or on High for 2 1/2 to 3 hours.

Drain liquid from slow cooker into medium bowl (see Note). Makes about 5 cups (1.25 L) beef mixture. Spoon beef mixture down centre of each tortilla.

Toss avocado and lemon juice in small bowl. Spoon over beef mixture on each tortilla.

Layer remaining 4 ingredients over avocado on each tortilla. Fold bottom ends of tortillas over filling. Fold in sides, slightly overlapping, leaving top ends open. Makes 10 fajitas.

*1 fajita: 428 Calories; 17.7 g Total Fat (5.0 g Mono, 1.4 g Poly, 5.7 g Sat); 40 mg Cholesterol; 46 g Carbohydrate; 3 g Fibre; 22 g Protein; 819 mg Sodium*

Pictured at right.

**Note:** The remaining liquid can be frozen and used for soup or to replace broth in another recipe.

# Chili

*A rich chili you can easily customize to your own heat preference. Mild as is, but you can add more chili powder to boost the fire factor.*

| | | |
|---|---|---|
| Cooking oil | 2 tsp. | 10 mL |
| Lean ground beef | 1 lb. | 454 g |
| Chopped onion | 1 cup | 250 mL |
| Green pepper, chopped | 1 | 1 |
| Can of red kidney beans (with liquid) | 14 oz. | 398 mL |
| Can of condensed tomato soup | 10 oz. | 284 mL |
| Can of sliced mushrooms, drained | 10 oz. | 284 mL |
| Chili powder | 1 tsp. | 5 mL |
| Granulated sugar | 1 tsp. | 5 mL |
| Seasoned salt | 1/4 tsp. | 1 mL |
| Salt | 1/2 tsp. | 2 mL |
| Pepper | 1/8 tsp. | 0.5 mL |

Heat cooking oil in large frying pan on medium. Add beef. Scramble-fry for about 10 minutes until no longer pink. Drain.

Layer onion and green pepper, in order given, in 3 1/2 to 4 quart (3.5 to 4 L) slow cooker.

Combine remaining 8 ingredients in medium bowl. Add beef. Stir. Pour over green pepper. Cook, covered, on Low for 6 to 7 hours or on High for 3 to 3 1/2 hours. Makes about 5 1/2 cups (1.4 L).

*1 cup (250 mL): 286 Calories; 9.5 g Total Fat (3.9 g Mono, 1.2 g Poly, 2.9 g Sat); 45 mg Cholesterol; 26 g Carbohydrate; 7 g Fibre; 24 g Protein; 984 mg Sodium*

# Beefy Bun Topping

*Forget the tidy beef patty, and get downright sloppy with this saucy topping. Add some slices of cucumber and tomato, and serve on open-faced, toasted hamburger buns.*

| | | |
|---|---|---|
| Cooking oil | 2 tsp. | 10 mL |
| Lean ground beef | 2 lbs. | 900 g |
| Large onion, chopped | 1 | 1 |
| Can of diced tomatoes (with juice) | 14 oz. | 398 mL |
| Can of tomato paste | 5 1/2 oz. | 156 mL |
| Brown sugar, packed | 1 1/2 tbsp. | 25 mL |
| Chili powder | 1 tbsp. | 15 mL |
| Beef bouillon powder | 2 tsp. | 10 mL |
| Dry mustard | 1/2 tsp. | 2 mL |
| Pepper | 1/4 tsp. | 1 mL |

*(continued on next page)*

Heat cooking oil in large frying pan on medium. Add beef. Scramble-fry for about 10 minutes until no longer pink. Drain.

Put onion into 3 1/2 to 4 quart (3.5 to 4 L) slow cooker. Add beef.

Combine remaining 7 ingredients in medium bowl. Add to slow cooker. Stir. Cook, covered, on Low for 5 to 6 hours or on High for 2 1/2 to 3 hours. Makes about 6 cups (1.5 L).

*1/2 cup (125 mL): 158 Calories; 6.8 g Total Fat (3.0 g Mono, 0.5 g Poly, 2.5 g Sat); 42 mg Cholesterol; 7 g Carbohydrate; 1 g Fibre; 17 g Protein; 356 mg Sodium*

Pictured below.                                    Beefy Bun Topping, page 66

*Lasagna without the layering. Once again our readers have spoken and voted this recipe one of their all-time slow cooker favourites.*

## about garnishes

The slow cooking process often drains foods of their vibrant colours, so to add a dash of panache to your finished recipes, consider garnishing your slow cooker masterpieces with sprinkles of vibrant fresh veggies like chopped green onion and diced tomato, or give fresh herbs a try.

# Lasagna

|  | | |
|---|---|---|
| Water | 12 cups | 3 L |
| Salt | 1 1/2 tsp. | 7 mL |
| Lasagna noodles, broken up | 8 | 8 |
| Cooking oil | 2 tsp. | 10 mL |
| Lean ground beef | 1 1/2 lbs. | 680 g |
| Cans of diced tomatoes (with juice), 14 oz. (398 mL) each | 2 | 2 |
| Grated mozzarella cheese | 2 cups | 500 mL |
| 2% cottage cheese | 1 cup | 250 mL |
| Finely chopped onion | 3/4 cup | 175 mL |
| Can of tomato paste | 5 1/2 oz. | 156 mL |
| Granulated sugar | 2 tsp. | 10 mL |
| Parsley flakes | 1 tsp. | 5 mL |
| Dried oregano | 1/2 tsp. | 2 mL |
| Salt | 1 1/4 tsp. | 6 mL |
| Pepper | 1/2 tsp. | 2 mL |
| Dried basil | 1/4 tsp. | 1 mL |
| Garlic powder | 1/4 tsp. | 1 mL |

Combine water and salt in Dutch oven. Bring to a boil. Add noodles. Boil, uncovered, for 12 to 14 minutes, stirring occasionally, until tender but firm. Drain.

Heat cooking oil in large frying pan on medium. Add beef. Scramble-fry for about 10 minutes until no longer pink. Drain. Transfer to 3 1/2 to 4 quart (3.5 to 4 L) slow cooker.

Add remaining 12 ingredients. Stir. Add noodles. Stir. Cook, covered, on Low for 7 to 9 hours or on High for 3 1/2 to 4 1/2 hours. Makes about 10 cups (2.5 L).

*1 cup (250 mL): 320 Calories; 12.0 g Total Fat (4.4 g Mono, 0.7 g Poly, 5.7 g Sat); 58 mg Cholesterol; 27 g Carbohydrate; 2 g Fibre; 26 g Protein; 747 mg Sodium*

# Bolognese Sauce

| | | |
|---|---|---|
| Olive (or cooking) oil | 2 tsp. | 10 mL |
| Chopped pancetta (or regular bacon) | 4 oz. | 113 g |
| Lean ground beef | 2 lbs. | 900 g |
| Finely chopped carrot | 2 cups | 500 mL |
| Finely chopped celery | 2 cups | 500 mL |
| Finely chopped onion | 1 1/2 cups | 375 mL |
| Cans of tomato sauce (14 oz., 398 mL, each) | 2 | 2 |
| Prepared beef broth | 2 cups | 500 mL |
| Dry (or alcohol-free) white wine | 1 cup | 250 mL |
| Can of evaporated milk | 5 1/2 oz. | 160 mL |

Heat olive oil in large frying pan on medium. Add bacon. Cook for about 4 minutes, stirring occasionally, until almost crisp. Increase heat to medium-high.

Add next 4 ingredients. Scramble-fry for about 10 minutes until beef is no longer pink. Drain. Transfer to 4 to 5 quart (4 to 5 L) slow cooker.

Add next 3 ingredients. Stir. Cook, covered, on Low for 6 to 8 hours or on High for 3 to 4 hours. Skim and discard fat from surface of liquid in slow cooker.

Add evaporated milk. Stir. Cook, covered, on High for about 10 minutes until heated through. Makes about 10 2/3 cups (2.7 L).

*1 cup (250 mL): 237 Calories; 9.8 g Total Fat (4.9 g Mono, 0.8 g Poly, 4.3 g Sat); 52 mg Cholesterol; 13 g Carbohydrate; 2 g Fibre; 21 g Protein; 808 mg Sodium*

*We've put a glamorous twist on Bolognese by adding pancetta, white wine and evaporated milk to make a decadently creamy mixture.*

## about pancetta

Pancetta (pronounced pan-CHEH-tuh) is an Italian variety of bacon that has been cured with spices but not smoked like most other types of bacon. It is usually rolled into a sausage-like shape, and when sliced is patterned with swirls. It will keep in the fridge for up to three weeks and in the freezer for up to six months.

*This perennial potluck pleaser also makes a great kid-pleasing entrée when served over rice.*

## "Sweetish" Meatballs

| | | |
|---|---|---|
| Box of frozen cooked meatballs | 2 1/4 lbs. | 1 kg |
| Salt, sprinkle | | |
| Pepper, sprinkle | | |
| Can of condensed tomato soup | 10 oz. | 284 mL |
| Brown sugar, packed | 3/4 cup | 175 mL |
| White vinegar | 1/2 cup | 125 mL |

Put meatballs into 4 to 5 quart (4 to 5 L) slow cooker. Sprinkle with salt and pepper.

Combine remaining 3 ingredients in medium bowl. Add to slow cooker. Stir until coated. Cook, covered, on Low for 5 to 6 hours or on High for 2 1/2 to 3 hours. Serves 8.

*1 serving: 411 Calories; 20.6 g Total Fat (0.1 g Mono, 0.3 g Poly, 8.3 g Sat); 55 mg Cholesterol; 32 g Carbohydrate; trace Fibre; 24 g Protein; 1006 mg Sodium*

*Ground beef? Steak? Too much work. Ready-made meatballs are the ultimate stew-starting time saver—perfect in this creamy dill-flavoured, chock-full-of-veggies dinner delight.*

## Meatball Stew

| | | |
|---|---|---|
| Chopped onion | 1 1/2 cups | 375 mL |
| Baby carrots | 3 1/2 cups | 875 mL |
| Baby potatoes, larger ones cut in half | 2 lbs. | 900 g |
| Dried dillweed | 1 1/2 tsp. | 7 mL |
| Pepper | 1/2 tsp. | 2 mL |
| Box of frozen cooked meatballs | 2 1/4 lbs. | 1 kg |
| Can of condensed cream of mushroom soup | 10 oz. | 284 mL |
| Prepared beef broth | 1 cup | 250 mL |
| Water | 1/2 cup | 125 mL |
| Worcestershire sauce | 2 tsp. | 10 mL |
| Frozen peas | 1 1/2 cups | 375 mL |

Layer first 3 ingredients, in order given, in 5 to 7 quart (5 to 7 L) slow cooker.

Sprinkle with dill and pepper. Arrange meatballs over top.

Combine next 4 ingredients in medium bowl. Pour over meatballs. Cook, covered, on Low for 8 to 10 hours or on High for 4 to 5 hours.

*(continued on next page)*

Add peas. Stir. Cook, covered, on High for about 5 minutes until heated through. Serves 8.

*1 serving: 506 Calories; 22.8 g Total Fat (0.1 g Mono, 0.3 g Poly, 8.8 g Sat); 56 mg Cholesterol; 45 g Carbohydrate; 5 g Fibre; 29 g Protein; 1288 mg Sodium*

Pictured below.

Meatball Stew, page 70

*Sounds fancy, tastes like it too, but it's easy to prepare this delicious French stew! Coq is chicken, vin is wine—supper's ready—come, let's dine!*

## about cleaning mushrooms

Are you one of those people who actually peel their mushrooms? Stop wasting your time! Mushrooms are actually quite delicate and all they need is a gentle brushing to get them suitably clean. Only wash your mushrooms just before using them. You can use a special mushroom brush to gently remove any dirt and then quickly rinse under water to avoid waterlogging. Don't have a mushroom brush? A soft-bristled toothbrush works just as well.

# Coq Au Vin

| | | |
|---|---|---|
| Bacon slices, diced | 6 | 6 |
| All-purpose flour | 1/4 cup | 60 mL |
| Paprika | 1/4 tsp. | 1 mL |
| Boneless, skinless chicken thighs (about 3 oz., 85 g, each) | 12 | 12 |
| Halved fresh white mushrooms | 4 cups | 1 L |
| Chopped onion | 1 cup | 250 mL |
| Garlic clove, minced (or 1/4 tsp., 1 mL, powder) | 1 | 1 |
| Can of condensed cream of mushroom soup | 10 oz. | 284 mL |
| Dry (or alcohol-free) red wine | 1/2 cup | 125 mL |
| Prepared chicken broth | 1/2 cup | 125 mL |
| Bay leaves | 2 | 2 |
| Dried thyme | 1/2 tsp. | 2 mL |

Chopped fresh parsley, for garnish

Cook bacon in large frying pan on medium until crisp. Transfer with slotted spoon to paper towel-lined plate to drain. Set aside.

Heat 1 tbsp. (15 mL) drippings in same frying pan on medium. Combine flour and paprika in large resealable freezer bag. Add half of chicken. Seal bag. Toss until coated. Repeat with remaining chicken. Discard any remaining flour mixture. Add chicken to frying pan in 2 batches. Cook for 8 to 10 minutes per batch, turning occasionally, until browned. Transfer to 3 1/2 to 4 quart (3.5 to 4 L) slow cooker.

Add next 3 ingredients to same frying pan. Cook for about 2 minutes, scraping any brown bits from bottom of pan, until onion starts to soften.

Add next 5 ingredients and bacon. Heat and stir for about 2 minutes until mixture just starts to boil. Pour over chicken. Cook, covered, on Low for 7 to 8 hours or on High for 3 1/2 to 4 hours. Discard bay leaves. Transfer chicken mixture to serving platter.

Garnish with parsley. Serves 6.

*1 serving: 361 Calories; 18.2 g Total Fat (6.3 g Mono, 3.1 g Poly, 5.2 g Sat); 108 mg Cholesterol; 13 g Carbohydrate; 1 g Fibre; 31 g Protein; 694 mg Sodium*

Pictured at right.

*These succulent drumsticks are cooked in a deep, rich gravy that's great served over mashed potatoes.*

## Drumstick Bake

| | | |
|---|---|---|
| Chicken drumsticks, skin removed (3 – 5 oz., 85 – 140 g, each), see Note | 12 | 12 |
| Can of condensed cream of chicken soup | 10 oz. | 284 mL |
| Onion flakes | 2 tbsp. | 30 mL |
| Liquid gravy browner (optional) | 1/2 tsp. | 2 mL |

Arrange drumsticks in 3 1/2 to 4 quart (3.5 to 4 L) slow cooker.

Combine remaining 3 ingredients in small bowl. Pour over chicken. Cook, covered, on Low for 6 to 7 hours or on High for 3 to 3 1/2 hours. Serves 6.

*1 serving: 200 Calories; 7.0 g Total Fat (1.3 g Mono, 1.1 g Poly, 1.9 g Sat); 99 mg Cholesterol; 6 g Carbohydrate; trace Fibre; 27 g Protein; 446 mg Sodium*

**Note:** When removing skin from drumsticks, grasp it with a paper towel. This will give a good grip on the otherwise slippery skin.

*This tomato-based chicken and vegetable sauce is easy to prepare and always a great favourite. Serve over spaghetti and add crusty rolls on the side.*

## Chicken Cacciatore

| | | |
|---|---|---|
| Chopped onion | 1 1/2 cups | 375 mL |
| Chopped celery | 1 1/2 cups | 375 mL |
| Chopped green pepper | 1 1/2 cups | 375 mL |
| Boneless, skinless chicken breast halves, halved | 1 lb. | 454 g |
| Boneless, skinless chicken thighs | 1 lb. | 454 g |
| Can of crushed tomatoes | 14 oz. | 398 mL |
| Can of stewed tomatoes, chopped (see Note) | 14 oz. | 398 mL |
| Garlic cloves, minced (or 1/2 tsp., 2 mL, powder) | 2 | 2 |
| Dried oregano | 1 1/2 tsp. | 7 mL |
| Bay leaf | 1 | 1 |
| Dried basil | 1 tsp. | 5 mL |
| Dried rosemary, crushed | 1/2 tsp. | 2 mL |
| Granulated sugar | 1/2 tsp. | 2 mL |
| Salt | 1/2 tsp. | 2 mL |
| Pepper | 1/4 tsp. | 1 mL |

*(continued on next page)*

Layer first 5 ingredients, in order given, in 4 to 5 quart (4 to 5 L) slow cooker.

Combine next 10 ingredients in medium bowl. Pour over chicken. Cook, covered, on Low for 8 to 10 hours or on High for 4 to 5 hours. Discard bay leaf. Serves 8.

*1 serving: 202 Calories; 6.3 g Total Fat (2.3 g Mono, 1.5 g Poly, 1.7 g Sat); 70 mg Cholesterol; 12 g Carbohydrate; 2 g Fibre; 24 g Protein; 407 mg Sodium*

Pictured below.

**Note:** Cut tomatoes with a paring knife or kitchen shears while still in the can.

Chicken Cacciatore, page 74

*Got a ragin' Cajun hunger? With a pot of this hearty sausage and chicken stew, Mardi Gras is just a slow cooker away. Serve over rice.*

## food fun

Creole and Cajun food are two types of cuisine popular in Louisiana. Although they share some of the same ingredients, their origins are quite different. Creole and Cajun are not just types of cuisine, they also represent cultural heritage. A person who is Creole has a multi-racial heritage with African and Caribbean roots. A person who claims Cajun ancestry has ties to the French Acadians who originally settled in modern-day Nova Scotia and moved south. Although both groups relocated to Southern Louisiana, their origins are very different and their cooking is influenced by their original heritage and the local foodstuffs available in Louisiana.

# Cajun Chicken

| | | |
|---|---|---|
| Cooking oil | 2 tbsp. | 30 mL |
| Chopped onion | 1 1/2 cups | 375 mL |
| Chopped red pepper | 1 cup | 250 mL |
| Chopped celery | 1/3 cup | 75 mL |
| Garlic cloves, minced (or 1 tsp., 5 mL, powder) | 4 | 4 |
| All-purpose flour | 2 tbsp. | 30 mL |
| Sliced green onion | 1/3 cup | 75 mL |
| Lean kielbasa (or smoked ham) sausage ring, cut into 6 pieces and halved lengthwise | 10 oz. | 285 g |
| Boneless, skinless chicken thighs (about 3 oz., 85 g, each) | 10 | 10 |
| Bay leaf | 1 | 1 |
| Can of condensed chicken broth | 10 oz. | 284 mL |
| Chili sauce | 1/2 cup | 125 mL |
| Chili powder | 1 1/2 tsp. | 7 mL |
| Dried basil | 1/2 tsp. | 2 mL |
| Dried oregano | 1/2 tsp. | 2 mL |
| Ground thyme | 1/4 tsp. | 1 mL |
| Pepper | 1/4 tsp. | 1 mL |

Heat cooking oil in large frying pan on medium-high. Add next 4 ingredients. Cook for 3 to 4 minutes, stirring often, until onion is softened.

Sprinkle with flour. Heat and stir for 1 minute. Transfer to 4 to 5 quart (4 to 5 L) slow cooker.

Layer next 3 ingredients, in order given, over vegetable mixture. Add bay leaf.

Combine next 7 ingredients in same frying pan. Heat and stir on medium for 5 minutes, scraping any brown bits from bottom of pan. Pour over chicken. Cook, covered, on Low for 7 to 8 hours or on High for 3 1/2 to 4 hours. Serves 8.

*1 serving: 275 Calories; 13.8 g Total Fat (4.7 g Mono, 2.7 g Poly, 2.3 g Sat); 63 mg Cholesterol; 13 g Carbohydrate; 1 g Fibre; 24 g Protein; 1106 mg Sodium*

Pictured at right.

*Roll out the slow cooker, and we'll have a slow cooker of fun! OK, our polka may not be up to snuff, but these ham and chicken rolls, covered in Swiss cheese, are sure to put the oompahpah into your dinner.*

### about swiss cheese

Ever wondered what gives Swiss cheese its characteristic holes or "eyes?" During the fermentation process carbon dioxide is released, which creates the bubbles that later form the holes in the cheese. The Swiss cheese we are familiar with in North America is quite mild tasting because it is only aged for about four months. The real Swiss cheeses that hail from the land of neutrality, Emmenthal and Gruyère, although similar in colour, are aged longer and have a stronger flavour. All three cheeses melt well and are great in fondues.

## Stuffed Chicken Rolls

| | | |
|---|---|---|
| Boneless, skinless chicken breast halves (4 – 6 oz., 113 – 170 g, each) | 6 | 6 |
| Thin deli ham slices (about 4 oz., 113 g) | 6 | 6 |
| Dry (or alcohol-free) white wine | 1/2 cup | 125 mL |
| Hot water | 1/2 cup | 125 mL |
| Chicken bouillon powder | 2 tsp. | 10 mL |
| Dried marjoram | 1/2 tsp. | 2 mL |
| Salt | 1/2 tsp. | 2 mL |
| Pepper | 1/4 tsp. | 1 mL |
| Liquid gravy browner (optional) | 1 tsp. | 5 mL |
| Grated Swiss cheese | 1 cup | 250 mL |
| Water | 2 1/2 tbsp. | 37 mL |
| Cornstarch | 1 tbsp. | 15 mL |

Place chicken breasts between 2 sheets of plastic wrap. Pound with mallet or rolling pin to 1/2 inch (12 mm) thickness. Place 1 ham slice on each chicken breast. Roll up tightly, jelly roll-style. Secure with wooden picks. Arrange in 3 1/2 to 4 quart (3.5 to 4 L) slow cooker.

Combine next 7 ingredients in small bowl. Pour over rolls. Cook, covered, on Low for 8 to 9 hours or on High for 4 to 4 1/2 hours. Transfer rolls to serving dish using slotted spoon.

Sprinkle cheese over rolls. Cover to keep warm.

Stir water into cornstarch in small cup. Add to slow cooker. Stir. Cook, covered, on High for about 15 minutes until boiling and slightly thickened. Serve with rolls. Serves 6.

*1 serving: 414 Calories; 10.0 g Total Fat (1.1 g Mono, 1.0 g Poly, 4.5 g Sat); 182 mg Cholesterol; 3 g Carbohydrate; trace Fibre; 69 g Protein; 1057 mg Sodium*

Pictured at right.

# Chicken And Stuffing Meal

| | | |
|---|---|---|
| Baby carrots, sliced lengthwise | 1/2 lb. | 225 g |
| Baby potatoes, larger ones cut in half | 1 lb. | 454 g |
| Boneless, skinless chicken breast halves, cut into bite-sized pieces | 1 1/2 lbs. | 680 g |
| Can of condensed cream of chicken soup | 10 oz. | 284 mL |
| Frozen peas | 2 cups | 500 mL |
| Hot water | 1/2 cup | 125 mL |
| Butter (or hard margarine) | 2 tbsp. | 30 mL |
| Box of stove-top stuffing mix | 4 1/4 oz. | 120 g |

Layer first 3 ingredients, in order given, in 3 1/2 to 4 quart (3.5 to 4 L) slow cooker.

Whisk soup in small bowl until smooth. Add peas. Stir. Spoon over chicken.

Stir hot water and butter in medium heatproof bowl until butter is melted. Add stuffing mix and seasoning packet. Stir. Spoon over chicken mixture. Cook, covered, on Low for 8 to 9 hours or on High for 4 to 4 1/2 hours. Serves 6.

*1 serving:* 407 Calories; 10.9 g Total Fat (1.5 g Mono, 0.7 g Poly, 3.7 g Sat); 80 mg Cholesterol; 41 g Carbohydrate; 5 g Fibre; 34 g Protein; 828 mg Sodium

*Tender chicken and veggies with a creamy stuffing—the perfect Sunday night fare (made all the more perfect by its easy preparation).*

## tip

It is important to clean the cutting board and any utensils used to cut raw chicken or any other meat in hot, soapy water. This will prevent bacteria from spreading to other food.

Stuffed Chicken Rolls, page 78

*Strike up the band with these delicious savoury drumettes. Serve with fries on the side and call it a dinner well played.*

# Parmesan Chicken Drumettes

| | | |
|---|---|---|
| Plain yogurt | 3/4 cup | 175 mL |
| Chicken drumettes | 3 lbs. | 1.4 kg |
| (or split chicken wings, tips discarded) | | |
| Grated Parmesan cheese | 1 1/2 cups | 375 mL |
| Fine dry bread crumbs | 1/3 cup | 75 mL |
| Paprika | 1 1/2 tsp. | 7 mL |
| Parsley flakes | 1 1/2 tsp. | 7 mL |
| Seasoned salt | 1 1/2 tsp. | 7 mL |

Measure yogurt into extra-large bowl. Add chicken. Stir until coated.

Combine remaining 5 ingredients in large resealable freezer bag. Add 1/3 of chicken. Seal bag. Toss until coated. Repeat with remaining chicken. Put chicken into greased 3 1/2 to 4 quart (3.5 to 4 L) slow cooker. Discard any remaining yogurt and cheese mixture. Cook, covered, on Low for 8 to 9 hours or on High for 4 to 4 1/2 hours. Transfer chicken with slotted spoon to serving platter. Discard any remaining liquid in slow cooker. Makes about 24 drumettes (or 36 wing pieces).

*1 drumette: 159 Calories; 10.9 g Total Fat (3.7 g Mono, 2 g Poly, 3.5 g Sat); 48 mg Cholesterol; 1 g Carbohydrate; trace Fibre; 13 g Protein; 210 mg Sodium*

Pictured at right.

*A sure bet is that peanut butter will up the ante in this saucy chicken dish. Serve it over noodles, rice or couscous, and all the peanut lovers will cash in—big time!*

## about zucchini

Although a zucchini's outward appearance resembles a cucumber, the first is actually a squash, and the latter is a gourd. Zucchini's flowers, when cooked, are considered quite a delicacy. The zucchini is a favourite of gardeners because it does well in temperate climates and can grow to almost monstrous proportions—sometimes nearing three feet in length! However, outside the county fair, smaller zucchinis are preferable because they are more tender and less fibrous than larger ones. When storing zucchini, keep it in the crisper so it doesn't get too soft. And because zucchini has a high water content, it is not advisable to freeze it.

# Peanut Butter Chicken

| | | |
|---|---|---|
| Olive (or cooking) oil | 2 tsp. | 10 mL |
| Medium onions, sliced | 2 | 2 |
| Garlic cloves, minced (or 1/2 tsp., 2 mL, powder) | 2 | 2 |
| Baby carrots | 2 cups | 500 mL |
| Bone-in chicken parts, skin removed (see Note) | 3 1/2 lbs. | 1.6 kg |
| Can of tomato sauce | 7 1/2 oz. | 213 mL |
| Brown sugar, packed | 1 tbsp. | 15 mL |
| Curry powder | 1 tsp. | 5 mL |
| Peanut butter | 1/2 cup | 125 mL |
| Plain yogurt (not non-fat) | 1/2 cup | 125 mL |
| Olive (or cooking) oil | 2 tsp. | 10 mL |
| Medium zucchini (with peel), quartered lengthwise and cut crosswise into 3/4 inch (2 cm) slices | 2 | 2 |
| Coarsely chopped unsalted peanuts (optional) | 2 tbsp. | 30 mL |

Heat first amount of olive oil in large frying pan on medium. Add onion and garlic. Cook for about 10 minutes, stirring often, until onion is softened and starting to brown. Transfer to 3 1/2 to 4 quart (3.5 to 4 L) slow cooker.

Layer carrots and chicken, in order given, over onion mixture.

Combine next 3 ingredients in small bowl. Pour over chicken. Cook, covered, on Low for 7 to 8 hours or on High for 3 1/2 to 4 hours. Transfer chicken to serving dish using slotted spoon. Cover to keep warm.

Combine peanut butter and yogurt in small bowl. Add to slow cooker. Stir. Cook, covered, on Low for about 5 minutes until heated through.

Heat second amount of olive oil in large frying pan on medium-high. Add zucchini. Cook for about 5 minutes, stirring often, until starting to brown. Add to slow cooker. Stir. Pour over chicken.

Sprinkle with peanuts. Serves 6.

*(continued on next page)*

*1 serving:* 644 Calories; 32.6 g Total Fat (13.0 g Mono, 7.7 g Poly, 7.7 g Sat); 170 mg Cholesterol;
23 g Carbohydrate; 4 g Fibre; 65 g Protein; 474 mg Sodium

Pictured below.

**Note:** Use whichever cuts of chicken you prefer as long as the weight used
is equal to that listed.

*Mama mia! A proper parmigiana in a slow cooker? Sì, certo (yes, of course)! This dish is simple to prepare and simply superb to dine on.*

# Chicken Parmigiana

| | | |
|---|---|---|
| Medium eggplant (with peel), cut into 3/4 inch (2 cm) slices | 1 | 1 |
| Boneless, skinless chicken breast halves (4 – 6 oz., 113 – 170 g, each) | 6 | 6 |
| Cans of pizza sauce (7 1/2 oz., 213 mL, each) | 2 | 2 |
| Salt | 1 tsp. | 5 mL |
| Pepper | 1/4 tsp. | 1 mL |
| Grated part-skim mozzarella cheese | 1 1/2 cups | 375 mL |
| Grated Parmesan cheese | 1 tbsp. | 15 mL |

Layer eggplant and chicken, in order given, in 5 to 7 quart (5 to 7 L) slow cooker.

Combine next 3 ingredients in small bowl. Pour over chicken. Cook, covered, on Low for 6 to 7 hours or on High for 3 to 3 1/2 hours.

Sprinkle with mozzarella and Parmesan cheese. Cook, covered, on High for about 5 minutes until cheese is melted. Serves 6.

*1 serving: 552 Calories; 17.3 g Total Fat (5.6 g Mono, 4.1 g Poly, 5.2 g Sat); 159 mg Cholesterol; 12 g Carbohydrate; 5 g Fibre; 79 g Protein; 1140 mg Sodium*

Pictured at right.

*Rah, rah raspberry! Three cheers for this MVI (most valuable ingredient). Sweet yet tangy, all the stats agree— this dish is a sure winner! (Remember to allow plenty of time for the chicken to properly marinate.)*

# Raspberry Chicken

| | | |
|---|---|---|
| Raspberry jam | 1 cup | 250 mL |
| Dry (or alcohol-free) white wine | 2/3 cup | 150 mL |
| Raspberry red wine vinegar | 1/2 cup | 125 mL |
| Soy sauce | 2 tbsp. | 30 mL |
| Dijon mustard | 2 tsp. | 10 mL |
| Garlic cloves, minced (or 1/2 tsp., 2 mL, powder) | 2 | 2 |
| Chicken legs, back attached (11 – 12 oz., 310 – 340 g, each), skin removed | 8 | 8 |
| Water | 1/4 cup | 60 mL |
| Cornstarch | 2 tbsp. | 30 mL |
| Chopped fresh parsley, for garnish | | |

*(continued on next page)*

Combine first 6 ingredients in small bowl. Transfer to large resealable freezer bag.

Add chicken. Turn until coated. Let stand, covered, in refrigerator for at least 4 hours or overnight, turning occasionally. Transfer chicken with raspberry mixture to 4 to 5 quart (4 to 5 L) slow cooker. Cook, covered, on Low for 8 to 9 hours or on High for 4 to 4 1/2 hours. Transfer chicken to serving dish using slotted spoon. Skim and discard fat from surface of liquid in slow cooker.

Stir water into cornstarch in small cup. Add to slow cooker. Stir. Cook, covered, on High for about 5 minutes until boiling and thickened. Pour over chicken.

Garnish with parsley. Serves 8.

*1 serving: 265 Calories; 3.4 g Total Fat (1.1 g Mono, 0.9 g Poly, 0.9 g Sat); 108 mg Cholesterol; 29 g Carbohydrate; trace Fibre; 26 g Protein; 334 mg Sodium*

Pictured below.

Top: Raspberry Chicken, page 84
Bottom: Chicken Parmigiana, page 84

*Slow-simmered with a hint of smokiness from the bacon and a touch of tanginess from the sour cream, this tender chicken dish could be considered a delicious embarrassment of riches. Serve over potatoes or pasta.*

# Rich Chicken Stew

|  | | |
|---|---|---|
| Bacon slices, diced | 2 | 2 |
| Medium onion, sliced | 1 | 1 |
| Chopped fresh white mushrooms | 1 cup | 250 mL |
| All-purpose flour | 2 tbsp. | 30 mL |
| Diced carrot | 1 1/2 cups | 375 mL |
| Diced celery (with leaves) | 1 1/2 cups | 375 mL |
| Bone-in chicken parts, skin removed (see Note) | 3 lbs. | 1.4 kg |
| Can of condensed chicken broth | 10 oz. | 284 mL |
| Parsley flakes | 1 tbsp. | 15 mL |
| Dried sage | 1/2 tsp. | 2 mL |
| Dried thyme | 1/2 tsp. | 2 mL |
| Salt | 1/4 tsp. | 1 mL |
| Pepper | 1/4 tsp. | 1 mL |
| Sour cream | 2/3 cup | 150 mL |
| All-purpose flour | 2 tbsp. | 30 mL |

Cook bacon in large frying pan on medium-high until crisp. Add onion and mushrooms. Cook for 3 to 4 minutes, stirring often, until onion starts to brown.

Sprinkle with first amount of flour. Heat and stir for 1 minute. Transfer to 4 to 5 quart (4 to 5 L) slow cooker.

Layer next 3 ingredients, in order given, over mushroom mixture.

Combine next 6 ingredients in same frying pan. Heat and stir on medium for 5 minutes, scraping any brown bits from bottom of pan. Pour over chicken. Cook, covered, on Low for 7 to 8 hours or on High for 3 1/2 to 4 hours. Transfer chicken to serving dish using slotted spoon. Cover to keep warm.

Stir sour cream into second amount of flour in small bowl until smooth. Add to slow cooker. Stir. Cook, covered, on High for about 5 minutes until slightly thickened. Pour over chicken. Serves 6.

*1 serving: 405 Calories; 15.5 g Total Fat (5.8 g Mono, 2.6 g Poly, 6.6 g Sat); 177 mg Cholesterol; 12 g Carbohydrate; 2 g Fibre; 52 g Protein; 685 mg Sodium*

**Note:** Use whichever cuts of chicken you prefer as long as the weight used is equal to that listed.

# Orange Chicken

| | | |
|---|---|---|
| Hot water | 1/4 cup | 60 mL |
| Chicken bouillon powder | 1 tsp. | 5 mL |
| Reserved mandarin orange juice | | |
| | | |
| Orange juice | 1 cup | 250 mL |
| Finely chopped fresh rosemary | 2 tsp. | 10 mL |
|    (or 1/2 tsp., 2 mL, dried, crushed) | | |
| Lemon pepper | 1 tsp. | 5 mL |
| Paprika | 1/2 tsp. | 2 mL |
| Salt (optional) | 1/4 tsp. | 1 mL |
| | | |
| Bone-in chicken parts, skin removed | 3 lbs. | 1.4 kg |
|    (see Note) | | |
| | | |
| Water | 2 tbsp. | 30 mL |
| Cornstarch | 2 tbsp. | 30 mL |
| | | |
| Can of mandarin orange segments, | 10 oz. | 284 mL |
|    drained and juice reserved | | |

Chopped fresh rosemary, for garnish

Stir hot water into bouillon powder in small bowl until dissolved. Add mandarin orange juice.

Add next 5 ingredients. Stir. Transfer to 3 1/2 quart (3.5 L) slow cooker.

Add chicken, pressing into juice mixture. Cook, covered, on Low for 7 to 8 hours or on High for 3 1/2 to 4 hours.

Stir water into cornstarch in small bowl. Add to slow cooker. Stir. Cook, covered, on High for about 15 minutes until boiling and thickened.

Add orange segments. Stir gently.

Garnish with rosemary. Serves 4.

*1 serving: 477 Calories; 10.8 g Total Fat (3.1 g Mono, 2.6 g Poly, 2.7 g Sat); 238 mg Cholesterol; 17 g Carbohydrate; 1 g Fibre; 74 g Protein; 637 mg Sodium*

Pictured on page 89.

**Note:** Use whichever cuts of chicken you prefer as long as the weight used is equal to that listed.

*A guaranteed hit with the kids, this dish has no onions or green bits, but plenty of sweet orange pieces. Even adults will love the succulent citrus flavour. Serve over rice.*

*Cardamom and cinnamon unite with a variety of spices to produce a spicy, yet subtly sweet taste reminiscent of many Moroccan dishes. Serve over rice or couscous.*

# Moroccan Chicken

| | | |
|---|---|---|
| Cooking oil | 2 tsp. | 10 mL |
| Thinly sliced onion | 2 cups | 500 mL |
| Garlic cloves, minced | 2 | 2 |
| (or 1/2 tsp., 2 mL, powder) | | |
| Finely grated gingerroot | 1/2 tsp. | 2 mL |
| Chili powder | 1/2 tsp. | 2 mL |
| Ground coriander | 1/2 tsp. | 2 mL |
| Ground cumin | 1/2 tsp. | 2 mL |
| Boneless, skinless chicken thighs, halved | 1 lb. | 454 g |
| Dry white wine (or prepared chicken broth) | 1/2 cup | 125 mL |
| Liquid honey | 2 tbsp. | 30 mL |
| Cinnamon stick (4 inches, 10 cm) | 1 | 1 |
| Whole green cardamom, bruised | 6 | 6 |
| (see Tip), or 1/4 tsp. (1 mL) ground | | |
| Salt, sprinkle | | |
| Orange juice | 1/4 cup | 60 mL |
| Cornstarch | 2 tsp. | 10 mL |
| Slivered almonds, toasted | 3 tbsp. | 50 mL |
| (see Tip), optional | | |

Heat cooking oil in large frying pan on medium. Add next 3 ingredients. Cook for 5 to 10 minutes, stirring often, until onion is softened and starting to brown.

Add next 3 ingredients. Heat and stir for 1 to 2 minutes until fragrant. Transfer to 3 1/2 quart (3.5 L) slow cooker.

Add next 6 ingredients. Stir. Cook, covered, on Low for 7 to 8 hours or on High for 3 1/2 to 4 hours.

Stir orange juice into cornstarch in small bowl. Add to slow cooker. Stir. Cook, covered, on High for about 15 minutes until boiling and thickened. Remove and discard cinnamon stick and cardamom pods.

Sprinkle with almonds. Serves 4.

*1 serving: 288 Calories; 11.0 g Total Fat (4.6 g Mono, 2.7 g Poly, 2.6 g Sat); 74 mg Cholesterol; 20 g Carbohydrate; 1 g Fibre; 21 g Protein; 77 mg Sodium*

Pictured at right.

Top: Orange Chicken, page 87
Bottom: Moroccan Chicken, above

*Free up some time in your evening—make dinner in the morning instead! This delicious sauce cooks while you're out and about. Put some pasta on when you get home and dinner's on the table in minutes!*

# Mushroom Chicken Sauce

| | | |
|---|---|---|
| Bacon slices, diced | 6 | 6 |
| Cooking oil | 1 tbsp. | 15 mL |
| Chopped onion | 1 cup | 250 mL |
| Sliced fresh white mushrooms | 3 cups | 750 mL |
| Garlic cloves, minced (or 1/2 tsp., 2 mL, powder) | 2 | 2 |
| Paprika | 1 tsp. | 5 mL |
| All-purpose flour | 3 tbsp. | 50 mL |
| Salt | 1/4 tsp. | 1 mL |
| Pepper | 1/4 tsp. | 1 mL |
| Boneless, skinless chicken thighs, cut into 3/4 inch (2 cm) cubes | 1 1/2 lbs. | 680 g |
| Dry (or alcohol-free) white wine | 1/2 cup | 125 mL |
| Prepared chicken broth | 1/2 cup | 125 mL |
| Frozen peas | 1/2 cup | 125 mL |
| Chopped fresh parsley (or 1 tbsp., 15 mL, flakes) | 1/4 cup | 60 mL |
| Sour cream | 1/4 cup | 60 mL |

Cook bacon in large frying pan on medium for about 5 minutes until almost crisp. Transfer with slotted spoon to paper towel-lined plate to drain. Drain and discard drippings from pan.

Heat cooking oil in same frying pan on medium. Add onion. Cook for 5 to 10 minutes, stirring often, until softened.

Add next 3 ingredients. Cook for about 5 minutes, stirring occasionally, until mushrooms are softened. Add bacon. Stir. Spread evenly in 3 1/2 quart (3.5 L) slow cooker.

Combine next 3 ingredients in large resealable freezer bag. Add chicken. Seal bag. Toss until coated. Arrange chicken over mushroom mixture. Discard any remaining flour mixture.

Pour wine and broth over chicken. Cook, covered, on Low for 8 to 9 hours or on High for 4 to 4 1/2 hours.

*(continued on next page)*

Add remaining 3 ingredients. Stir. Cook, covered, on High for about 10 minutes until heated through. Makes about 5 1/4 cups (1.3 L).

*1 cup (250 mL): 333 Calories; 17.7 g Total Fat (7.2 g Mono, 3.5 g Poly, 5.2 g Sat); 98 mg Cholesterol; 10 g Carbohydrate; 1 g Fibre; 29 g Protein; 526 mg Sodium*

# Curious Chicken Chili

| | | |
|---|---|---|
| Cooking oil | 2 tsp. | 10 mL |
| Boneless, skinless chicken thighs,<br>    cut into 1/2 inch (12 mm) pieces | 1 lb. | 454 g |
| Chopped onion | 1 1/2 cups | 375 mL |
| Chopped green pepper | 1 cup | 250 mL |
| Diced jalapeño pepper (see Tip) | 1 tbsp. | 15 mL |
| Garlic cloves, minced<br>    (or 1/2 tsp., 2 mL, powder) | 2 | 2 |
| Salt | 1 tsp. | 5 mL |
| Can of diced tomatoes (with juice) | 14 oz. | 398 mL |
| Can of pineapple chunks (with juice) | 14 oz. | 398 mL |
| Can of red kidney beans, rinsed and drained | 14 oz. | 398 mL |
| Hot (or cold) strong prepared coffee | 1 cup | 250 mL |
| Can of diced green chilies | 4 oz. | 113 g |
| Tomato paste (see Tip) | 3 tbsp. | 50 mL |
| Chili powder | 2 tbsp. | 30 mL |
| Semi-sweet chocolate baking square<br>    (1 oz., 28 g), grated | 1 | 1 |
| Ground cumin | 1 tsp. | 5 mL |

Heat cooking oil in large frying pan on medium-high. Add chicken. Cook for about 5 minutes, stirring often, until browned.

Add next 5 ingredients. Cook for about 5 minutes, stirring often, until onion starts to soften. Transfer to 3 1/2 to 4 quart (3.5 to 4 L) slow cooker.

Add remaining 9 ingredients. Stir. Cook, covered, on Low for 4 hours or on High for 2 hours. Makes about 8 cups (2 L).

*1 cup (250 mL): 349 Calories; 7.5 g Total Fat (2.4 g Mono, 1.8 g Poly, 2.1 g Sat); 37 mg Cholesterol; 50 g Carbohydrate; 10 g Fibre; 23 g Protein; 516 mg Sodium*

Pictured on page 93.

*Curious as to why this chili is such a curiosity? It's all in the ingredients—coffee, chocolate, jalapeño and pineapple. This is a chili you just have to taste. Go ahead, we know you want to.*

### tip

If a recipe calls for less than an entire can of tomato paste, freeze the unopened can for 30 minutes. Open both ends and push the contents through one end. Slice off only what you need and freeze the remaining paste in a resealable freezer bag or plastic wrap for future use.

### tip

Hot peppers contain capsaicin in the seeds and ribs. If you like less spice in your food, removing the seeds and ribs will reduce the heat. Wear rubber gloves when handling hot peppers and avoid touching your eyes—and always wash your hands well afterwards.

*Get ready to wow the crowd with these beautiful bright red peppers stuffed with black beans, corn, chicken and couscous.*

# Corn And Bean-Stuffed Peppers

| | | |
|---|---|---|
| Large red peppers | 6 | 6 |
| Long grain white (or brown) rice | 1/4 cup | 60 mL |
| Cooking oil | 1 tsp. | 5 mL |
| Lean ground chicken | 3/4 lb. | 340 g |
| Canned black beans, rinsed and drained | 1 cup | 250 mL |
| Frozen kernel corn | 1 cup | 250 mL |
| Sliced green onion | 1/4 cup | 60 mL |
| Garlic clove, minced | 1 | 1 |
| (or 1/4 tsp., 1 mL, powder), optional | | |
| Seasoned salt | 1/2 tsp. | 2 mL |
| Dried basil | 1/4 tsp. | 1 mL |
| Dried oregano | 1/4 tsp. | 1 mL |
| Pepper | 1/4 tsp. | 1 mL |
| Can of diced tomatoes (with juice) | 14 oz. | 398 mL |
| Couscous, approximately | 2/3 cup | 150 mL |
| Chopped fresh parsley (or cilantro), for garnish | | |

Trim 1/4 inch (6 mm) slice from top of each red pepper. Remove and discard seeds and ribs. Sprinkle 2 tsp. (10 mL) rice into each red pepper. Place red peppers upright in 5 to 7 quart (5 to 7 L) slow cooker.

Heat cooking oil in large frying pan on medium-high. Add chicken. Scramble-fry for about 5 minutes until no longer pink. Remove from heat.

Add next 8 ingredients. Stir. Spoon into red peppers.

Pour tomatoes with juice over red peppers. Cook, covered, on Low for 5 hours or on High for 2 1/2 hours. Transfer red peppers to serving dish. Cover to keep warm.

Pour liquid from slow cooker into 2 cup (500 mL) liquid measure. Add equal amount of couscous to liquid. Stir. Let stand, covered, for about 5 minutes until liquid is absorbed. Spoon couscous into red peppers.

Garnish with parsley. Serves 6.

*1 serving: 312 Calories; 8.4 g Total Fat (trace Mono, 0.3 g Poly, 0.1 g Sat); 0 mg Cholesterol; 45 g Carbohydrate; 7 g Fibre; 17 g Protein; 512 mg Sodium*

Pictured at right.

Top: Corn And Bean-Stuffed Peppers, page 92
Bottom: Curious Chicken Chili, page 91

*Got a hankerin' for some good
old southwestern sandwich flavour?
Then, yee doggies, this is the meal
for you! Sweet and tangy with an
authentic taste.*

# Pulled Tex Turkey

| | | |
|---|---|---|
| Sliced onion | 1 1/2 cups | 375 mL |
| Barbecue sauce | 1 cup | 250 mL |
| Can of tomato sauce | 7 1/2 oz. | 213 mL |
| Can of diced green chilies | 4 oz. | 113 g |
| Chili powder | 1 tbsp. | 15 mL |
| Dried oregano | 1 tsp. | 5 mL |
| Ground cumin | 1/2 tsp. | 2 mL |
| Ground cinnamon | 1/4 tsp. | 1 mL |
| Boneless, skinless turkey thighs | 1 3/4 lbs. | 790 g |
| Kaiser rolls, split (toasted, optional) | 6 | 6 |

Combine first 8 ingredients in 3 1/2 to 4 quart (3.5 to 4 L) slow cooker.
Add turkey. Spoon barbecue sauce mixture over turkey to cover. Cook,
covered, on Low for 7 to 8 hours or on High for 3 1/2 to 4 hours. Remove
turkey to cutting board using tongs. Shred turkey using 2 forks. Add to sauce
mixture. Stir. Makes about 4 cups (1 L) turkey mixture.

Serve turkey mixture in rolls. Makes 6 sandwiches.

*1 sandwich: 534 Calories; 22.5 g Total Fat (1.0 g Mono, 1.4 g Poly, 6.9 g Sat); 126 mg Cholesterol;
44 g Carbohydrate; 5 g Fibre; 39 g Protein; 981 mg Sodium*

*We're not full of beans but this
delicious, mildly curry-flavoured delight
has four kinds of them—and some
peaches for good measure!*

# Full-Of-Beans Turkey Pot

| | | |
|---|---|---|
| Cans of sliced peaches in light syrup (with syrup), 14 oz. (398 mL) each | 2 | 2 |
| Boneless, skinless turkey thighs, cut into 1 inch (2.5 cm) pieces | 1 1/2 lbs. | 680 g |
| Can of black beans, rinsed and drained | 19 oz. | 540 mL |
| Can of red kidney beans, rinsed and drained | 19 oz. | 540 mL |
| Can of white kidney beans, rinsed and drained | 19 oz. | 540 mL |
| Can of baked beans in tomato sauce | 14 oz. | 398 mL |
| Chopped green pepper | 1 cup | 250 mL |
| Chopped onion | 1 cup | 250 mL |
| Sweet (or regular) chili sauce | 1/2 cup | 125 mL |
| Curry powder | 1 tsp. | 5 mL |

*(continued on next page)*

Combine all 10 ingredients in 4 to 5 quart (4 to 5 L) slow cooker. Cook, covered, on Low for 8 to 10 hours or on High for 4 to 5 hours. Makes about 12 cups (3 L).

*1 cup (250 mL): 329 Calories; 8.9 g Total Fat (trace Mono, trace Poly, 2.7 g Sat); 54 mg Cholesterol; 43 g Carbohydrate; 11 g Fibre; 22 g Protein; 678 mg Sodium*

Pictured below.

Full-Of-Beans Turkey Pot, page 94

*Take turkey back from the holidays and start making it weekday fare. This turkey roast cooks up juicy and tender in the slow cooker. And the leftovers make amazing sandwiches.*

## about cleaning slow cookers

Keeping your cooker clean is always very important. Any missed debris may become baked on the next time you use it and can be almost impossible to remove. Some slow cookers come with removable liners that can be popped directly into the sink or dishwasher. Or you can line your slow cooker with a heatproof plastic cooking bag for speedy cleanups when pressed for time. And need we say it? Never submerge the electric components of your slow cooker!

# Turkey Roast Supreme

| | | |
|---|---|---|
| Baby carrots | 2 cups | 500 mL |
| Sliced celery | 1 2/3 cups | 400 mL |
| Olive (or cooking) oil | 1 tbsp. | 15 mL |
| Sliced onion | 1 1/2 cups | 375 mL |
| Garlic cloves, minced (or 1/2 tsp., 2 mL, powder) | 2 | 2 |
| Olive (or cooking) oil | 1 tsp. | 5 mL |
| Paprika | 1 tsp. | 5 mL |
| Pepper | 1 tsp. | 5 mL |
| Turkey breast roast | 2 1/2 lbs. | 1.1 kg |
| Prepared chicken broth | 1 cup | 250 mL |
| Italian no-salt seasoning | 2 tsp. | 10 mL |
| Evaporated milk | 3/4 cup | 175 mL |
| All-purpose flour | 2 tbsp. | 30 mL |

Layer carrots and celery, in order given, in 3 1/2 to 4 quart (3.5 to 4 L) slow cooker.

Heat first amount of olive oil in large frying pan on medium. Add onion. Cook for about 10 minutes, stirring often, until onion is softened and starting to brown. Add to slow cooker.

Combine next 4 ingredients in small dish.

Rub spice mixture on roast. Place over onion in slow cooker.

Pour broth around roast. Sprinkle with seasoning. Cook, covered, on Low for 7 to 8 hours or on High for 3 1/2 to 4 hours. Transfer roast to cutting board. Cover with foil. Let stand for 10 minutes.

Stir evaporated milk into flour in small bowl until smooth. Add to slow cooker. Stir. Cook, covered, on High for about 15 minutes until boiling and slightly thickened. Cut roast into thin slices. Arrange on serving platter. Spoon vegetables and sauce over top. Serves 8.

*1 serving: 249 Calories; 4.2 g Total Fat (2.1 g Mono, 0.7 g Poly, 1.0 g Sat); 90 mg Cholesterol; 13 g Carbohydrate; 2 g Fibre; 38 g Protein; 323 mg Sodium*

Pictured at right.

*You don't need meat for a rich hearty stew. The firm, meaty texture of eggplant acts as a satisfying meat replacement in this veggie-laden dish.*

# Ratatouille

| | | |
|---|---|---|
| Sliced zucchini (with peel), 1/4 inch (6 mm) thick | 3 cups | 750 mL |
| Small eggplant (with peel), cut into 1/2 inch (12 mm) cubes | 1 | 1 |
| Can of diced tomatoes (with juice) | 14 oz. | 398 mL |
| Chopped celery | 1 cup | 250 mL |
| Finely chopped onion | 1 cup | 250 mL |
| Medium green (or red) pepper, chopped | 1 | 1 |
| Ketchup | 1/4 cup | 60 mL |
| Granulated sugar | 2 tsp. | 10 mL |
| Parsley flakes | 1 tsp. | 5 mL |
| Dried basil | 1/2 tsp. | 2 mL |
| Dried oregano | 1/2 tsp. | 2 mL |
| Garlic powder | 1/4 tsp. | 1 mL |
| Salt | 1/2 tsp. | 2 mL |
| Pepper | 1/8 tsp. | 0.5 mL |

Combine all 14 ingredients in 3 1/2 to 4 quart (3.5 to 4 L) slow cooker. Cook, covered, on Low for 8 to 9 hours or on High for 4 to 4 1/2 hours. Makes about 6 1/2 cups (1.6 L).

*1 cup (250 mL): 72 Calories; 0.4 g Total Fat (trace Mono, 0.2 g Poly, 0.1 g Sat); 0 mg Cholesterol; 17 g Carbohydrate; 5 g Fibre; 3 g Protein; 480 mg Sodium*

Pictured on page 101.

*The enticing Italian flavour in this subtly spiced, meatless stew makes it particularly pleasing—and the dumplings finish it off perfectly!*

# Squash And Dumplings

| | | |
|---|---|---|
| Cans of Italian-style stewed tomatoes (14 oz., 398 mL, each) | 2 | 2 |
| Can of mixed beans, rinsed and drained | 19 oz. | 540 mL |
| Small fresh whole white mushrooms, halved | 2 cups | 500 mL |
| Butternut squash, cut into 1/2 inch (12 mm) pieces (see Tip, page 99) | 3/4 lb. | 340 g |
| Water | 1 cup | 250 mL |
| Garlic cloves, minced (or 1/2 tsp., 2 mL, powder) | 2 | 2 |
| Italian seasoning | 2 tsp. | 10 mL |
| Pepper | 1/4 tsp. | 1 mL |

*(continued on next page)*

**DUMPLINGS**

| | | |
|---|---|---|
| All-purpose flour | 1/2 cup | 125 mL |
| Yellow cornmeal | 1/3 cup | 75 mL |
| Grated Parmesan cheese | 2 tbsp. | 30 mL |
| Baking powder | 1 tsp. | 5 mL |
| Paprika | 1/8 tsp. | 0.5 mL |
| Large egg | 1 | 1 |
| Cooking oil | 2 tbsp. | 30 mL |
| Milk | 2 tbsp. | 30 mL |
| Basil pesto | 1 tsp. | 5 mL |

tip

Some people have an allergic reaction to raw squash flesh, so wear rubber gloves when cutting or handling raw butternut squash or acorn squash.

Combine first 8 ingredients in 4 to 5 quart (4 to 5 L) slow cooker. Cook, covered, on Low for 8 to 9 hours or on High for 4 to 4 1/2 hours. Bring to a boil on High.

**Dumplings:** Measure first 5 ingredients into medium bowl. Stir. Make a well in centre.

Beat remaining 4 ingredients with fork in small bowl. Add to well. Stir until just moistened. Spoon mounds of batter, using 2 tbsp. (30 mL) for each, in single layer over squash mixture. Cook, covered, on High for 40 to 50 minutes until wooden pick inserted in centre of dumpling comes out clean. Serves 6.

*1 serving: 271 Calories; 7.0 g Total Fat (3.2 g Mono, 1.7 g Poly, 1.0 g Sat); 33 mg Cholesterol; 43 g Carbohydrate; 8 g Fibre; 11 g Protein; 506 mg Sodium*

Pictured below.

Squash And Dumplings, page 98

*This mellow yellow dish gets its colour from curry powder and its distinctive flavour from ginger and coconut milk. The mellow part? That's you getting a little R 'n' R while it cooks!*

## about slow cooker cookery

Don't assume that just any recipe can go in the slow cooker. Liquids will never reach a full boil in the slow cooker and any ground meat needs to be browned before going in for safety reasons. Also, you need to consider that some vegetables will cook faster than others and may end up soggy if put in too early. To take advantage of the ease of the slow cooker, it's best to use recipes that are specially designed for them.

# Vegetable Curry

| | | |
|---|---|---|
| Can of coconut milk | 14 oz. | 398 mL |
| All-purpose flour | 1 1/2 tbsp. | 25 mL |
| Curry powder | 2 tsp. | 10 mL |
| Cauliflower florets | 3 cups | 750 mL |
| Chopped peeled potato | 3 cups | 750 mL |
| Can of chickpeas (garbanzo beans), rinsed and drained | 19 oz. | 540 mL |
| Chopped carrot | 2 cups | 500 mL |
| Chopped onion | 1 2/3 cups | 400 mL |
| Finely grated gingerroot | 1 tbsp. | 15 mL |
| Garlic cloves, minced (or 1/2 tsp., 2 mL, powder) | 2 | 2 |
| Salt | 1 tsp. | 5 mL |
| Frozen peas | 1/2 cup | 125 mL |

Whisk first 3 ingredients in small bowl until smooth.

Put next 8 ingredients in 5 to 7 quart (5 to 7 L) slow cooker. Add coconut milk mixture. Stir. Cook, covered, on Low for 7 to 8 hours or on High for 3 1/2 to 4 hours.

Add peas. Stir gently. Cook, covered, on High for about 5 minutes until heated through. Makes about 8 1/2 cups (2.1 L).

*1 cup (250 mL): 258 Calories; 11.4 g Total Fat (0.7 g Mono, 0.8 g Poly, 8.9 g Sat); 0 mg Cholesterol; 35 g Carbohydrate; 8 g Fibre; 8 g Protein; 403 mg Sodium*

Pictured at right.

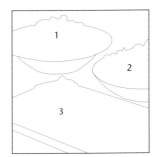

1. Ratatouille, page 98
2. Vegetable Curry, above
3. Lentil Rice Rolls, page 104

*Serve this spicy bean treat with tortilla chips, salsa and sour cream on the side for your own flavour fiesta.*

## tip

Chipotle chili peppers are smoked jalapeño peppers so, just as with fresh jalapeños, be sure to wash your hands after handling.
To store any leftover chipotle chili peppers, divide into recipe-friendly portions and freeze, with sauce, in airtight containers for up to one year.

## easy burritos

Turn Spicy Beans And Rice into super-simple burritos by spooning about 1/2 cup (125 mL) of Spicy Beans And Rice down the centre of each of 8 flour tortillas (9 inch, 22 cm, diameter). Add chopped or torn lettuce, sour cream, salsa, grated Cheddar cheese and chopped tomato. Fold in sides and roll up from the bottoms to enclose filling.

Pictured at right.

# Spicy Beans And Rice

|  | | |
|---|---|---|
| Can of red kidney beans, rinsed and drained | 19 oz. | 540 mL |
| Prepared vegetable broth | 1 1/4 cups | 300 mL |
| Chopped onion | 1 cup | 250 mL |
| Chopped red pepper | 1 cup | 250 mL |
| Chopped tomato | 1 cup | 250 mL |
| Chopped celery | 1/2 cup | 125 mL |
| Chili powder | 1 tsp. | 5 mL |
| Chopped chipotle pepper in adobo sauce (see Tip) | 1 tsp. | 5 mL |
| Dried oregano | 1 tsp. | 5 mL |
| Salt | 1/2 tsp. | 2 mL |
| Pepper | 1/4 tsp. | 1 mL |
| Converted white rice | 1/2 cup | 125 mL |
| Chopped green onion | 1/3 cup | 75 mL |
| Chopped fresh parsley (or 1 1/2 tsp., 7 mL, flakes) | 2 tbsp. | 30 mL |
| Lime juice | 1 tbsp. | 15 mL |

Combine first 11 ingredients in 3 1/2 quart (3.5 L) slow cooker. Cook, covered, on Low for 7 to 8 hours or on High for 3 1/2 to 4 hours.

Add rice. Stir. Cook, covered, on High for about 30 minutes until rice is tender.

Add remaining 3 ingredients. Stir gently. Makes about 4 cups (1 L).

*1 cup (250 mL): 238 Calories; 1.3 g Total Fat (0.1 g Mono, 0.2 g Poly, 0.1 g Sat); 0 mg Cholesterol; 46 g Carbohydrate; 15 g Fibre; 12 g Protein; 466 mg Sodium*

Pictured at right.

Left: Easy Burritos, this page
Top Right: Spicy Beans And Rice, above

*These ravishing roll-ups get exotic with lentils and a hint of sweetness from raisins, brown sugar and cinnamon.*

## tip

When a recipe calls for grated lemon zest and juice, it's easier to grate the lemon first, then juice it. Be careful not to grate down to the pith (the white part of the peel), which is bitter and best avoided.

# Lentil Rice Rolls

| | | |
|---|---|---|
| Medium head of green cabbage (about 3 lbs., 1.4 kg) | 1 | 1 |
| Boiling water, to cover | | |
| Can of lentils, rinsed and drained | 19 oz. | 540 mL |
| Can of tomato sauce | 7 1/2 oz. | 213 mL |
| Finely chopped carrot | 1/2 cup | 125 mL |
| Finely chopped celery | 1/2 cup | 125 mL |
| Finely chopped onion | 1/2 cup | 125 mL |
| Long grain brown (or white) rice | 1/2 cup | 125 mL |
| Garlic clove, minced (or 1/4 tsp., 1 mL, powder) | 1 | 1 |
| Dried oregano | 1/2 tsp. | 2 mL |
| Can of tomato sauce | 25 oz. | 680 mL |
| Raisins | 1/4 cup | 60 mL |
| Lemon juice | 3 tbsp. | 50 mL |
| Brown sugar, packed | 2 tbsp. | 30 mL |
| Grated lemon zest (see Tip) | 2 tsp. | 10 mL |
| Ground cinnamon | 1/2 tsp. | 2 mL |

Remove core from cabbage. Trim about 1/2 inch (12 mm) slice from bottom. Place, cut-side down, in Dutch oven or large pot. Cover with boiling water. Cover Dutch oven with foil. Let stand for 5 minutes. Drain. Let stand until cool enough to handle. Carefully remove 10 large outer leaves from cabbage. Cut 'V' shape along tough ribs of leaves to remove. Discard ribs. Set leaves aside. Shred remaining cabbage. Put into 5 to 7 quart (5 to 7 L) slow cooker.

Combine next 8 ingredients in large bowl. Place about 1/3 cup (75 mL) lentil mixture on centre of 1 cabbage leaf. Fold in sides. Roll up tightly from bottom to enclose filling. Repeat with remaining lentil mixture and cabbage leaves.

Combine remaining 6 ingredients in medium bowl. Add 1 1/2 cups (375 mL) to slow cooker. Stir. Spread evenly. Arrange rolls, seam-side down, over top. Pour remaining tomato sauce mixture over rolls. Cook, covered, on Low for 8 to 10 hours or on High for 4 to 5 hours. Carefully transfer rolls to plate. Transfer cabbage mixture to large serving platter. Arrange rolls over top. Makes 10 rolls.

*1 roll: 176 Calories; 0.5 g Total Fat (0.1 g Mono, 0.2 g Poly, 0.1 g Sat); 0 mg Cholesterol; 37 g Carbohydrate; 9 g Fibre; 7 g Protein; 664 mg Sodium*

Pictured on page 101.

# Chili Black Beans

| | | |
|---|---|---|
| Cans of black beans (19 oz., 540 mL, each), rinsed and drained | 2 | 2 |
| Chopped butternut squash (see Tip, page 99) | 2 cups | 500 mL |
| Can of diced tomatoes (with juice) | 14 oz. | 398 mL |
| Chopped onion | 1 1/2 cups | 375 mL |
| Prepared vegetable broth | 1/2 cup | 125 mL |
| Finely chopped fresh jalapeño pepper (with seeds), see Tip | 2 tbsp. | 30 mL |
| Chili powder | 1 tbsp. | 15 mL |
| Bay leaves | 2 | 2 |
| Garlic cloves, minced (or 1/2 tsp., 2 mL, powder) | 2 | 2 |
| Salt | 1/4 tsp. | 1 mL |
| Chopped green pepper | 1 cup | 250 mL |

Combine first 10 ingredients in 3 1/2 to 4 quart (3.5 to 4 L) slow cooker. Cook, covered, on Low for 8 to 10 hours or on High for 4 to 5 hours.

Add green pepper. Stir gently. Cook, covered, on High for about 20 minutes until green pepper is tender-crisp. Discard bay leaves. Makes about 6 cups (1.5 L).

*1 cup (250 mL): 176 Calories; 0.4 g Total Fat (0.1 g Mono, 0.2 g Poly, 0.1 g Sat); 0 mg Cholesterol; 43 g Carbohydrate; 12 g Fibre; 9 g Protein; 1070 mg Sodium*

Pictured below.

*Bean looking for a great vegetarian entrée? Look no further—this spicy blend of beans and veggies is sure to win over even the most dedicated meat lover. Top with sour cream, salsa or green onion, if you desire.*

### tip

Hot peppers contain capsaicin in the seeds and ribs. If you like less spice in your food, removing the seeds and ribs will reduce the heat. Wear rubber gloves when handling hot peppers and avoid touching your eyes—and always wash your hands well afterwards.

*This big-batch delight of tender pork in a sweet orange sauce makes enough for a crowd of eight.*

# Pork With Orange Sauce

| | | |
|---|---|---|
| Apricot jam, warmed | 1/4 cup | 60 mL |
| Dijon mustard (with whole seeds) | 2 tbsp. | 30 mL |
| Salt, sprinkle | | |
| Pepper, sprinkle | | |
| Pork sirloin (or boneless loin) roast | 3 lbs. | 1.4 kg |
| ORANGE SAUCE | | |
| Hard margarine (or butter) | 1 tsp. | 5 mL |
| Finely chopped onion | 1/4 cup | 60 mL |
| Brandy (or 1 tsp., 5 mL, brandy extract) | 3 tbsp. | 50 mL |
| Orange juice | 1 cup | 250 mL |
| Prepared chicken broth | 1 cup | 250 mL |
| Dijon mustard (with whole seeds) | 1 tbsp. | 15 mL |
| Water | 1 tbsp. | 15 mL |
| Cornstarch | 2 tsp. | 10 mL |

Combine first 4 ingredients in small cup.

Brush jam mixture over roast. Place in 4 to 5 quart (4 to 5 L) slow cooker. Cook, covered, on Low for 8 hours or on High for 4 hours. Transfer roast to cutting board. Cover with foil. Let stand for 10 minutes.

**Orange Sauce:** Melt margarine in medium saucepan on medium. Add onion. Cook for 5 to 10 minutes, stirring often, until softened and starting to brown.

Add brandy. Heat and stir for about 2 minutes until liquid is almost evaporated.

Add next 3 ingredients. Stir. Bring to a boil on medium-high. Boil, uncovered, for about 5 minutes until slightly reduced. Reduce heat to medium.

Stir water into cornstarch in small cup. Add to orange juice mixture. Heat and stir for about 5 minutes until boiling and thickened. Makes about 1 1/3 cups (325 mL) sauce. Cut roast into thin slices. Serve with Orange Sauce. Serves 8.

*1 serving: 316 Calories; 11.9 g Total Fat (5.2 g Mono, 1.3 g Poly, 3.8 g Sat); 109 mg Cholesterol; 12 g Carbohydrate; trace Fibre; 36 g Protein; 396 mg Sodium*

Pictured at right.

*Built to feed and please a hungry crowd, these pulled pork sandwiches have a down-home barbecue flavour.*

# Barbecue Shredded Pork Sandwiches

| | | |
|---|---|---|
| Boneless pork shoulder butt roast | 3 lbs. | 1.4 kg |
| Can of tomato sauce | 14 oz. | 398 mL |
| Brown sugar, packed | 1/2 cup | 125 mL |
| Ketchup | 1/2 cup | 125 mL |
| Medium onion, chopped | 1 | 1 |
| Apple cider vinegar | 1/3 cup | 75 mL |
| Garlic cloves, minced (or 1 tsp., 5 mL, powder) | 4 | 4 |
| Worcestershire sauce | 1 tbsp. | 15 mL |
| Chili powder | 2 tsp. | 10 mL |
| Dry mustard | 2 tsp. | 10 mL |
| Salt | 1 tsp. | 5 mL |
| Pepper | 1/2 tsp. | 2 mL |
| Dried crushed chilies | 1/2 tsp. | 2 mL |
| Crusty rolls, split (toasted, optional) | 12 | 12 |

Place roast in 3 1/2 to 4 quart (3.5 to 4 L) slow cooker.

Combine next 12 ingredients in medium bowl. Pour over roast. Cook, covered, on Low for 10 to 12 hours or on High for 5 to 6 hours. Transfer roast to cutting board. Cool slightly. Shred roast with 2 forks. Skim and discard fat from surface of liquid in slow cooker. Pour remaining liquid into large frying pan. Bring to a boil on medium. Boil gently, uncovered, for 12 to 15 minutes until thickened to a pasta sauce consistency. Add pork. Stir.

Serve pork mixture in rolls. Makes 12 sandwiches.

*1 sandwich: 311 Calories; 6.1 g Total Fat (2.3 g Mono, 0.6 g Poly, 1.7 g Sat); 71 mg Cholesterol; 36 g Carbohydrate; 2 g Fibre; 29 g Protein; 843 mg Sodium*

Pictured at right.

# Cherry Pork Chops

| | | |
|---|---|---|
| Bone-in pork chops, trimmed of fat | 6 | 6 |
| Liquid gravy browner (optional) | 1 tsp. | 5 mL |
| Salt, sprinkle | | |
| Pepper, sprinkle | | |
| | | |
| Cherry pie filling | 1 cup | 250 mL |
| Apple cider vinegar | 1 1/2 tsp. | 7 mL |
| Prepared mustard | 1 tsp. | 5 mL |
| Ground cloves, sprinkle | | |

Brush both sides of pork with gravy browner. Sprinkle with salt and pepper.

Combine remaining 4 ingredients in small bowl. Layer pork and cherry mixture in 5 to 7 quart (5 to 7 L) slow cooker. Cook, covered, on Low for 8 to 9 hours or on High for 4 to 4 1/2 hours. Transfer pork to serving plate. Spoon cherry mixture over top. Serves 6.

*1 serving: 201 Calories; 6.0 g Total Fat (2.7 g Mono, 0.4 g Poly, 2.2 g Sat); 61 mg Cholesterol; 12 g Carbohydrate; trace Fibre; 23 g Protein; 62 mg Sodium*

Pictured below.

*Sweet cherry adds a delectable flavour twist to tender, savoury pork. Consider this dish a sweet surprise.*

Top: Cherry Pork Chops, above
Bottom: Barbecue Shredded Pork Sandwiches, page 108

*Tender pork and potatoes in a creamy celery-flavoured sauce make for a comforting home dinner. Double the amount of chicken spice to add a bit more kick.*

# Celery-Sauced Chops

| | | |
|---|---|---|
| Red baby potatoes, larger ones cut in half | 2 lbs. | 900 g |
| Salt, sprinkle | | |
| Pepper, sprinkle | | |
| Boneless pork loin chops, trimmed of fat | 6 | 6 |
| Montreal chicken spice | 1/2 tsp. | 2 mL |
| Pepper, just a pinch | | |
| Cans of condensed cream of celery soup (10 oz., 284 mL, each) | 2 | 2 |
| Water (1 soup can) | 10 oz. | 284 mL |

Put potatoes into 4 to 5 quart (4 to 5 L) slow cooker. Sprinkle with salt and pepper.

Arrange pork over potatoes. Sprinkle with chicken spice and pepper.

Combine soup and water in medium bowl. Pour over pork. Cook, covered, on Low for 8 to 10 hours or on High for 4 to 5 hours. Transfer pork and potatoes to serving platter using slotted spoon. Carefully process liquid in slow cooker with hand blender or in blender until smooth (see Safety Tip). Serve with pork and potatoes. Serves 6.

*1 serving: 352 Calories; 10.6 g Total Fat (2.7 g Mono, 0.4 g Poly, 3.3 g Sat); 65 mg Cholesterol; 34 g Carbohydrate; 3 g Fibre; 27 g Protein; 760 mg Sodium*

Pictured at right.

**Safety Tip:** Follow manufacturer's instructions for processing hot liquids.

*Meaty chops slowly cooked in a sweet and savoury combination of peppery applesauce and creamy soup make for exquisite fare when served over noodles, rice or mashed potatoes.*

# Pork Chops Normandy

| | | |
|---|---|---|
| Medium peeled cooking apples (such as McIntosh), quartered | 3 | 3 |
| Boneless pork loin chops, trimmed of fat | 6 | 6 |
| Water | 1 1/2 cups | 375 mL |
| Can of condensed cream of mushroom soup | 10 oz. | 284 mL |
| Envelope of peppercorn sauce mix | 1 1/4 oz. | 38 g |

Put apple into 4 to 5 quart (4 to 5 L) slow cooker. Arrange pork over apple.

*(continued on next page)*

Combine remaining 3 ingredients in medium bowl. Pour over pork. Cook, covered, on Low for 8 to 10 hours or on High for 4 to 5 hours. Transfer pork to serving platter. Carefully process liquid in slow cooker with hand blender or in blender until smooth. Serve with pork. Serves 6.

*1 serving: 239 Calories; 9.3 g Total Fat (2.7 g Mono, 0.5 g Poly, 2.8 g Sat); 63 mg Cholesterol; 16 g Carbohydrate; 1 g Fibre; 24 g Protein; 755 mg Sodium*

Pictured below.

Top: Pork Chops Normandy, page 110
Bottom: Celery-Sauced Chops, page 110

*Guard your plate closely because sharing's out of the question when it comes to these brown sugar-glazed beauties.*

## Sweet-And-Sour Ribs

| | | |
|---|---|---|
| Brown sugar, packed | 2 cups | 500 mL |
| All-purpose flour | 1/4 cup | 60 mL |
| Water | 1/3 cup | 75 mL |
| White vinegar | 1/2 cup | 125 mL |
| Ketchup | 2 tbsp. | 30 mL |
| Soy sauce | 2 tbsp. | 30 mL |
| Garlic powder | 1/4 tsp. | 1 mL |
| Ground ginger | 1/4 tsp. | 1 mL |
| Pork side ribs, cut into 2 or 3 bone portions | 3 lbs. | 1.4 kg |

Combine brown sugar and flour in medium saucepan. Add water. Stir. Add next 5 ingredients. Heat and stir on medium until boiling and thickened.

Layer ribs and brown sugar mixture in 5 to 7 quart (5 to 7 L) slow cooker. Cook, covered, on Low for 10 to 12 hours or on High for 5 to 6 hours. Serves 6.

*1 serving: 720 Calories; 32.0 g Total Fat (14.2 g Mono, 2.9 g Poly, 11.7 g Sat); 128 mg Cholesterol; 77 g Carbohydrate; trace Fibre; 32 g Protein; 449 mg Sodium*

Pictured at right.

*The heavenly aroma of these effortless ribs will have your whole family clamouring for a taste. For best results, use well-trimmed ribs.*

## Easiest Ribs

| | | |
|---|---|---|
| Fancy (mild) molasses | 1/3 cup | 75 mL |
| Low-sodium soy sauce | 1/3 cup | 75 mL |
| Garlic cloves, minced (or 3/4 tsp., 4 mL, powder) | 3 | 3 |
| Dried crushed chilies | 1/4 tsp. | 1 mL |
| Sweet-and-sour-cut pork ribs, trimmed of fat and cut into 1 bone portions | 3 1/2 lbs. | 1.6 kg |

Combine first 4 ingredients in 3 1/2 to 4 quart (3.5 to 4 L) slow cooker.

Add ribs. Stir until coated. Cook on Low for 7 to 8 hours or on High for 3 1/2 to 4 hours, stirring occasionally. Serves 6.

*1 serving: 527 Calories; 38.8 g Total Fat (16.8 g Mono, 3.6 g Poly, 14.7 g Sat); 128 mg Cholesterol; 14 g Carbohydrate; trace Fibre; 29 g Protein; 561 mg Sodium*

Pictured at right.

Left: Sweet-And-Sour Ribs, page 112
Right: Easiest Ribs, page 112

*The saltiness of tender ham is perfectly complemented by a tangy citrus-flavoured sauce.*

# Slow Cooker Baked Ham

| | | |
|---|---|---|
| Cooked boneless ham (not frozen, see Note) | 3 lbs. | 1.4 kg |
| Brown sugar, packed | 1/2 cup | 125 mL |
| Frozen concentrated orange juice, thawed | 2 tbsp. | 30 mL |
| Dijon mustard (with whole seeds) | 1 tbsp. | 15 mL |
| Prepared horseradish | 2 tsp. | 10 mL |
| Water | 2/3 cup | 150 mL |
| Lemon juice | 3 tbsp. | 50 mL |
| Cornstarch | 2 tbsp. | 30 mL |

Place ham in 3 1/2 to 4 quart (3.5 to 4 L) slow cooker.

Combine next 4 ingredients in small dish. Pour over ham. Cook, covered, on Low for 5 hours or on High for 2 1/2 hours. Transfer ham to cutting board. Cut into thin slices. Arrange on serving platter. Cover to keep warm.

Pour liquid from slow cooker into small saucepan. Add water.

Stir lemon juice into cornstarch in small cup. Slowly add to brown sugar mixture. Heat and stir on medium until boiling and thickened. Drizzle over ham slices. Serves 8.

*1 serving: 363 Calories; 14.3 g Total Fat (6.8 g Mono, 1.7 g Poly, 4.7 g Sat); 99 mg Cholesterol; 18 g Carbohydrate; trace Fibre; 38 g Protein; 1696 mg Sodium*

**Note:** A ham that's been frozen adds too much moisture, resulting in boiling instead of cooking.

# Sausage And Potato Stew

| | | |
|---|---|---|
| Italian sausages, casing removed and cut into 1 inch (2.5 cm) slices | 8 | 8 |
| Chopped onion | 1 cup | 250 mL |
| Peeled sweet potatoes, cut into 3/4 inch (2 cm) cubes | 1 lb. | 454 g |
| Large peeled potato, cut into 1/2 inch (12 mm) cubes | 1 | 1 |
| Large carrot, chopped | 1 | 1 |
| Medium parsnips, chopped | 2 | 2 |
| Can of diced tomatoes (with juice) | 28 oz. | 796 mL |
| Prepared chicken broth | 1 cup | 250 mL |
| Granulated sugar | 1/2 tsp. | 2 mL |
| Pepper | 1/4 tsp. | 1 mL |
| Sour cream | 1/4 cup | 60 mL |
| Instant potato flakes | 2 tbsp. | 30 mL |
| Chopped fresh oregano | 1 tbsp. | 15 mL |

Heat large frying pan on medium-high. Add sausage. Cook for about 10 minutes, turning occasionally, until browned. Transfer with slotted spoon to paper towel-lined plate to drain.

Layer next 5 ingredients, in order given, in 5 to 7 quart (5 to 7 L) slow cooker. Arrange sausage over top.

Combine next 4 ingredients in small bowl. Pour over sausage. Cook, covered, on Low for 8 to 10 hours or on High for 4 to 5 hours.

Add remaining 3 ingredients. Stir. Makes about 11 1/2 cups (2.9 L).

*1 cup (250 mL): 272 Calories; 13.4 g Total Fat (6.0 g Mono, 1.7 g Poly, 4.9 g Sat); 39 mg Cholesterol; 26 g Carbohydrate; 3 g Fibre; 12 g Protein; 846 mg Sodium*

*Sweet potatoes, spicy sausage and tangy sour cream combine in this one-pot slow cooker feast.*

*With spicy sausage, tomatoes and a tender polenta topping, this crock-pot pie has all the best flavours of Italy.*

### about slow cooker leftovers

If you have leftovers that you want to save for the next day, remove them from your slow cooker as soon as possible and refrigerate. Because the walls of the slow cooker are so thick, food can't cool down quickly and safely enough in it.

# Corny Shepherd's Pie

| | | |
|---|---|---|
| Cooking oil | 1 tsp. | 5 mL |
| Hot Italian sausage, casing removed and chopped | 1 lb. | 454 g |
| Lean ground pork | 1 lb. | 454 g |
| Chopped celery | 1/2 cup | 125 mL |
| Chopped onion | 1/2 cup | 125 mL |
| Cans of diced tomatoes (with juice), 14 oz. (398 mL) each | 2 | 2 |
| Frozen kernel corn | 1 cup | 250 mL |
| Dried oregano | 1 tsp. | 5 mL |
| TOPPING | | |
| Water | 3 cups | 750 mL |
| Butter (or hard margarine) | 1 tbsp. | 15 mL |
| Pepper | 1/4 tsp. | 1 mL |
| Yellow cornmeal | 1 cup | 250 mL |
| Grated Parmesan cheese | 1/2 cup | 125 mL |
| Parsley flakes | 2 tsp. | 10 mL |

Heat cooking oil in large frying pan on medium. Add next 4 ingredients. Scramble-fry for 8 to 10 minutes until sausage and pork are no longer pink. Drain. Transfer to 3 1/2 to 4 quart (3.5 to 4 L) slow cooker.

Add next 3 ingredients. Stir.

**Topping:** Measure water into medium saucepan. Bring to a boil. Reduce heat to low. Add butter and pepper. Stir. Slowly add cornmeal, stirring constantly, until water is absorbed. Cook for 2 to 3 minutes, stirring occasionally, until mixture is very thick.

Add cheese and parsley. Stir. Spread evenly over sausage mixture. Cook, covered, on Low for 8 to 9 hours or on High for 4 to 4 1/2 hours. Serves 8.

*1 serving: 513 Calories; 33.9 g Total Fat (14.2 g Mono, 3.7 g Poly, 12.8 g Sat); 105 mg Cholesterol; 23 g Carbohydrate; 2 g Fibre; 29 g Protein; 870 mg Sodium*

Pictured at right.

*Don't worry, eat curry! With its mild coconut flavour and big pieces of lamb and vegetables, this delectable offering is sure to make all your troubles go away. Serve over rice or potatoes. (You'll be able to find coconut cream in the import section of larger grocery stores.)*

## about cauliflower

In case you were wondering, cauliflower comes by its floral name honestly—the white head is actually a mass of flower buds. When shopping for this awesome blossom, look for heads that are white rather than yellowish. If leaves are attached, they should look fresh and green. When home, remove the leaves and wrap the cauliflower in a plastic bag, and it will keep in your crisper for several days.

# Slow Cooker Lamb Curry

| | | |
|---|---|---|
| All-purpose flour | 2 tbsp. | 30 mL |
| Seasoned salt | 1 tsp. | 5 mL |
| Cayenne pepper | 1/4 tsp. | 1 mL |
| Stewing lamb, trimmed of fat | 1 lb. | 454 g |
| Cooking oil | 2 tbsp. | 30 mL |
| Sliced carrot | 1 1/2 cups | 375 mL |
| Cauliflower florets | 1 cup | 250 mL |
| Coarsely chopped green pepper | 1 cup | 250 mL |
| Medium onion, coarsely chopped | 1 | 1 |
| Curry powder | 1 tbsp. | 15 mL |
| Garlic cloves, minced (or 1/2 tsp., 2 mL, powder) | 2 | 2 |
| Can of condensed chicken broth | 10 oz. | 284 mL |
| Reserved pineapple juice | 1/4 cup | 60 mL |
| Can of pineapple chunks, drained and juice reserved | 14 oz. | 398 mL |
| Grated solid coconut cream (half of 7 1/2 oz., 200 g, package) | 2/3 cup | 150 mL |
| Plain yogurt | 1/2 cup | 125 mL |
| All-purpose flour | 2 tbsp. | 30 mL |
| Chopped fresh cilantro (or mint), optional | 2 tbsp. | 30 mL |

Combine first 3 ingredients in large resealable freezer bag. Add lamb. Seal bag. Toss until coated.

Heat cooking oil in large frying pan on medium-high. Add lamb. Discard any remaining flour mixture. Cook for about 5 minutes, stirring often, until browned. Transfer to 3 1/2 to 4 quart (3.5 to 4 L) slow cooker.

Add next 3 ingredients. Stir.

Add next 3 ingredients to same frying pan. Cook on medium for about 5 minutes until onion is softened.

*(continued on next page)*

Add broth and pineapple juice. Heat and stir for about 5 minutes, scraping any brown bits from bottom of pan, until boiling. Add to slow cooker. Stir. Cook, covered, on Low for 6 hours or on High for 3 hours.

Add pineapple and coconut cream. Stir.

Stir yogurt into second amount of flour in small bowl until smooth. Add to slow cooker. Stir. Cook, covered, on High for about 1 hour until sauce is boiling and thickened.

Sprinkle with cilantro. Makes about 6 1/2 cups (1.6 L).

*1 cup (250 mL): 291 Calories; 15.0 g Total Fat (4.6 g Mono, 1.8 g Poly, 7.1 g Sat); 51 mg Cholesterol; 23 g Carbohydrate; 3 g Fibre; 18 g Protein; 527 mg Sodium*

Pictured below.

*Serve this hearty stew with the tanginess of sun-dried tomato and a hint of honey sweetness over mashed potatoes or couscous.*

### time-saving tip

To save time during the morning rush, prepare the onion mixture the night before and chill in a covered bowl. Then assemble and cook as directed in the morning. Dinner will be ready by the time you come home from work.

# Sun-Dried Tomato Lamb

| | | |
|---|---|---|
| All-purpose flour | 3 tbsp. | 50 mL |
| Stewing lamb, trimmed of fat | 2 lbs. | 900 g |
| Prepared chicken broth | 1 1/2 cups | 375 mL |
| Medium onions, cut into 8 wedges each | 2 | 2 |
| Medium carrot, chopped | 1 | 1 |
| Sun-dried tomatoes in oil, blotted dry, chopped | 1/2 cup | 125 mL |
| Liquid honey | 2 tbsp. | 30 mL |
| Salt | 1/4 tsp. | 1 mL |
| Chopped fresh parsley | 2 tbsp. | 30 mL |

Measure flour into large resealable freezer bag. Add half of lamb. Seal bag. Toss until coated. Repeat with remaining lamb. Transfer to 3 1/2 to 4 quart (3.5 to 4 L) slow cooker. Sprinkle with any remaining flour.

Add next 6 ingredients. Stir. Cook, covered, on Low for 8 to 10 hours or on High for 4 to 5 hours. Skim and discard fat from surface of liquid in slow cooker.

Add parsley. Stir. Makes about 6 cups (1.5 L).

*1 cup (250 mL): 283 Calories; 9.6 g Total Fat (4.1 g Mono, 1.0 g Poly, 3.1 g Sat); 98 mg Cholesterol; 16 g Carbohydrate; 1 g Fibre; 32 g Protein; 600 mg Sodium*

Pictured at right.

*The slow-braised lamb in this warmly-spiced stew is sure to tempt and tantalize the taste buds. Serve over couscous or steamed rice and garnish with lemon zest.*

## about browning

It is important to brown some meats before they go into the slow cooker. Browning adds colour and seals in flavour but is also very important for safety reasons. Ground meats should never be put into a slow cooker without first being properly browned.

# Moroccan Lamb Stew

| | | |
|---|---|---|
| Medium carrots, cut into 1 inch (2.5 cm) pieces | 4 | 4 |
| Cooking oil | 2 tbsp. | 30 mL |
| Stewing lamb, trimmed of fat | 2 lbs. | 900 g |
| Cooking oil | 1 tbsp. | 15 mL |
| Thinly sliced onion | 2 cups | 500 mL |
| Garlic cloves, minced (or 1 tsp., 5 mL, powder) | 4 | 4 |
| Ground cumin | 2 tsp. | 10 mL |
| Ground coriander | 1 tsp. | 5 mL |
| Ground ginger | 1 tsp. | 5 mL |
| Dried crushed chilies | 1/2 tsp. | 2 mL |
| Ground cinnamon | 1/2 tsp. | 2 mL |
| Dry (or alcohol-free) white wine | 1/2 cup | 125 mL |
| Orange juice | 1/2 cup | 125 mL |
| Brown sugar, packed | 1 tbsp. | 15 mL |
| Salt | 1/4 tsp. | 1 mL |
| Liquid honey | 1 tbsp. | 15 mL |
| Grated orange zest | 1/2 tsp. | 2 mL |
| Large pitted green olives, halved (optional) | 12 | 12 |
| Water | 1 tbsp. | 15 mL |
| Cornstarch | 1 tbsp. | 15 mL |

Put carrot into 3 1/2 to 4 quart (3.5 to 4 L) slow cooker.

Heat first amount of cooking oil in large frying pan on medium-high. Add lamb in 2 batches. Cook for 8 to 10 minutes per batch, stirring occasionally, until browned. Spread evenly over carrot.

Heat second amount of cooking oil in same frying pan on medium. Add onion. Cook for 5 to 10 minutes, stirring often, until softened.

Add next 6 ingredients. Heat and stir for about 1 minute until fragrant. Spread evenly over lamb.

*(continued on next page)*

Combine next 4 ingredients in small bowl. Pour over onion mixture. Cook, covered, on Low for 8 to 10 hours or on High for 4 to 5 hours.

Add next 3 ingredients. Stir.

Stir water into cornstarch in small cup. Add to slow cooker. Stir. Cook, covered, on High for 5 to 10 minutes until boiling and slightly thickened. Makes about 5 1/2 cups (1.4 L).

*1 cup (250 mL): 390 Calories; 16.6 g Total Fat (7.9 g Mono, 3.1 g Poly, 3.7 g Sat); 107 mg Cholesterol; 21 g Carbohydrate; 3 g Fibre; 35 g Protein; 250 mg Sodium*

Pictured below.

Throughout this book measurements are given in Conventional and Metric measure. To compensate for differences between the two measurements due to rounding, a full metric measure is not always used. The cup used is the standard 8 fluid ounce. Temperature is given in degrees Fahrenheit and Celsius. Baking pan measurements are in inches and centimetres as well as quarts and litres. An exact metric conversion is given on this page as well as the working equivalent (Metric Standard Measure).

## Pans

| Conventional – Inches | Metric – Centimetres |
|---|---|
| 8 × 8 inch | 20 × 20 cm |
| 9 × 9 inch | 23 × 23 cm |
| 9 × 13 inch | 23 × 33 cm |
| 10 × 15 inch | 25 × 38 cm |
| 11 × 17 inch | 28 × 43 cm |
| 8 × 2 inch round | 20 × 5 cm |
| 9 × 2 inch round | 23 × 5 cm |
| 10 × 4 1/2 inch tube | 25 × 11 cm |
| 8 × 4 × 3 inch loaf | 20 × 10 × 7.5 cm |
| 9 × 5 × 3 inch loaf | 23 × 12.5 × 7.5 cm |

## Oven Temperatures

| Fahrenheit (°F) | Celsius (°C) | Fahrenheit (°F) | Celsius (°C) |
|---|---|---|---|
| 175° | 80° | 350° | 175° |
| 200° | 95° | 375° | 190° |
| 225° | 110° | 400° | 205° |
| 250° | 120° | 425° | 220° |
| 275° | 140° | 450° | 230° |
| 300° | 150° | 475° | 240° |
| 325° | 160° | 500° | 260° |

## Spoons

| Conventional Measure | Metric Exact Conversion Millilitre (mL) | Metric Standard Measure Millilitre (mL) |
|---|---|---|
| 1/8 teaspoon (tsp.) | 0.6 mL | 0.5 mL |
| 1/4 teaspoon (tsp.) | 1.2 mL | 1 mL |
| 1/2 teaspoon (tsp.) | 2.4 mL | 2 mL |
| 1 teaspoon (tsp.) | 4.7 mL | 5 mL |
| 2 teaspoons (tsp.) | 9.4 mL | 10 mL |
| 1 tablespoon (tbsp.) | 14.2 mL | 15 mL |

## Cups

| | | |
|---|---|---|
| 1/4 cup (4 tbsp.) | 56.8 mL | 60 mL |
| 1/3 cup (5 1/3 tbsp.) | 75.6 mL | 75 mL |
| 1/2 cup (8 tbsp.) | 113.7 mL | 125 mL |
| 2/3 cup (10 2/3 tbsp.) | 151.2 mL | 150 mL |
| 3/4 cup (12 tbsp.) | 170.5 mL | 175 mL |
| 1 cup (16 tbsp.) | 227.3 mL | 250 mL |
| 4 1/2 cups | 1022.9 mL | 1000 mL (1 L) |

## Dry Measurements

| Conventional Measure Ounces (oz.) | Metric Exact Conversion Grams (g) | Metric Standard Measure Grams (g) |
|---|---|---|
| 1 oz. | 28.3 g | 28 g |
| 2 oz. | 56.7 g | 57 g |
| 3 oz. | 85.0 g | 85 g |
| 4 oz. | 113.4 g | 125 g |
| 5 oz. | 141.7 g | 140 g |
| 6 oz. | 170.1 g | 170 g |
| 7 oz. | 198.4 g | 200 g |
| 8 oz. | 226.8 g | 250 g |
| 16 oz. | 453.6 g | 500 g |
| 32 oz. | 907.2 g | 1000 g (1 kg) |

## Casseroles

| Canada & Britain | | United States | |
|---|---|---|---|
| Standard Size Casserole | Exact Metric Measure | Standard Size Casserole | Exact Metric Measure |
| 1 qt. (5 cups) | 1.13 L | 1 qt. (4 cups) | 900 mL |
| 1 1/2 qts. (7 1/2 cups) | 1.69 L | 1 1/2 qts. (6 cups) | 1.35 L |
| 2 qts. (10 cups) | 2.25 L | 2 qts. (8 cups) | 1.8 L |
| 2 1/2 qts. (12 1/2 cups) | 2.81 L | 2 1/2 qts. (10 cups) | 2.25 L |
| 3 qts. (15 cups) | 3.38 L | 3 qts. (12 cups) | 2.7 L |
| 4 qts. (20 cups) | 4.5 L | 4 qts. (16 cups) | 3.6 L |
| 5 qts. (25 cups) | 5.63 L | 5 qts. (20 cups) | 4.5 L |

# Tip Index

# Recipe Index

*most loved*

# Soups

**Pictured on divider:**
Cream of Carrot Soup, page 88

*We gratefully acknowledge the following
suppliers for their generous support of our
Test and Photography Kitchens:*

*Broil King Barbecues*
*Corelle®*
*Hamilton Beach® Canada*
*Lagostina®*
*Proctor Silex® Canada*
*Tupperware®*

*Our special thanks to the following business
for providing props for photography:*

*Stokes*

Pictured from left: Coconut Shrimp Soup, page 41; Scotch Broth, page 75;
Pineapple Mango Soup and West Indies Summer Soup, page 118; Sweet Potato Vichyssoise, page 106

# table of contents

## the Company's Coming story

Jean Paré (pronounced "jeen PAIR-ee") grew up understanding that the combination of family, friends and home cooking is the best recipe for a good life. From her mother, she learned to appreciate good cooking, while her father praised even her earliest attempts in the kitchen. When Jean left home, she took with her a love of cooking, many family recipes and an intriguing desire to read cookbooks as if they were novels!

When her four children had all reached school age, Jean volunteered to cater the 50th anniversary celebration of the Vermilion School of Agriculture, now Lakeland College, in Alberta, Canada. Working out of her home, Jean prepared a dinner for more than 1,000 people, launching a flourishing catering operation that continued for over 18 years. During that time, she had countless opportunities to test new ideas with immediate feedback—resulting in empty plates and contented customers! Whether preparing cocktail sandwiches for a house party or serving a hot meal for 1,500 people, Jean Paré earned a reputation for great food, courteous service and reasonable prices.

As requests for her recipes increased, Jean was often asked the question, "Why don't you write a cookbook?" Jean responded by teaming up with her son, Grant Lovig, in the fall of 1980 to form Company's Coming Publishing Limited. The publication of *150 Delicious Squares* on April 14, 1981 marked the debut of what would soon become one of the world's most popular cookbook series.

The company has grown since those early days when Jean worked from a spare bedroom in her home. Nowadays every Company's Coming recipe is *kitchen-tested* before it is approved for publication.

Company's Coming cookbooks are distributed in Canada, the United States, Australia and other world markets. Bestsellers many times over in English, Company's Coming cookbooks have also been published in French and Spanish.

Familiar and trusted in home kitchens around the world, Company's Coming cookbooks are offered in a variety of formats. Highly regarded as kitchen workbooks, the softcover Original Series, with its lay-flat plastic comb binding, is still a favourite among readers.

Jean Paré's approach to cooking has always called for *quick and easy recipes* using *everyday ingredients.* That view has served her well. The recipient of many awards, including the Queen Elizabeth Golden Jubilee Medal, Jean was appointed Member of the Order of Canada, her country's highest lifetime achievement honour.

Jean continues to share what she calls The Golden Rule of Cooking: *Never share a recipe you wouldn't use yourself.* It's an approach that has worked—*millions of times over!*

*"Never share a recipe you wouldn't use yourself."*

# foreword

Homemade soups radiate comfort, and tucking into a bowl can brighten an otherwise grey day. The aroma of a simmering pot of homemade soup has the power to bring back all kinds of memories and make us feel relaxed and happy. In this new collection of soups, we've selected all of our favourite soup recipes from the Company's Coming library so you'll have the best of the best in one handy volume.

Soup isn't just about comfort though. Light, clear soups such as Beef Wine Consommé make elegant dinner starters. Chilled savoury soups like Gazpacho or Vichyssoise work well as refreshing and light summer meals. Hearty Minestrone and Manhattan Clam Chowder are nutritious meals in a bowl. And chilled sweet soups such as Cherry Soup make for delicious and novel desserts. One of the great things about soup is how varied it can be and how well it can fit into any menu.

In *Most Loved Soups* you'll find not only a wide range of delicious soup recipes to choose from, but also two flavourful stock recipes, one for beef (page 6) and one for chicken (page 26), which can be used to make many of the other soups in the book. By making large batches of these two recipes periodically, and then freezing them, you'll have the base for all kinds of other great soups on hand. Add some noodles to the stocks themselves and you'll have light, heartwarming soups sure to make you feel better.

Making soup at home allows you to select more healthful ingredients and control the salt and fat in what you eat. Much of the fat in stock, or any broth-based soup, can be removed by skimming it off the surface. Puréeing or adding potatoes or onions will thicken a soup without the need to add cream. Using reduced-sodium prepared broths or making your own stock at home helps control salt levels. Adding beans and legumes increases protein, fibre and nutrients while adding minimal calories, salt and fat.

Discover the wonders of soups with *Most Loved Soups* and you'll be sitting down to a steaming, delicious bowl of something "souper" before you know it!

*Jean Paré*

## nutrition information

Each recipe is analyzed using the most current version of the Canadian Nutrient File from Health Canada, which is based on the United States Department of Agriculture (USDA) Nutrient Database.

- If more than one ingredient is listed (such as "butter or hard margarine"), or if a range is given (1 – 2 tsp., 5 – 10 mL), only the first ingredient or first amount is analyzed.

- For meat, poultry and fish, the serving size per person is based on the recommended 4 oz. (113 g) uncooked weight (without bone), which is 2 – 3 oz. (57 – 85 g) cooked weight (without bone)— approximately the size of a deck of playing cards.

- Milk used is 1% M.F. (milk fat), unless otherwise stated.

- Cooking oil used is canola oil, unless otherwise stated.

- Ingredients indicating "sprinkle," "optional," or "for garnish" are not included in the nutrition information.

- The fat in recipes and combination foods can vary greatly depending on the sources and types of fats used in each specific ingredient. For these reasons, the amount of saturated, monounsaturated and polyunsaturated fats may not add up to the total fat content.

Vera C. Mazurak, Ph.D.
Nutritionist

*Good things come to those who wait, and a long simmering time really brings out the flavour in this beef barley soup. The beef bones make this stock deliciously rich and savoury.*

## about stock

There are several different sources of broth if you don't have the time to make your own stock. Store-bought broth comes in a ready-to-use form in cans or cartons. You can also mix bouillon cubes, pastes or powders with hot water to create instant broth in a pinch. For any recipe in this book that requires stock, you may use either store-bought broth or homemade stock. However, if you're concerned about keeping your salt intake low, then homemade stock is preferable to store-bought broths. For more stock tips, see page 26.

# Old-Fashioned Barley Soup

**BEEF STOCK**

| | | |
|---|---|---|
| Beef neck bones | 3 lbs. | 1.4 kg |
| Bone-in beef shanks | 1 lb. | 454 g |
| Cold water | 16 cups | 4 L |
| Celery ribs, with leaves, halved | 6 | 6 |
| Medium onions, halved | 2 | 2 |
| Medium carrot, halved | 1 | 1 |
| Bay leaves | 2 | 2 |
| Whole black peppercorns | 10 | 10 |

**SOUP**

| | | |
|---|---|---|
| Diced peeled potato | 2 cups | 500 mL |
| Can of condensed tomato soup | 10 oz. | 284 mL |
| Chopped onion | 1 cup | 250 mL |
| Chopped celery | 1 cup | 250 mL |
| Diced carrot | 1 cup | 250 mL |
| Diced parsnip (optional) | 1 cup | 250 mL |
| Pearl barley | 2/3 cup | 150 mL |
| Salt | 1 tsp. | 5 mL |
| Pepper | 3/4 tsp. | 4 mL |

**Beef Stock:** Put first 3 ingredients into large pot. Bring to a boil. Boil, uncovered, for 5 minutes without stirring. Skim and discard foam from side of pot.

Add next 5 ingredients. Stir. Reduce heat to medium-low. Simmer, partially covered, for about 4 hours, stirring occasionally, until beef starts to fall off bones. Remove from heat. Remove bones and shanks to cutting board using slotted spoon. Remove beef from bones. Discard bones. Chop beef coarsely. Set aside. Strain stock through sieve into separate large pot. Discard solids. Makes about 10 cups (2.5 L) stock.

**Soup:** Add remaining 9 ingredients to stock in pot. Bring to a boil. Add beef. Reduce heat to medium-low. Simmer, partially covered, for about 45 minutes, stirring occasionally, until barley and vegetables are tender. Makes about 14 cups (3.5 L).

*1 cup (250 mL): 112 Calories; 2.1 g Total Fat (0.8 g Mono, 0.3 g Poly, 0.7 g Sat); 11 mg Cholesterol; 17 g Carbohydrate; 2 g Fibre; 6 g Protein; 345 mg Sodium*

Pictured at right.

## Beefy Vegetable Soup

*Tender beef and plenty of vegetables pair up in a dark, flavourful broth. This is a small-batch recipe, but it's easily doubled.*

| | | |
|---|---|---|
| Boneless beef, such as stew beef, diced | 1/4 lb. | 113 g |
| Water | 3 cups | 750 mL |
| Chopped onion | 1/2 cup | 125 mL |
| Medium carrot, diced | 1 | 1 |
| Diced turnip | 1/3 cup | 75 mL |
| Beef bouillon powder | 1 tbsp. | 15 mL |
| Small bay leaf | 1 | 1 |
| Parsley flakes, sprinkle | | |
| Ground sage, sprinkle | | |
| Pepper, sprinkle | | |

Cook beef in water slowly in covered saucepan for 1 hour.

Add remaining 8 ingredients. Cover. Boil gently for about 30 minutes until vegetables are tender. Discard bay leaf. Makes about 4 cups (1 L).

*1 cup (250 mL): 77 Calories; 3.9 g Total Fat (1.7 g Mono, 0.2 g Poly, 1.5 g Sat); 18 mg Cholesterol; 5 g Carbohydrate; 1 g Fibre; 6 g Protein; 828 mg Sodium*

## Hamburger Soup

*A Classic!*

*Hearty vegetables and a robust tomato herb broth transform hamburger into a marvelous meal, ready in less than an hour!*

### make ahead

This soup freezes well, so pop some lunch-size portions in the freezer.

| | | |
|---|---|---|
| Cooking oil | 1 tsp. | 5 mL |
| Lean ground beef | 1 lb. | 454 g |
| Chopped onion | 1 cup | 250 mL |
| Diced carrot | 1 cup | 250 mL |
| Chopped celery | 1/2 cup | 125 mL |
| Can of diced tomatoes (with juice) | 14 oz. | 398 mL |
| Water | 1 1/2 cups | 375 mL |
| Can of condensed beef broth | 10 oz. | 284 mL |
| Frozen kernel corn | 1 cup | 250 mL |
| Can of tomato sauce | 7 1/2 oz. | 213 mL |
| Granulated sugar | 1 tsp. | 5 mL |
| Worcestershire sauce | 1 tsp. | 5 mL |
| Dried basil (optional) | 1/2 – 1 tsp. | 2 – 5 mL |
| Pepper | 1/4 tsp. | 1 mL |

*(continued on next page)*

Heat cooking oil in large saucepan on medium. Add ground beef. Scramble-fry for about 5 minutes until no longer pink. Drain.

Add onion, carrot and celery. Cook for about 5 minutes, stirring often, until onion is softened.

Add remaining 9 ingredients. Stir. Bring to a boil on medium-high. Reduce heat to medium-low. Cover. Simmer for about 45 minutes until vegetables are tender. Makes about 6 3/4 cups (1.7 L).

*1 cup (250 mL): 183 Calories; 6.9 g Total Fat (3.0 g Mono, 0.6 g Poly, 2.4 g Sat); 35 mg Cholesterol; 16 g Carbohydrate; 3 g Fibre; 16 g Protein; 634 mg Sodium*

Pictured below.

Hamburger Soup, left

*A satisfying and full-bodied soup that makes a real meal! Beef stock can be used in place of the bouillon cubes and water, and a can of chickpeas (garbanzo beans) can be used instead of kidney beans.*

## about minestrone

*Minestra* (mee-NES-trah) is the Italian word for soup, usually one of medium thickness containing meat and vegetables. *Minestrina* (mee-nes-TREE-nah), or "little soup," is a light broth containing thin or small pasta. *Minestrone* (mee-nes-TROH-neh), or "big soup," is filled with vegetables, pasta, meat and beans and intended to be a meal in a bowl.

## freezing

This recipe makes a big batch of soup, but leftovers can be frozen.

# Minestrone

*A Classic!*

| | | |
|---|---|---|
| Bacon slices, chopped | 4 | 4 |
| Chopped onion | 1 1/2 cups | 375 mL |
| Lean ground beef | 1 1/2 lbs. | 680 g |
| Beef bouillon cubes | 10 x 1/5 oz. | 10 x 6 g |
| Boiling water | 10 cups | 2.5 L |
| Can of plum tomatoes, broken up | 14 oz. | 398 mL |
| Chopped celery | 1 cup | 250 mL |
| Diced carrot | 1 cup | 250 mL |
| Diced potato | 1 1/2 cups | 375 mL |
| Chopped cabbage, packed | 1 cup | 250 mL |
| Salt | 1 tsp. | 5 mL |
| Pepper | 1/4 tsp. | 1 mL |
| Garlic powder | 1/4 tsp. | 1 mL |
| Dried basil | 1/2 tsp. | 2 mL |
| Dried oregano | 1/2 tsp. | 2 mL |
| Fusilli | 8 oz. | 225 g |
| Can of kidney beans, rinsed and drained | 14 oz. | 398 mL |

Scramble-fry bacon, onion and ground beef in Dutch oven to brown.

Dissolve bouillon cubes in boiling water. Add.

Add next 10 ingredients. Stir. Bring to a boil. Cover and simmer until vegetables are tender, about 25 minutes.

Add pasta and beans. Boil slowly, uncovered, for 10 minutes or until pasta is tender. Makes about 14 cups (3.5 L).

*1 cup (250 mL): 259 Calories; 10.8 g Total Fat (1.4 g Mono, 0.4 g Poly, 4.0 g Sat); 38 mg Cholesterol; 25 g Carbohydrate; 3 g Fibre; 15 g Protein; 1352 mg Sodium*

# Italian Meatball Soup

| | | |
|---|---|---|
| Large egg | 1 | 1 |
| Crushed seasoned croutons | 1/4 cup | 60 mL |
| Chopped fresh parsley | 2 tbsp. | 30 mL |
| (or 1 1/2 tsp., 7 mL, flakes) | | |
| Grated Parmesan cheese | 2 tbsp. | 30 mL |
| Garlic clove, minced | 1 | 1 |
| (or 1/4 tsp., 1 mL, powder) | | |
| Lean ground beef | 1 lb. | 454 g |
| Prepared beef broth | 7 cups | 1.75 L |
| Very small pasta (such as orzo | 2/3 cup | 150 mL |
| or alphabet) | | |
| Finely shredded fresh basil | 2 tbsp. | 30 mL |

Combine first 5 ingredients in medium bowl.

Add ground beef. Mix well. Roll into 3/4 inch (2 cm) balls. Arrange on greased baking sheet with sides. Bake in 350°F (175°C) oven for about 15 minutes until no longer pink inside. Makes about 65 meatballs. Transfer to paper towels to drain. Set aside.

Measure broth into large pot or Dutch oven. Bring to a boil on high. Add pasta. Stir. Reduce heat to medium. Boil gently, uncovered, for 5 to 6 minutes until pasta is tender but firm.

Add meatballs and basil. Heat and stir for about 1 minute until meatballs are heated through. Makes about 8 cups (2 L).

*1 cup (250 mL): 209 Calories; 7.1 g Total Fat (2.9 g Mono, 0.5 g Poly, 2.8 g Sat); 58 mg Cholesterol; 18 g Carbohydrate; 1 g Fibre; 17 g Protein; 817 mg Sodium*

*This tasty soup is a creative way to serve pasta with meatballs.*

## food fun

Some call Italian Meatball Soup by another name, Italian Wedding Soup, although it's not a dish traditionally served at Italian weddings. Food historians think the name came from the idea that the meat, cheese, pasta and herbs in the soup create a marriage of delicious flavours!

*A meal in a bowl. Sweet tomato broth with a dash of Parmesan cheese that will have everyone returning for seconds. A great choice for an Italian potluck.*

# Meatball Soup

| | | |
|---|---|---|
| Large egg | 1 | 1 |
| Lean ground beef | 1 lb. | 454 g |
| Long-grain white rice | 1/4 cup | 60 mL |
| Dried oregano | 1/2 tsp. | 2 mL |
| Cooking oil | 2 tsp. | 10 mL |
| Cooking oil | 1 tsp. | 5 mL |
| Diced carrot | 1 cup | 250 mL |
| Chopped onion | 1/2 cup | 125 mL |
| Water | 2 cups | 500 mL |
| Can of condensed tomato soup | 10 oz. | 284 mL |
| Prepared beef broth | 1 cup | 250 mL |
| Frozen peas | 1/2 cup | 125 mL |
| Grated Parmesan cheese | 1/4 cup | 60 mL |

Beat egg with fork in large bowl. Add ground beef, rice and oregano. Mix well. Roll into 1/2 inch (12 mm) balls.

*(continued on next page)*

Meatball Soup, above

Heat first amount of cooking oil in large saucepan on medium. Add meatballs. Cook for about 10 minutes, turning occasionally, until browned. Makes about 70 meatballs. Transfer to paper towels to drain.

Heat second amount of cooking oil in same large saucepan on medium. Add carrot and onion. Cook for 5 to 10 minutes, stirring often, until onion is softened.

Add next 3 ingredients. Stir. Add meatballs. Stir. Bring to a boil on medium-high. Reduce heat to medium-low. Cover. Simmer for about 30 minutes, stirring occasionally, until meatballs are no longer pink inside and rice is tender.

Add peas and Parmesan cheese. Heat and stir for about 2 minutes until heated through. Makes about 6 cups (1.5 L).

*1 cup (250 mL): 293 Calories; 16.9 g Total Fat (7.2 g Mono, 1.8 g Poly, 6.0 g Sat); 82 mg Cholesterol; 15 g Carbohydrate; 2 g Fibre; 20 g Protein; 663 mg Sodium*

Pictured at left.

## Beef Wine Consommé

| | | |
|---|---|---|
| Water | 3 cups | 750 mL |
| Onion slivers | 1 tbsp. | 15 mL |
| Carrot slivers | 1 tbsp. | 15 mL |
| Celery slivers | 1 tbsp. | 15 mL |
| Yellow turnip (or parsnip) slivers | 1 tbsp. | 15 mL |
| Chopped green onion | 1 tbsp. | 15 mL |
| Beef bouillon powder | 1 tbsp. | 15 mL |
| Granulated sugar | 1 1/2 tsp. | 7 mL |
| Lemon juice | 1/2 tsp. | 2 mL |
| Salt | 1/4 tsp. | 1 mL |
| Dry red (or alcohol-free) wine | 1/4 cup | 60 mL |

Place first 6 ingredients in medium saucepan. Bring to a boil. Cover. Simmer for about 5 minutes until vegetables are cooked.

Add remaining 5 ingredients. Stir. Simmer for about 1 minute. Makes 3 cups (750 mL). Serves 4.

*1 serving: 26 Calories; 0.2 g Total Fat (0.1 g Mono, trace Poly, 0.1 g Sat); trace Cholesterol; 3 g Carbohydrate; trace Fibre; trace Protein; 950 mg Sodium*

*A clear, richly flavoured starter soup with elegant vegetable slivers and a hint of red wine. This is easy to double to make more servings.*

### about consommé

Traditionally, consommé (CON-so-may) is a rich broth that can be served hot or cold or as a base for other soups or sauces. Double consommé is broth that has been reduced by half the volume, and as a result, it has twice the flavour of non-reduced consommé.

*Ban-foh-BOH is a common meal served in all Vietnamese homes. Street vendors in larger cities have this beef noodle soup available all day. Very good.*

## food fun

Believe it or not, there's an art to eating pho! Begin with a pair of chopsticks and a Chinese-style soup spoon. First add more garnishes to your soup such as basil or mint leaves, bean sprouts, cilantro and fresh chili peppers. Then add squirts of lime juice and fish sauce (hoisin or plum sauce are nice additions too). Using your chopsticks, pile some rice noodles, a piece of meat, some herbs and sprouts and a little broth onto the spoon, and then deliver the savoury bundle to your mouth.

# Banh Pho Bo

| | | |
|---|---|---|
| Diced onion | 1 cup | 250 mL |
| Cooking oil | 1 tbsp. | 15 mL |
| Finely grated ginger root (or 1/2 tsp., 2 mL, ground ginger) | 2 tsp. | 10 mL |
| Garlic clove, minced (or 1/4 tsp., 1 mL, powder) | 1 | 1 |
| Freshly ground pepper, sprinkle | | |
| Ground cinnamon, sprinkle | | |
| Cans of condensed chicken broth (10 oz., 284 mL, each) | 2 | 2 |
| Water | 3 cups | 750 mL |
| Beef bouillon powder | 2 tsp. | 10 mL |
| Grated carrot | 1/2 cup | 125 mL |
| Fresh small red chili (seeds and ribs removed for less heat), finely diced (see Tip, right) | 1 | 1 |
| Fish sauce | 3 tbsp. | 50 mL |
| Lime juice | 1 tbsp. | 15 mL |
| Beef tenderloin, very thinly sliced across the grain (see Tip, page 16) | 5 oz. | 140 g |
| Green onions, cut into 1 1/2 inch (3.8 cm) pieces and then cut julienne (see Tip, page 60) | 2 | 2 |
| Fresh bean sprouts | 3 oz. | 85 g |
| Small rice stick noodles | 8 oz. | 225 g |
| Boiling water, to cover | | |
| Shredded fresh basil (or cilantro), for garnish | | |

*(continued on next page)*

Sauté onion in cooking oil in large saucepan for about 3 minutes until soft.

Add ginger, garlic, pepper and cinnamon. Stir. Sauté for 3 minutes until onion is browned.

Add next 5 ingredients. Stir. Reduce heat. Cover. Simmer for 10 minutes.

Add fish sauce, lime juice, beef, green onion and bean sprouts. Stir. Bring to a simmer. Simmer until beef is cooked. Turn off heat. Cover to keep hot. Makes 7 cups (1.75 L) soup.

Cover noodles with boiling water in large heatproof bowl. Let stand for 3 minutes until softened. Drain. Divide noodles among 6 large individual soup bowls. Ladle soup over top.

Garnish with basil. Serves 6.

*1 serving:* 241 Calories; 4.5 g Total Fat (1.8 g Mono, 0.8 g Poly, 0.6 g Sat); 17 mg Cholesterol; 41 g Carbohydrate; 2 g Fibre; 9 g Protein; 1756 mg Sodium

Pictured below.

### tip

Hot peppers contain capsaicin in the seeds and ribs. Removing the seeds and ribs will reduce the heat. Wear rubber gloves when handling hot peppers and avoid touching your eyes. Wash your hands well afterwards.

*This quick soup is hearty, fragrant and just spicy enough! Make it a meal with bread sticks or a warm loaf of crusty bread.*

## Curried Lentil Beef Soup

| | | |
|---|---|---|
| Cooking oil | 1 tbsp. | 15 mL |
| Beef minute (or fast-fry) steak, thinly sliced (see Tip, left) | 1/2 lb. | 225 g |
| Chopped onion | 1 1/2 cups | 375 mL |
| Curry paste | 2 tbsp. | 30 mL |
| Prepared beef broth | 6 cups | 1.5 L |
| Can of lentils, rinsed and drained | 19 oz. | 540 mL |
| Frozen mixed vegetables | 1 1/2 cups | 375 mL |
| Pepper, sprinkle | | |

Heat cooking oil in large pot or Dutch oven on medium-high. Add steak. Cook for 4 to 5 minutes, stirring occasionally, until browned.

Add onion and curry paste. Heat and stir for 1 minute until fragrant.

Add broth and lentils. Stir. Bring to a boil. Reduce heat to medium-low. Cover. Simmer for 5 minutes, stirring occasionally, to blend flavours.

Add mixed vegetables and pepper. Stir. Bring to a boil on high. Reduce heat to medium. Cover. Simmer for about 5 minutes until vegetables are tender. Makes about 9 cups (2.25 L).

*1 cup (250 mL): 132 Calories; 3.3 g Total Fat (1.7 g Mono, 0.6 g Poly, 0.8 g Sat); 15 mg Cholesterol; 14 g Carbohydrate; 5 g Fibre; 12 g Protein; 731 mg Sodium*

Pictured at right.

*Earthy mushrooms and a pleasant hint of tarragon complement the nutty flavour of wild rice. Delicious.*

## Hearty Wild Rice Soup

| | | |
|---|---|---|
| Cooking oil | 2 tsp. | 10 mL |
| Chopped fresh white mushrooms | 2 cups | 500 mL |
| Lean ground beef | 1 lb. | 454 g |
| Chopped onion | 1 cup | 250 mL |
| Dried tarragon | 1 tsp. | 5 mL |
| All-purpose flour | 3 tbsp. | 50 mL |
| Prepared beef broth | 6 cups | 1.5 L |
| Wild rice | 2/3 cup | 150 mL |
| Grated carrot | 1/2 cup | 125 mL |

*(continued on next page)*

Heat cooking oil in large pot or Dutch oven on medium. Add next 4 ingredients. Scramble-fry for about 10 minutes until ground beef is no longer pink. Drain.

Add flour. Stir well. Add broth and rice. Stir until boiling. Reduce heat to medium-low. Simmer, covered, for about 50 minutes, stirring occasionally, until rice is tender.

Add carrot. Heat and stir for about 2 minutes until carrot is tender-crisp. Skim any fat from surface of soup. Makes about 8 cups (2 L).

*1 cup (250 mL): 187 Calories; 6.6 g Total Fat (2.9 g Mono, 0.7 g Poly, 2.2 g Sat); 29 mg Cholesterol; 16 g Carbohydrate; 2 g Fibre; 15 g Protein; 646 mg Sodium*

Pictured below.

Left: Curried Lentil Beef Soup, left
Right: Hearty Wild Rice Soup, left

### about wild rice

Wild rice is not a true rice, but the seed of a grass that grows naturally in the shallow waters and slow-flowing streams of temperate climates. Saskatchewan, California and Minnesota are the largest North American producers of wild rice today, but Native Americans have been harvesting the seed heads for centuries. Its distinctive nutty flavour, chewy texture and high nutritional value make wild rice a very healthy choice, and it tastes great mixed with other rices.

*This rich broth seasoned with cumin and coriander provides a spicy taste of the East.*

# Spiced Beef Soup

|  | | |
|---|---|---|
| Cooking oil | 1 tbsp. | 15 mL |
| Beef stew meat, cut into 1/2 inch (12 mm) pieces | 3/4 lb. | 340 g |
| Cooking oil | 2 tsp. | 10 mL |
| Chopped onion | 1 1/2 cups | 375 mL |
| Ground cumin | 2 tsp. | 10 mL |
| Ground coriander | 2 tsp. | 10 mL |
| Ground ginger | 1 tsp. | 5 mL |
| Dried crushed chilies | 1 tsp. | 5 mL |
| Can of diced tomatoes (with juice) | 28 oz. | 796 mL |
| Low-sodium prepared beef broth | 4 cups | 1 L |
| Can of chickpeas (garbanzo beans), rinsed and drained | 19 oz. | 540 mL |
| Medium zucchini (with peel), chopped | 1 | 1 |
| Chopped fresh mint leaves (or 1 1/2 tsp., 7 mL, dried) | 2 tbsp. | 30 mL |
| Liquid honey | 2 tsp. | 10 mL |
| Grated lemon zest | 1 tsp. | 5 mL |

Heat first amount of cooking oil in large pot or Dutch oven on medium-high. Add beef. Cook for 5 to 10 minutes, stirring occasionally, until browned. Transfer to large bowl. Cover to keep warm.

Heat second amount of cooking oil in same large pot on medium. Add onion. Cook for 5 to 10 minutes, stirring often, until softened.

Add next 4 ingredients. Heat and stir for about 1 minute until fragrant.

Add beef, tomatoes and broth. Stir. Bring to a boil on medium-high. Reduce heat to medium-low. Cover. Simmer for 20 minutes, stirring occasionally.

*(continued on next page)*

Add chickpeas. Stir. Cover. Simmer for about 20 minutes until beef is
very tender.

Add remaining 4 ingredients. Stir. Cook, uncovered, on medium for about
5 minutes until zucchini is tender. Makes 10 cups (2.5 L). Serves 8.

*1 serving: 200 Calories; 7.9 g Total Fat (3.5 g Mono, 1.5 g Poly, 1.8 g Sat); 24 mg Cholesterol;
19 g Carbohydrate; 3 g Fibre; 15 g Protein; 605 mg Sodium*

Pictured below.

*Wholesome tomatoes and potatoes in a simple beef broth.*

# Goulash Chowder

| | | |
|---|---|---|
| Chopped onion | 1/2 cup | 125 mL |
| Cooking oil | 1 tbsp. | 15 mL |
| All-purpose flour | 2 tbsp. | 30 mL |
| Boneless beef inside round (or blade or chuck) steak, trimmed of fat and cubed | 3/4 lb. | 340 g |
| Water | 4 cups | 1 L |
| Medium potatoes, diced | 4 | 4 |
| Can of diced tomatoes, with juice | 14 oz. | 398 mL |
| Frozen kernel corn | 1/2 cup | 125 mL |
| Paprika | 1/2 – 1 tsp. | 2 – 5 mL |
| Granulated sugar | 1/2 tsp. | 2 mL |
| Salt | 1 tsp. | 5 mL |
| Pepper | 1/4 tsp. | 1 mL |

Sauté onion in cooking oil in large pot or Dutch oven until soft and golden. Stir in flour until well mixed. Turn into small bowl. Set aside.

Put beef and water into same pot. Cover. Simmer for 1 to 1 1/2 hours until tender.

Add next 7 ingredients. Cook for 25 minutes. Add reserved onion mixture. Heat and stir until boiling and thickened. Makes 9 cups (2.25 L).

*1 cup (250 mL): 151 Calories; 5.6 g Total Fat (2.5 g Mono, 0.7 g Poly, 1.6 g Sat); 25 mg Cholesterol; 17 g Carbohydrate; 2 g Fibre; 10 g Protein; 390 mg Sodium*

Pictured at right.

*Why wait until Sunday for a pot roast dinner? This rich, stew-like soup is full of tender meat and vegetables for that feeling of savoury satisfaction, any day of the week.*

## tip

Try freezing tomato paste for 30 minutes before opening both ends and pushing the tube out. You'll be able to slice off what you need and wrap the rest for later.

# Pot Roast Soup

| | | |
|---|---|---|
| Cooking oil | 2 tsp. | 10 mL |
| Beef top sirloin steak, trimmed of fat and diced | 1 lb. | 454 g |
| Chopped onion | 1 cup | 250 mL |
| Garlic cloves, minced (or 1/2 tsp., 2 mL, powder) | 2 | 2 |
| Beef Stock (page 6), or prepared beef broth | 5 cups | 1.25 L |
| Cubed peeled potato | 2 cups | 500 mL |
| Baby carrots, halved | 1 cup | 250 mL |
| Tomato paste (see Tip, left) | 1 tbsp. | 15 mL |
| Worcestershire sauce | 1 tbsp. | 15 mL |
| Dried thyme | 1/4 tsp. | 1 mL |
| Salt | 1/4 tsp. | 1 mL |
| Water | 1/4 cup | 60 mL |
| All-purpose flour | 1/4 cup | 60 mL |
| Frozen peas | 1 cup | 250 mL |

Heat cooking oil in large saucepan on medium-high. Add beef. Cook for about 10 minutes, stirring often, until browned. Reduce heat to medium.

Add onion and garlic. Cook for 3 to 5 minutes, stirring occasionally, until onion is softened.

Add stock. Stir. Bring to a boil. Reduce heat to medium-low. Simmer, partially covered, for about 40 minutes until beef is tender.

Add next 6 ingredients. Bring to a boil.

Stir water into flour in small bowl until smooth. Slowly add to soup, stirring constantly, until boiling and thickened. Reduce heat to medium. Boil gently, covered, for 15 to 20 minutes, stirring occasionally, until vegetables are tender.

Add peas. Heat and stir for 3 to 5 minutes until peas are tender. Makes 8 cups (2 L). Serves 6.

*1 serving: 233 Calories; 4.8 g Total Fat (2.1 g Mono, 0.7 g Poly, 1.2 g Sat); 36 mg Cholesterol; 24 g Carbohydrate; 3 g Fibre; 23 g Protein; 931 mg Sodium*

Pictured at right.

*This soup hearty with pasta, beef and navy beans (fah-JOH-lee) is filling, easy to prepare and delicious—sure to become a favourite!*

# Pasta Fagioli Soup

|  | | |
|---|---|---|
| Olive (or cooking) oil | 1 tbsp. | 15 mL |
| Medium onion, chopped | 1 | 1 |
| Celery rib, finely diced | 1 | 1 |
| Garlic clove, minced (or 1/4 tsp., 1 mL, powder) | 1 | 1 |
| Extra lean ground beef | 6 oz. | 170 g |
| All-purpose flour | 1 tsp. | 5 mL |
| Salt | 1/2 tsp. | 2 mL |
| Coarse ground pepper | 1/2 tsp. | 2 mL |
| Cayenne pepper (optional) | 1/8 tsp. | 0.5 mL |
| Prepared beef broth | 3 2/3 cups | 900 mL |
| Cans of stewed tomatoes (14 oz., 398 mL, each) | 2 | 2 |
| Can of vegetable cocktail juice | 12 oz. | 340 mL |
| Coarsely grated carrot | 1/2 cup | 125 mL |
| Dried basil | 1 tsp. | 5 mL |
| Granulated sugar | 1/4 tsp. | 1 mL |
| Cans of navy beans (14 oz., 398 mL, each), rinsed and drained | 2 | 2 |
| Leftover cooked pasta, chopped if long or very large | 1 cup | 250 mL |

Heat olive oil in large pot or Dutch oven on medium. Add onion, celery and garlic. Cook for 5 to 10 minutes, stirring often, until onion and celery are softened.

Add ground beef. Scramble-fry for about 10 minutes until no longer pink.

Add next 4 ingredients. Stir.

Add next 6 ingredients. Stir.

*(continued on next page)*

Mash 1/2 cup (125 mL) beans in small bowl. Add to pot. Add remaining beans to pot. Bring to a boil. Reduce heat to medium-low. Simmer, uncovered, for 15 minutes.

Add pasta. Simmer, uncovered, for about 5 minutes until heated through. Makes 12 cups (3 L).

*1 cup (250 mL): 314 Calories; 3.0 g Total Fat (1.3 g Mono, 0.8 g Poly, 0.5 g Sat); 8 mg Cholesterol; 54 g Carbohydrate; 17 g Fibre; 20 g Protein; 695 mg Sodium*

Pictured below.

*There's nothing like a comforting bowl of chicken noodle soup to cure what ails you! This long-simmered, made-from-scratch soup is well worth the effort. Use whichever cuts of chicken you prefer, as long as the weight used is equal to that listed.*

## make ahead

Freeze homemade stock in differently sized containers to flavour not just soups but gravies, sauces, risottos and other dishes. For very small amounts, freeze stock in ice cube trays or muffin tins, then transfer the cubes to a plastic freezer bag. No time to make your own stock? See page 6 for information on stock alternatives.

## tip

To make stocks virtually fat-free, chill overnight and remove the solidified fat from the surface.

# Comfort Chicken Noodle Soup

 *A Classic!*

### CHICKEN STOCK

| | | |
|---|---|---|
| Bone-in chicken parts | 4 lbs. | 1.8 kg |
| Water | 10 cups | 2.5 L |
| Celery ribs, with leaves, halved | 2 | 2 |
| Large onion, quartered | 1 | 1 |
| Large carrot, halved | 1 | 1 |
| Sprigs of fresh thyme | 3 | 3 |
| Sprig of fresh parsley | 1 | 1 |
| Bay leaves | 2 | 2 |
| Garlic clove | 1 | 1 |
| Whole black peppercorns | 12 | 12 |

### SOUP

| | | |
|---|---|---|
| Cooking oil | 2 tsp. | 10 mL |
| Chopped onion | 1/2 cup | 125 mL |
| Chopped carrot | 1/2 cup | 125 mL |
| Chopped celery | 1/2 cup | 125 mL |
| Spaghetti, broken into about 3 inch (7.5 cm) pieces | 3 oz. | 85 g |
| Chopped fresh parsley | 1/4 cup | 60 mL |
| Salt | 3/4 tsp. | 4 mL |
| Pepper | 1/4 tsp. | 1 mL |

**Chicken Stock:** Put chicken and water into Dutch oven or large pot. Bring to a boil. Boil, uncovered, for 5 minutes without stirring. Skim and discard foam from side of pot.

Add next 8 ingredients. Stir. Bring to a boil. Reduce heat to medium-low. Simmer, uncovered, for about 3 hours, stirring occasionally, until chicken is tender and starts to fall off bones. Remove from heat. Remove chicken and bones to cutting board using slotted spoon. Remove chicken from bones. Discard bones and skin. Chop enough chicken to make 2 cups (500 mL). Reserve remaining chicken for another use. Strain stock through sieve into large bowl. Discard solids. Skim fat from stock. Makes about 6 1/2 cups (1.6 L) stock.

*(continued on next page)*

**Soup:** Heat cooking oil in large saucepan on medium. Add next 3 ingredients. Cook for 5 to 10 minutes, stirring often, until onion is softened. Add stock. Bring to a boil.

Add spaghetti. Cook, uncovered, for about 10 minutes, stirring occasionally, until spaghetti and vegetables are tender.

Add chicken and remaining 3 ingredients. Heat and stir until chicken is heated through. Makes about 7 1/2 cups (1.9 L).

*1 cup (250 mL): 137 Calories; 4.3 g Total Fat (1.8 g Mono, 1.1 g Poly, 0.9 g Sat); 34 mg Cholesterol; 11 g Carbohydrate; 1 g Fibre; 13 g Protein; 287 mg Sodium*

Pictured below.

*A hearty chicken soup that's on the table in half an hour! A standard in any cook's repertoire.*

# Chicken Pasta Soup

| | | |
|---|---|---|
| Cooking oil | 1 tsp. | 5 mL |
| Finely chopped onion | 1 cup | 250 mL |
| Lean ground chicken | 1/2 lb. | 225 g |
| Finely chopped celery | 1/4 cup | 60 mL |
| Precooked bacon slices, diced | 4 | 4 |
| Water | 5 cups | 1.25 L |
| Chicken bouillon powder | 1 tbsp. | 15 mL |
| Pepper | 1/4 tsp. | 1 mL |
| Frozen mixed vegetables | 1 cup | 250 mL |
| Tiny shell (or other very small) pasta | 1/2 cup | 125 mL |
| Parsley flakes (or 4 tsp., 20 mL, chopped fresh parsley) | 1 tsp. | 5 mL |

Heat cooking oil in large frying pan on medium-high. Add next 4 ingredients. Scramble-fry for 5 to 10 minutes, stirring occasionally, until ground chicken is no longer pink and onion is softened. Drain.

Combine next 3 ingredients in large saucepan. Bring to a boil on medium-high.

Add chicken mixture, mixed vegetables and pasta. Stir. Cover. Bring to a boil. Reduce heat to medium-low. Simmer for about 10 minutes, stirring occasionally, until pasta is tender but firm.

Add parsley. Stir. Makes about 7 cups (1.75 L).

*1 cup (250 mL): 145 Calories; 7.3 g Total Fat (1.4 g Mono, 0.6 g Poly, 0.8 g Sat); 3 mg Cholesterol; 11 g Carbohydrate; 1 g Fibre; 9 g Protein; 375 mg Sodium*

*Your standard chicken soup just went south of the border and came back with the exciting flavours of chipotle, lime and cilantro.*

# Chicken Corn Soup

| | | |
|---|---|---|
| Canola oil | 1 tsp. | 5 mL |
| Frozen kernel corn | 2 cups | 500 mL |
| Chopped onion | 1 cup | 250 mL |
| Garlic cloves, minced (or 1/2 tsp., 2 mL, powder) | 2 | 2 |
| Finely chopped chipotle pepper in adobo sauce (see Tip, right) | 1/2 tsp. | 2 mL |

*(continued on next page)*

| Low-sodium prepared chicken broth | 3 cups | 750 mL |
|---|---|---|
| Can of diced tomatoes (with juice) | 14 oz. | 398 mL |
| Pepper | 1/4 tsp. | 1 mL |
| Chopped cooked chicken (see Tip, page 36) | 2 cups | 500 mL |
| Chopped fresh cilantro | 1 tbsp. | 15 mL |
| Lime juice | 1 tbsp. | 15 mL |

Heat canola oil in large saucepan on medium-high. Add next 4 ingredients. Cook, uncovered, for about 4 minutes, stirring often, until onion is softened.

Add next 3 ingredients. Stir. Bring to a boil. Reduce heat to medium. Boil gently, covered, for 6 minutes to blend flavours.

Add chicken. Cook and stir for about 3 minutes until heated through.

Add cilantro and lime juice. Stir. Makes about 7 cups (1.75 L). Serves 6.

*1 serving: 201 Calories; 5.6 g Total Fat (1.8 g Mono, 1.1 g Poly, 1.1 g Sat); 58 mg Cholesterol; 16 g Carbohydrate; 1 g Fibre; 22 g Protein; 699 mg Sodium*

Pictured below.

Chicken Corn Soup, left

## about adobo sauce

Adobo is a thick, dark red Mexican sauce made of chilies, vinegar, herbs and spices. It's used as a marinade, sauce or as a condiment together with chipotle peppers.

## tip

Chipotle chili peppers are smoked jalapeño peppers. Be sure to wash your hands after handling. Store leftover chipotle chili peppers with sauce in airtight container in refrigerator for up to 1 year.

*Back bacon adds rich, smoky flavour to this light and colourful soup.*

serving suggestion

Make it a meal by adding a green salad and crusty bread.

# Chicken and Bacon Pea Soup

| | | |
|---|---|---|
| Cooking oil | 2 tsp. | 10 mL |
| Chopped red pepper | 1 cup | 250 mL |
| Chopped green onion | 1 cup | 250 mL |
| Boneless, skinless chicken thighs, cut into 1/2 inch (12 mm) pieces | 6 oz. | 170 g |
| Chopped lean back bacon | 1/3 cup | 75 mL |
| Paprika | 1/2 tsp. | 2 mL |
| Pepper | 1/2 tsp. | 2 mL |
| All-purpose flour | 2 tbsp. | 30 mL |
| Milk | 2 cups | 500 mL |
| Low-sodium prepared chicken broth | 2 cups | 500 mL |
| Frozen peas | 1 cup | 250 mL |
| Light sour cream | 2 tbsp. | 30 mL |

Heat cooking oil in large saucepan on medium. Add next 6 ingredients. Cook for 5 to 10 minutes, stirring occasionally, until chicken is no longer pink inside.

Add flour. Heat and stir for 1 minute.

Slowly add milk and broth, stirring constantly. Heat and stir until boiling and thickened. Reduce heat to medium-low. Simmer, uncovered, for 10 minutes, stirring occasionally.

Add peas and sour cream. Stir. Cover. Simmer for about 5 minutes, stirring occasionally, until peas are heated through. Makes 5 1/2 cups (1.4 L). Serves 6.

*1 serving: 149 Calories; 5 g Total Fat (2.1 g Mono, 1.0 g Poly, 1.7 g Sat); 33 mg Cholesterol; 13 g Carbohydrate; 2 g Fibre; 13 g Protein; 361 mg Sodium*

Pictured at right.

*It's not a lie—everything but the chicken is blended smooth! This creamy, golden soup has a wonderful medley of vegetable and chicken flavours.*

# Only Chicken Soup

| | | |
|---|---|---|
| Chopped onion | 1 cup | 250 mL |
| Chopped celery | 1 cup | 250 mL |
| Garlic clove, minced (or 1/4 tsp., 1 mL, powder) | 1 | 1 |
| Cooking oil | 1 tbsp. | 15 mL |

(continued on next page)

| | | |
|---|---|---|
| Water | 6 cups | 1.5 L |
| Chopped carrot (about 2 medium) | 1 cup | 250 mL |
| Medium potatoes, peeled and cut into 8 chunks | 2 | 2 |
| Peeled diced zucchini | 1 1/2 cups | 375 mL |
| Boneless, skinless chicken breast halves (about 2) | 8 oz. | 225 g |
| Chicken bouillon powder | 3 tbsp. | 50 mL |
| Parsley flakes | 2 tsp. | 10 mL |
| Bay leaf | 1 | 1 |
| Alphabet pasta, uncooked (optional) | 1/2 cup | 125 mL |

Sauté onion, celery and garlic in cooking oil in large uncovered pot or Dutch oven until onion is soft and clear.

Stir in remaining 9 ingredients. Cover. Simmer for 1 hour. Remove chicken to cutting board. Remove and discard bay leaf. Purée soup, in 2 batches, in blender or with hand blender until smooth (see Safety Tip). Return to pot. Cut chicken into bite-sized pieces. Return to soup. Makes 10 2/3 cups (2.7 L).

*1 cup (250 mL): 77 Calories; 1.9 g Total Fat (0.9 g Mono, 0.5 g Poly, 0.2 g Sat); 13 mg Cholesterol; 10 g Carbohydrate; 1 g Fibre; 6 g Protein; 961 mg Sodium*

Pictured below.

**Safety Tip:** Follow manufacturer's instructions for processing hot liquids.

## freezing

If you want to freeze Only Chicken Soup or any other containing pasta or potatoes, keep in mind that those ingredients do not freeze well, so you may want to consider adding them after thawing. Rice will soften after thawing; undercooking it slightly before freezing will prevent this from happening.

Left: Chicken and Bacon Pea Soup, left
Right: Only Chicken Soup, left

*This filling Chinese-inspired soup has lots of corn, ham, chicken and cooked egg threads. A hint of sherry complements the flavours nicely.*

## about slurry

A slurry is a mixture of cold liquid and flour or cornstarch that is useful for thickening soup and other dishes. It's usually added slowly to hot ingredients and then cooked gently until boiling and thickened to eliminate any raw taste from the flour or cornstarch.

# Sweet Corn Chicken Soup

| | | |
|---|---|---|
| Water | 3 cups | 750 mL |
| Can of cream-style corn | 14 oz. | 398 mL |
| Slice of deli ham, diced | 1 | 1 |
| Boneless, skinless chicken breast halves (about 2), cooked and chopped | 1/2 lb. | 225 g |
| Soy sauce | 1/2 tsp. | 2 mL |
| Chicken bouillon powder | 1 tbsp. | 15 mL |
| Chopped fresh chives | 2 tsp. | 10 mL |
| Salt | 1/8 tsp. | 0.5 mL |
| Pepper | 1/8 tsp. | 0.5 mL |
| Water | 2 tbsp. | 30 mL |
| Cornstarch | 1 tbsp. | 15 mL |
| Sherry (optional) | 1 tbsp. | 15 mL |
| Large egg, fork-beaten | 1 | 1 |

Combine first 9 ingredients in large saucepan. Heat and stir until boiling.

Stir second amount of water into cornstarch in small cup until smooth. Stir into chicken mixture until boiling and thickened.

Add sherry. Stir. Add egg in a very fine stream, stirring constantly. Makes 5 1/4 cups (1.3 L).

*1 cup (250 mL): 136 Calories; 2.0 g Total Fat (0.6 g Mono, 0.3 g Poly, 0.5 g Sat); 68 mg Cholesterol; 15 g Carbohydrate; 1 g Fibre; 13 g Protein; 1080 mg Sodium*

*A thick, attractively sage-coloured soup complete with generous amounts of chicken and the freshness of broccoli.*

# Broccoli Chicken Chowder

| | | |
|---|---|---|
| Packages of frozen cut broccoli (10 oz., 300 g, each) | 2 | 2 |
| Water | 1 cup | 250 mL |
| Milk | 1 cup | 250 mL |
| Can of skim evaporated milk | 13 1/2 oz. | 385 mL |
| Cans of condensed cream of chicken soup (10 oz., 284 mL, each) | 2 | 2 |
| Chicken bouillon powder | 1 tbsp. | 15 mL |
| Ground oregano | 1/2 tsp. | 2 mL |

*(continued on next page)*

| | | |
|---|---|---|
| Boneless, skinless chicken breast halves (about 2), diced | 1/2 lb. | 225 g |
| Hard margarine (or butter) | 1 tbsp. | 15 mL |

Cook broccoli in water in large saucepan until tender. Do not drain. Purée broccoli with liquid in blender (see Safety Tip). Return to saucepan.

Add both milks, chicken soup, bouillon powder and oregano. Stir.

Sauté chicken in margarine in frying pan until tender and no longer pink inside. Add to broccoli mixture. Simmer for about 5 minutes, stirring occasionally. Makes 9 cups (2.25 L).

*1 cup (250 mL): 167 Calories; 6.2 g Total Fat (1.6 g Mono, 1.4 g Poly, 2.1 g Sat); 24 mg Cholesterol; 15 g Carbohydrate; 2 g Fibre; 13 g Protein; 966 mg Sodium*

**Safety Tip:** Follow manufacturer's instructions for processing hot liquids.

## Cock-a-Leekie Soup

*A Classic!*

| | | |
|---|---|---|
| Chicken Stock (page 26), or prepared chicken broth | 10 cups | 2.5 L |
| Leeks, white part only, chopped | 8 | 8 |
| Long-grain rice, uncooked | 1/4 cup | 60 mL |
| Quartered pitted dried prunes | 1 1/2 cups | 375 mL |
| Parsley flakes | 1/2 tsp. | 2 mL |
| Ground thyme | 1/8 tsp. | 0.5 mL |
| Salt | 1/2 tsp. | 2 mL |
| Pepper | 1/4 tsp. | 1 mL |
| Diced cooked chicken (see Tip, page 36) | 3 cups | 750 mL |

Combine first 8 ingredients in large pot. Bring to a boil. Cook slowly for about 30 minutes.

Add chicken. Cover. Cook for another 10 minutes. Makes about 14 cups (3.5 L).

*1 cup (250 mL): 125 Calories; 2.4 g Total Fat (0.9 g Mono, 0.5 g Poly, 0.7 g Sat); 27 mg Cholesterol; 15 g Carbohydrate; 1 g Fibre; 10 g Protein; 935 mg Sodium*

*A chicken and leek soup that was served in Scotland as early as the 16th century—it's sure to bring out the Scot in anyone! This version includes the traditional ingredient of dried prunes, which adds a rich flavour.*

### time-saving tip

If you've no time to make stock from scratch, make a quick substitute by using 10 cups (2.5 L) water plus 3 1/2 tbsp. (57 mL) chicken bouillon powder, or substitute an equal amount of store-bought chicken broth.

*This is a full-bodied gumbo thickened with rice and vegetables. The okra gives it an authentic Southern feel!*

## about gumbo

Perhaps one of the most famous dishes to have come out of the United States, gumbo originated in Louisiana, but the word itself is thought to be derived from an African word for okra. Gumbo can contain many different kinds of vegetables, meats and shellfish, but all gumbos are thickened either with okra or a roux. In the southern U.S., fresh okra is the preferred thickener, and it's available year-round. Elsewhere it is in season from about May to October.

*Plan for two days to create this rich and flavourful turkey soup—one day to boil, strain and chill the broth, and the next day to finish the soup.*

## about celery hearts

The celery heart is the very centre of a celery bunch, the inner ribs so to speak, including the small, pale-coloured stalks with leaves. Celery hearts are available in ready-to-use packages from the produce section in grocery stores.

# Chicken Gumbo

| | | |
|---|---|---|
| Chicken Stock (page 26), or prepared chicken broth | 8 cups | 2 L |
| Chopped onion | 1 cup | 250 mL |
| Canned tomatoes, broken up | 14 oz. | 398 mL |
| Sliced okra | 1 cup | 250 mL |
| Small green pepper, seeded and chopped | 1 | 1 |
| Finely chopped celery | 1/4 cup | 60 mL |
| Long-grain rice, uncooked | 1/2 cup | 125 mL |
| Granulated sugar | 1 tsp. | 5 mL |
| Salt | 1 tsp. | 5 mL |
| Pepper | 1/4 tsp. | 1 mL |
| Diced cooked chicken (see Tip, page 36) | 2 cups | 500 mL |

Put first 10 ingredients into large pot. Cover. Bring to a boil, stirring often. Boil gently for about 20 minutes until rice is cooked.

Add chicken. Cook until heated through. Makes about 10 cups (2.5 L).

*1 cup (250 mL): 134 Calories; 3.3 g Total Fat (1.2 g Mono, 0.7 g Poly, 0.9 g Sat); 25 mg Cholesterol; 12 g Carbohydrate; 1 g Fibre; 13 g Protein; 932 mg Sodium*

# Meaty Turkey Rice Soup

**DAY 1**

| | | |
|---|---|---|
| Water | 12 cups | 3 L |
| Turkey parts, with skin | 6 lbs. | 2.7 kg |
| Whole celery heart | 1 | 1 |
| Medium onions, halved | 2 | 2 |
| Large carrot, halved | 1 | 1 |
| Bay leaves | 2 | 2 |
| Peppercorns | 10 | 10 |
| Fresh parsley sprigs | 2 | 2 |
| Salt | 1 tbsp. | 15 mL |

**DAY 2**

| | | |
|---|---|---|
| Water | | |
| Chopped onion | 1 cup | 250 mL |
| Chopped celery | 1 cup | 250 mL |
| Diced carrot | 1 cup | 250 mL |

*(continued on next page)*

| | | |
|---|---|---|
| Reserved cooked turkey | 4 cups | 1 L |
| Cooked long-grain white rice | 1 1/2 cups | 375 mL |
| (about 1/2 cup, 125 mL, uncooked) | | |
| Frozen peas | 1 cup | 250 mL |
| Chopped fresh parsley | 1/4 cup | 60 mL |
| (or 1 tbsp., 15 mL, flakes) | | |
| Salt, to taste | | |
| Pepper, to taste | | |

**Day 1:** Combine water and turkey parts in at least 6 quart (6 L) Dutch oven or stockpot. Bring to a boil. Boil, uncovered, for 5 minutes. Remove from heat. Carefully spoon off and discard foam from surface. Bring to a boil.

Add next 7 ingredients. Reduce heat. Simmer, partially covered, for about 3 hours until meat is falling off bones. Pour through sieve over large liquid measure. Remove meat from turkey bones as soon as cool enough to handle. Dice meat. Reserve 4 cups (1 L). Cover. Chill. Discard skin, turkey bones and strained solids. Chill broth overnight until fat comes to surface and solidifies.

**Day 2:** Carefully spoon off and discard fat from surface of broth. Add water, if necessary, to make 10 cups (2.5 L). Pour into Dutch oven or stockpot. Bring to a boil. Add onion, celery and carrot. Reduce heat. Simmer, partially covered, for 1 hour.

Add remaining 6 ingredients. Cook gently for about 10 minutes until heated through. Makes about 10 1/2 cups (2.6 L).

*1 cup (250 mL): 147 Calories; 2.9 g Total Fat (0.6 g Mono, 0.8 g Poly, 0.9 g Sat); 41 mg Cholesterol; 12 g Carbohydrate; 2 g Fibre; 18 g Protein; 745 mg Sodium*

Pictured below.

## tip

If you're watching your weight, soup can make a nutritious, filling meal. To reduce calories even further, trim the fat off any meat you use, or drain it away if you're searing it first. You can further reduce the fat of broth-based soups by placing a coffee filter on the soup's surface and blotting it up. Or, if you let the soup chill in the refrigerator overnight, the fat will harden on the surface, making it easy to lift out.

Meaty Turkey Rice Soup, left

*Who says chicken soup has the cure-all market cornered? This slow-cooker turkey soup is so comforting, and has just the right blend of spicy and sour ingredients to perk you up in no time.*

## tip

Don't have any leftover chicken or turkey? Start with 2 boneless, skinless chicken breasts (4 – 6 oz., 113 – 117 g, each) or 1 boneless, skinless turkey breast (about 10 oz., 285 g). Place in large frying pan with 1 cup (250 mL) water or chicken broth. Simmer, covered, for 12 to 14 minutes until no longer pink inside. Drain. Chop. Makes about 2 cups (500 mL).

# Hot and Sour Turkey Pot Soup

| | | |
|---|---|---|
| Chinese dried mushrooms | 6 | 6 |
| Boiling water | 1 cup | 250 mL |
| Prepared chicken broth | 4 cups | 1 L |
| Diced cooked turkey (see Tip, left) | 2 cups | 500 mL |
| Sliced carrot | 2 cups | 500 mL |
| Cubed firm tofu | 1 cup | 250 mL |
| Sliced celery | 1 cup | 250 mL |
| Soy sauce | 1/4 cup | 60 mL |
| Rice vinegar | 2 tbsp. | 30 mL |
| Chili paste (sambal oelek) | 1 tsp. | 5 mL |
| Prepared chicken broth | 1/4 cup | 60 mL |
| Cornstarch | 2 tbsp. | 30 mL |
| Sesame oil (optional) | 1 tsp. | 5 mL |
| Chopped baby bok choy | 2 cups | 500 mL |
| Thinly sliced green onion | 1/4 cup | 60 mL |
| Rice vinegar | 1 tbsp. | 15 mL |

Put mushrooms into small heatproof bowl. Add boiling water. Stir. Let stand for about 20 minutes until softened. Drain. Remove and discard stems. Slice into thin strips. Transfer to 3 1/2 to 4 quart (3.5 to 4 L) slow cooker.

Add next 8 ingredients. Stir well. Cook, covered, on Low for 4 to 6 hours or High for 2 to 3 hours until carrot is tender.

Combine next 3 ingredients in small bowl. Add to slow cooker. Stir.

Add bok choy and green onion. Stir well. Cook, covered, on High for about 5 minutes until slightly thickened.

Stir in second amount of vinegar. Makes about 8 cups (2 L).

*1 cup (250 mL): 118 Calories; 2.1 g Total Fat (0.6 g Mono, 0.6 g Poly, 0.6 g Sat); 34 mg Cholesterol; 9 g Carbohydrate; 2 g Fibre; 15 g Protein; 1142 mg Sodium*

Pictured at right.

*This delectable chowder is thick and almost stew-like. For an extra-special occasion, add shrimp, scallops or lobster.*

## make ahead

This hearty chowder is easy to make ahead and freeze in air-tight containers.

# Clam Chowder  *A Classic!*

| | | |
|---|---|---|
| Large potatoes, cubed | 3 | 3 |
| Large carrots, cut into 1 inch (2.5 cm) pieces | 3 | 3 |
| Boiling water, to cover | | |
| Bacon slices, diced | 10 – 12 | 10 – 12 |
| Large green pepper, diced | 1 | 1 |
| Chopped celery | 1 1/2 cups | 375 mL |
| Chopped onion | 1 1/2 cups | 375 mL |
| Reserved clam liquid | | |
| Cans of condensed cream of potato soup (10 oz., 284 mL, each) | 2 | 2 |
| Lemon pepper | 1/4 tsp. | 1 mL |
| Salt | 1 tsp. | 5 mL |
| Pepper | 1/8 tsp. | 0.5 mL |
| Cans of baby clams, drained, liquid reserved (5 oz., 142 g, each) | 2 | 2 |
| Canned stewed tomatoes | 14 oz. | 398 mL |
| Milk | 1 1/2 cups | 375 mL |

*(continued on next page)*

Clam Chowder, above

Cook potato and carrot in boiling water in large saucepan until tender. Do not drain.

Fry bacon until crisp. Remove to dish. Discard fat except for 1 tbsp. (15 mL).

Add green pepper, celery and onion to frying pan. Sauté until soft. Add to potato mixture along with bits from pan. Add bacon.

Add liquid from clams, potato soup, lemon pepper, salt and pepper. Stir. Boil gently for 10 to 15 minutes.

Add clams, tomatoes and milk. Heat through, without boiling, to prevent curdling. Makes 20 cups (5 L) chowder.

*1 cup (250 mL): 128 Calories; 3.4 g Total Fat (1.0 g Mono, 0.3 g Poly, 1.4 g Sat); 19 mg Cholesterol; 19 g Carbohydrate; 2 g Fibre; 6 g Protein; 546 mg Sodium*

Pictured at left.

## Tuna Corn Chowder

| | | |
|---|---|---|
| Hard margarine (or butter) | 1 tbsp. | 15 mL |
| Chopped onion | 1/3 cup | 75 mL |
| Chopped celery | 1/4 cup | 60 mL |
| Water | 1 1/2 cups | 375 mL |
| Diced peeled potato | 1 cup | 250 mL |
| Chicken bouillon powder | 1 tsp. | 5 mL |
| Dill weed | 1/2 tsp. | 2 mL |
| Salt | 1/2 tsp. | 2 mL |
| Pepper | 1/4 tsp. | 1 mL |
| Can of cream-style corn | 14 oz. | 398 mL |
| Milk | 1 cup | 250 mL |
| Can of flaked tuna, drained | 6 oz. | 170 g |

*A simple can of tuna turns corn chowder into a complete meal! A pleasantly creamy soup with a hint of dill.*

### make ahead

This recipe freezes well, so why not make a batch or two on the weekend and freeze it in dinner-sized portions for quick weeknight meals? Use airtight containers to reduce freezer burn.

Melt margarine in large saucepan on medium. Add onion and celery. Cook for 5 to 10 minutes, stirring often, until onion is softened.

Add next 6 ingredients. Stir. Bring to a boil on medium-high. Reduce heat to medium-low. Cover. Simmer for about 10 minutes until potato is tender.

Add corn, milk and tuna. Heat for about 10 minutes, stirring occasionally, until heated through. Do not boil. Makes about 5 cups (1.25 L).

*1 cup (250 mL): 176 Calories; 4.3 g Total Fat (2.1 g Mono, 0.8 g Poly, 1.2 g Sat); 15 mg Cholesterol; 25 g Carbohydrate; 2 g Fibre; 11 g Protein; 787 mg Sodium*

*Traditionally served with a pat of butter or swirls of whipping cream, this Scottish smoked fish soup makes a great cold-day supper.*

## about cullen skink

This soup is named for the town of Cullen in Morayshire, Scotland. "Skink" is a Scottish word meaning "beef shank," but the term is also used more generally to mean "soup."

## variation

If smoked haddock is hard to find, substitute smoked cod.

*This Thai-influenced soup has a wonderful combination of curry spice and herb freshness. Adjust the amount of green curry paste to suit your heat preference.*

## make ahead

Curries often improve in flavour if the spices are left to mellow for a day, so you may find that your curry soup actually tastes better the next day.

# Cullen Skink

|  | | |
|---|---|---|
| Finnan haddie (smoked haddock) | 1 lb. | 454 g |
| Medium onion, chopped | 1 | 1 |
| Water | 3 cups | 750 mL |
| Mashed potatoes | 2 1/2 cups | 625 mL |
| Skim evaporated milk | 2/3 cup | 150 mL |
| Milk | 1 3/4 cups | 425 mL |
| Chopped fresh parsley | 1 1/2 tbsp. | 25 mL |
| (or 1 tsp., 5 mL, flakes) | | |
| Pepper | 1/8 tsp. | 0.5 mL |

Cook fish and onion in water in large saucepan for 20 minutes. Do not drain. Remove fish. Remove bones, flaking flesh from skin. Return fish to saucepan.

Add remaining 5 ingredients. Stir well. Bring to a boil, stirring frequently. Makes 8 cups (2 L).

*1 cup (250 mL): 175 Calories; 2.0 g Total Fat (0.6 g Mono, 0.4 g Poly, 0.8 g Sat); 48 mg Cholesterol; 19 g Carbohydrate; trace Fibre; 20 g Protein; 660 mg Sodium*

# Coconut Shrimp Soup

|  | | |
|---|---|---|
| Finely grated ginger root | 2 tsp. | 10 mL |
| (or 1/2 tsp., 2 mL, ground ginger) | | |
| Garlic cloves, minced | 2 | 2 |
| (or 1/2 tsp., 2 mL, powder) | | |
| Green curry paste | 1 tbsp. | 15 mL |
| Cooking oil | 2 tsp. | 10 mL |
| Cans of light coconut milk | 2 | 2 |
| (14 oz., 398 mL, each) | | |
| Prepared chicken broth | 1 cup | 250 mL |
| Stalk of lemon grass, halved | 1 | 1 |
| Fish sauce | 2 tsp. | 10 mL |
| Brown sugar, packed | 2 tsp. | 10 mL |
| Fresh snow peas, trimmed, | 4 oz. | 113 g |
| thinly sliced lengthwise | | |

*(continued on next page)*

| Raw medium shrimp, peeled and deveined | 1 lb. | 454 g |
| Chopped fresh basil | 3 tbsp. | 50 mL |
|   (or 2 1/4 tsp., 11 mL, dried) | | |
| Chopped fresh cilantro (or parsley) | 3 tbsp. | 50 mL |

Sauté ginger, garlic and curry paste in cooking oil in large saucepan for 1 to 2 minutes until fragrant.

Add next 6 ingredients. Stir. Bring to a boil on medium-high. Cover. Reduce heat to medium. Simmer for 2 minutes to blend flavours.

Add remaining 3 ingredients. Reduce heat to medium-low. Heat and stir for 3 to 5 minutes until shrimp are just pink. Remove and discard lemon grass. Makes 6 cups (1.5 L).

*1 cup (250 mL):* 255 Calories; 16.2 g Total Fat (1.2 g Mono, 1.1 g Poly, 12.9 g Sat); 115 mg Cholesterol; 8 g Carbohydrate; 1 g Fibre; 18 g Protein; 476 mg Sodium

Pictured below.

## about green curry

Curries are a major part of Thai cuisine, and they're often named by their colour—yellow, red and green. Yellow is the mildest and green is the hottest. Green curry paste and green curries get their colour from the green chilies used to make them.

Coconut Shrimp Soup, left

*This deliciously simple and elegant soup is creamy white with mild and delicate flavours.*

### time-saving tip

When making this soup, try mixing just 1 cup (250 mL) of the milk with the flour, bouillon powder and pepper, and let this come to a boil before adding the remaining 3 cups (750 mL) of milk. The milk will boil much faster this way than if you try boiling all 4 cups (1 L) at once.

## Simple Crab Soup

| | | |
|---|---|---|
| Butter (or hard margarine) | 1/3 cup | 75 mL |
| All-purpose flour | 1/3 cup | 75 mL |
| Chicken bouillon powder | 1 tbsp. | 15 mL |
| Pepper (white is best for colour) | 1/8 tsp. | 0.5 mL |
| Milk | 4 cups | 1 L |
| Crabmeat (or 4 1/4 oz., 120 g, can, drained, cartilage removed) | 1 cup | 250 mL |
| Sherry | 1 1/2 tbsp. | 25 mL |

Chopped chives, for garnish

Melt butter in saucepan. Mix in flour, bouillon powder and pepper. Stir in milk until it boils and thickens.

Add crabmeat and sherry. Heat through but do not boil.

Sprinkle each serving with chives. Makes 5 cups (1.25 L).

*1 cup (250 mL): 255 Calories; 14.6 g Total Fat (4.1 g Mono, 0.6 g Poly, 9.0 g Sat); 66 mg Cholesterol; 18 g Carbohydrate; trace Fibre; 13 g Protein; 956 mg Sodium*

*A lovely soup with plenty of leafy spinach and sweet shrimp. The rich broth, perfectly accented with white wine, makes this soup a special treat.*

## Spinach and Shrimp Soup

| | | |
|---|---|---|
| Uncooked medium shrimp (with shells) | 1 lb. | 454 g |
| Water | 7 cups | 1.75 L |
| Dry white (or alcohol-free) wine | 1 cup | 250 mL |
| Chopped onion | 1/2 cup | 125 mL |
| Chopped carrot | 1/2 cup | 125 mL |
| Olive (or canola) oil | 1 tbsp. | 15 mL |
| Chopped onion | 1 cup | 250 mL |
| Garlic cloves, minced (or 1 tsp., 5 mL, powder) | 4 | 4 |
| All-purpose flour | 1 tbsp. | 15 mL |
| Fresh spinach, stems removed, coarsely chopped, lightly packed | 6 cups | 1.5 L |
| Chopped fresh parsley (or 1 1/2 tsp., 7 mL, flakes) | 2 tbsp. | 30 mL |
| Salt | 1 tsp. | 5 mL |
| Can of evaporated milk | 5 1/2 oz. | 160 mL |

*(continued on next page)*

Peel and devein shrimp, reserving shells and tails. Coarsely chop shrimp. Transfer to medium bowl. Set aside.

Put reserved shells and tails into large pot or Dutch oven. Add next 4 ingredients. Stir. Bring to a boil on medium-high. Reduce heat to medium. Simmer, uncovered, for 20 minutes, stirring occasionally. Strain through sieve into large bowl. Discard solids. Set liquid aside.

Heat olive oil in same pot on medium. Add second amount of onion. Cook for 5 to 10 minutes, stirring often, until softened.

Add garlic. Heat and stir for 1 to 2 minutes until fragrant.

Add flour. Heat and stir for 1 minute. Slowly add reserved liquid, stirring constantly until boiling and slightly thickened. Reduce heat to medium-low. Simmer, uncovered, for 5 minutes, stirring occasionally.

Add spinach, parsley and salt. Heat and stir for about 3 minutes until spinach is wilted.

Add shrimp and evaporated milk. Heat and stir on medium-high for about 2 minutes until shrimp turn pink. Makes about 8 cups (2 L) soup. Serves 6.

*1 serving:* 202 Calories; 6.1 g Total Fat (2.6 g Mono, 0.9 g Poly, 2.0 g Sat); 110 mg Cholesterol; 12 g Carbohydrate; 3 g Fibre; 18 g Protein; 581 mg Sodium

Pictured below.

Spinach and Shrimp Soup, left

*Though people often expect shellfish to be the base ingredient in bisques, this version uses basa instead. We've also used evaporated milk as a lower-fat alternative to the traditional cream.*

### about bisque

On the soup family tree, bisque is a close relative of chowder. Both are rich, thick soups often made with a seafood base, the main difference being that chowders are chunky while bisques are smooth. Several hundred years ago, the term "bisque" was used to describe a spicy dish of meat or game birds. By the 1700s, crayfish became the dominant ingredient, and from that point on bisque became known mainly as a seafood-based soup, although bisques can also feature meat or vegetables as a main ingredient.

# Basa Bisque

| | | |
|---|---|---|
| Cooking oil | 1 tsp. | 5 mL |
| Chopped onion | 1 cup | 250 mL |
| Chopped celery | 1/2 cup | 125 mL |
| Garlic cloves, minced (or 1/2 tsp., 2 mL, powder) | 2 | 2 |
| Water | 2 1/2 cups | 625 mL |
| Chopped peeled potatoes | 2 cups | 500 mL |
| Can of cut yellow wax beans (with liquid) | 14 oz. | 398 mL |
| Chopped carrot | 1 cup | 250 mL |
| Frozen kernel corn | 1/2 cup | 125 mL |
| Bay leaf | 1 | 1 |
| Can of evaporated milk | 13 1/2 oz. | 385 mL |
| Milk | 1 cup | 250 mL |
| All-purpose flour | 1/4 cup | 60 mL |
| Salt | 1 1/2 tsp. | 7 mL |
| Pepper | 1/2 tsp. | 2 mL |
| Ground nutmeg | 1/8 tsp. | 0.5 mL |
| Basa fillets, any small bones removed, cut into 1 inch (2.5 cm) pieces | 1 lb. | 454 g |

Heat cooking oil in Dutch oven on medium. Add next 3 ingredients. Cook for 5 to 10 minutes, stirring often, until onion is softened.

Add next 6 ingredients. Stir. Bring to a boil. Reduce heat to medium-low. Simmer, covered, for about 20 minutes, stirring occasionally, until vegetables are soft.

Whisk next 6 ingredients in small bowl until smooth. Add to vegetables. Stir well on medium until boiling and thickened slightly.

Add fish. Simmer for 5 minutes, stirring occasionally, until fish flakes easily when tested with fork. Remove and discard bay leaf. Carefully process, in 3 batches, in blender (see Safety Tip). Makes about 9 1/4 cups (2.3 L).

*1 cup (250 mL): 194 Calories; 5.6 g Total Fat (1.0 g Mono, 0.3 g Poly, 3.0 g Sat); 37 mg Cholesterol; 24 g Carbohydrate; 3 g Fibre; 12 g Protein; 705 mg Sodium*

Pictured at right.

**Safety Tip:** Follow manufacturer's instructions for processing hot liquids.

## Simple Seafood Bisque

| | | |
|---|---|---|
| Can of ready-to-serve New England clam chowder | 19 oz. | 540 mL |
| Can of condensed tomato soup | 10 oz. | 284 mL |
| Can of crabmeat, drained, cartilage removed, flaked | 6 oz. | 170 g |
| Water | 1 cup | 250 mL |
| Medium sherry | 2 tbsp. | 30 mL |

Process chowder in blender or food processor until smooth. Transfer to medium saucepan.

Add soup. Stir. Add crabmeat and water. Stir well. Heat on medium-low, stirring often, until boiling. Remove from heat.

Add sherry. Stir. Makes about 4 3/4 cups (1.2 L).

*1 cup (250 mL): 148 Calories; 4.4 g Total Fat (1.3 g Mono, 1.0 g Poly, 1.6 g Sat); 11 mg Cholesterol; 17 g Carbohydrate; 1 g Fibre; 10 g Protein; 1130 mg Sodium*

Pictured below.

*Sherry provides a subtle sweetness to this creamy combination of just a few simple ingredients. Garnish with green onion to add a special touch.*

Left: Simple Seafood Bisque, above
Right: Basa Bisque, left

*A chunky crab soup with colourful tomatoes and vegetables—so tasty!*

variation

Turn Crab Soup into tuna soup by using canned tuna with liquid instead of crabmeat.

# Crab Soup

| | | |
|---|---|---|
| Canned stewed tomatoes | 14 oz. | 398 mL |
| Chopped onion | 1 cup | 250 mL |
| Chopped celery | 1/2 cup | 125 mL |
| Grated potato | 1 1/2 cups | 375 mL |
| Grated carrot | 1/2 cup | 125 mL |
| Water | 3 cups | 750 mL |
| Milk | 1/2 cup | 125 mL |
| All-purpose flour | 1/4 cup | 60 mL |
| Chicken bouillon powder | 1 tbsp. | 15 mL |
| Salt | 1 tsp. | 5 mL |
| Pepper | 1/8 – 1/4 tsp. | 0.5 – 1 mL |
| Can of evaporated skim milk (or light cream) | 13 1/2 oz. | 385 mL |
| Can of crabmeat, with liquid, cartilage removed | 4 1/4 oz. | 120 g |

Combine first 6 ingredients in saucepan. Cover. Cook until vegetables are tender.

Measure next 5 ingredients into small bowl. Whisk until no lumps remain. Stir into tomato mixture until it boils and thickens.

Add evaporated milk and crabmeat. Heat slowly, stirring often, until steaming hot, but not boiling. Makes 8 cups (2 L).

*1 cup (250 mL): 119 Calories; 0.5 g Total Fat (0.1 g Mono, 0.1 g Poly, 0.2 g Sat); 13 mg Cholesterol; 21 g Carbohydrate; 1 g Fibre; 8 g Protein; 940 mg Sodium*

Pictured at right.

*This traditional gumbo will have you feeling like you're down on the bayou. Full of rice, vegetables and seafood, it will satisfy any appetite.*

serving suggestion

Serve with a bottle of hot sauce for those who want to up the spice factor!

# Seafood Gumbo

| | | |
|---|---|---|
| Cooking oil | 1 tbsp. | 15 mL |
| Chopped celery | 1 cup | 250 mL |
| Chopped onion | 1 cup | 250 mL |
| Cajun seasoning | 1 1/2 tsp. | 7 mL |
| Garlic clove, minced (or 1/4 tsp., 1 mL, powder) | 1 | 1 |
| Dried thyme | 1/4 tsp. | 1 mL |
| Pepper | 1/4 tsp. | 1 mL |

*(continued on next page)*

| | | |
|---|---|---|
| All-purpose flour | 2 tbsp. | 30 mL |
| Prepared vegetable broth | 3 cups | 750 mL |
| Can of diced tomatoes (with juice) | 14 oz. | 398 mL |
| Fresh (or frozen) okra, chopped (optional) | 1 cup | 250 mL |
| Long-grain white rice | 1/2 cup | 125 mL |
| Bay leaves | 2 | 2 |
| Cod fillets, any small bones removed, cut into 1 inch (2.5 cm) pieces | 1 cup | 250 mL |
| Frozen seafood mix, thawed | 1 cup | 250 mL |

Heat cooking oil in large saucepan or Dutch oven on medium. Add next 6 ingredients. Cook for about 10 minutes, stirring occasionally, until onion is browned.

Add flour. Heat and stir for about 5 minutes until flour starts to turn brown. Slowly add broth, stirring constantly and scraping any brown bits from bottom of pan, until boiling and thickened.

Add next 4 ingredients. Stir. Bring to a boil. Cook, covered, for about 15 minutes until rice is almost tender. Remove and discard bay leaves.

Add fish and seafood mix. Stir. Cook, covered, for about 10 minutes until fish flakes easily when tested with fork and rice is tender. Makes about 6 cups (1.5 L).

*1 cup (250 mL): 172 Calories; 3.1 g Total Fat (1.4 g Mono, 0.9 g Poly, 0.3 g Sat); 65 mg Cholesterol; 23 g Carbohydrate; 1 g Fibre; 14 g Protein; 667 mg Sodium*

## about roux

Gumbos often use a roux (ROO) as a thickener. To make a traditional roux, heat butter or other fat and stir in an equal amount of flour. Cook the flour in the fat for a few minutes until it starts to lightly brown. Once the roux is made, add liquid to it slowly while stirring and heat it to a boil. Make sure to stir continuously to prevent lumps from forming as you proceed with your recipe.

Crab Soup, left

This soup is a lightened-up version of cioppino (cho-PEE-no), a classic stew containing fish, seafood and often shell-on shellfish, in a broth of tomato and fish stock.

## serving suggestion

Serve with a thick slice of fresh sourdough or garlic bread for a hearty and delicious lunch.

# Tomato Seafood Soup    *A Classic!*

| | | |
|---|---|---|
| Olive (or cooking) oil | 2 tbsp. | 30 mL |
| Chopped fennel bulb (white part only) | 1 cup | 250 mL |
| Chopped onion | 1 cup | 250 mL |
| Garlic clove, minced (or 1/4 tsp., 1 mL, powder) | 1 | 1 |
| Dried crushed chilies | 1/4 tsp. | 1 mL |
| Dry (or alcohol-free) white wine | 1/2 cup | 125 mL |
| Clam tomato beverage | 3 cups | 750 mL |
| Prepared vegetable broth | 3 cups | 750 mL |
| Can of diced tomatoes (with juice) | 14 oz. | 398 mL |
| Bay leaf | 1 | 1 |
| Can of whole baby clams (with liquid) | 5 oz. | 142 g |
| Halibut fillet, any small bones removed, cut into 3/4 inch (2 cm) pieces | 4 oz. | 113 g |
| Small bay scallops | 4 oz. | 113 g |
| Uncooked medium shrimp (peeled and deveined) | 4 oz. | 113 g |
| Chopped fresh parsley | 1 tbsp. | 15 mL |
| Chopped fresh thyme | 2 tsp. | 10 mL |

Heat olive oil in large saucepan or Dutch oven on medium. Add fennel and onion. Cook for about 10 minutes, stirring often, until onion is softened and starting to brown.

Add garlic and chilies. Heat and stir for 1 minute. Add wine. Simmer until liquid is reduced by half.

Add next 4 ingredients. Stir. Bring to a boil. Reduce heat to medium-low. Cook, partially covered, for 30 minutes to blend flavours. Remove and discard bay leaf.

Add remaining 6 ingredients. Stir. Cook for about 3 minutes, stirring frequently, until shrimp turn pink and scallops are opaque. Makes about 10 2/3 cups (2.7 L).

*1 cup (250 mL): 134 Calories; 3.9 g Total Fat (2.0 g Mono, 0.6 g Poly, 0.6 g Sat); 34 mg Cholesterol; 14 g Carbohydrate; 1 g Fibre; 10 g Protein; 590 mg Sodium*

Pictured at right.

*A favourite variation of clam chowder, with a rich red-orange broth and wonderful flavours.*

## food fun

Just in case you can't keep them straight, Manhattan clam chowder is tomato-based while New England-style clam chowder is made with milk or cream. Manhattan-style is said to have been created by Portuguese immigrants and named after New York by New Englanders, who were scornful of what they thought was an inferior soup (and an inferior locale)! It's said that many restaurants will feature one chowder or the other on their menus, but not both types.

# Manhattan Clam Chowder

| | | |
|---|---|---|
| Bacon slices, diced | 4 | 4 |
| Chopped onion | 1 cup | 250 mL |
| Medium potatoes, peeled and diced | 2 | 2 |
| Canned tomatoes, broken up | 14 oz. | 398 mL |
| Finely diced celery | 1 cup | 250 mL |
| Chicken bouillon powder | 1 tbsp. | 15 mL |
| Salt | 1/2 tsp. | 2 mL |
| Pepper | 1/4 tsp. | 1 mL |
| Ground thyme | 1/4 tsp. | 1 mL |
| Cayenne pepper (optional but good) | 1/8 tsp. | 0.5 mL |
| Water | 3 cups | 750 mL |
| All-purpose flour | 1/4 cup | 60 mL |
| Water | 1 cup | 250 mL |
| Can of baby clams, with liquid, chopped | 5 oz. | 142 g |

Fry bacon and onion in Dutch oven until bacon is cooked and onion is clear.

Add next 9 ingredients. Bring to a boil. Boil gently, covered, for about 25 minutes until vegetables are tender.

Mix flour and second amount of water until smooth. Stir into boiling mixture until it returns to a boil and thickens.

Add clams and liquid. Heat through. Makes 7 1/3 cups (1.8 L).

*1 cup (250 mL): 155 Calories; 6.4 g Total Fat (2.5 g Mono, 0.7 g Poly, 2.1 g Sat); 24 mg Cholesterol; 18 g Carbohydrate; 2 g Fibre; 7 g Protein; 1062 mg Sodium*

Pictured at right.

*This quick and easy soup covers all your bases with a good helping of broccoli, pasta and fish—great to serve for a light yet satisfying meal.*

## Broccoli and Haddock Soup

| | | |
|---|---|---|
| Prepared chicken broth | 4 cups | 1 L |
| Water | 2 cups | 500 mL |
| Garlic clove, minced | 1 | 1 |
| (or 1/4 tsp., 1 mL, powder) | | |
| Tiny shell pasta | 1 cup | 250 mL |
| Chopped broccoli | 2 cups | 500 mL |
| Haddock fillets, any small bones removed, | 1 lb. | 454 g |
| cut into bite-sized pieces | | |
| Lemon juice | 1 tbsp. | 15 mL |
| Salt | 1/2 tsp. | 2 mL |
| Pepper | 1/2 tsp. | 2 mL |

Combine first 3 ingredients in large saucepan or Dutch oven. Bring to a boil. Add pasta. Reduce heat to medium. Boil gently, uncovered, for 8 minutes, stirring occasionally, until pasta is almost tender.

Add broccoli and fish. Cook for about 5 minutes until broccoli and pasta are tender.

Add remaining 3 ingredients. Stir. Makes about 8 cups (2 L).

*1 cup (250 mL): 110 Calories; 1.2 g Total Fat (0.3 g Mono, 0.4 g Poly, 0.3 g Sat); 32 mg Cholesterol; 11 g Carbohydrate; 1 g Fibre; 13 g Protein; 931 mg Sodium*

*Sweet-and-sour soup gently accented with ginger—an enticing combination.*

## Pineapple Shrimp Soup

| | | |
|---|---|---|
| Uncooked medium shrimp | 1 lb. | 454 g |
| (peeled and deveined) | | |
| Soy sauce | 1 tbsp. | 15 mL |
| Granulated sugar | 1 tbsp. | 15 mL |
| Garlic cloves, minced | 2 | 2 |
| (or 1/2 tsp., 2 mL, powder) | | |
| Finely grated, peeled ginger root | 1 tsp. | 5 mL |
| (or 1/4 tsp., 1 mL, ground ginger) | | |
| Pepper | 1/2 tsp. | 2 mL |

*(continued on next page)*

| | | |
|---|---|---|
| Cooking oil | 2 tsp. | 10 mL |
| Medium onion, cut into 12 wedges | 1 | 1 |
| Prepared chicken broth | 4 cups | 1 L |
| Can of pineapple tidbits (with juice) | 14 oz. | 398 mL |
| Medium tomatoes, quartered, seeds removed, diced | 2 | 2 |
| Green onions, cut into 1 inch (2.5 cm) pieces | 2 | 2 |
| Finely shredded basil (or 1 tbsp., 15 mL, dried) | 1/4 cup | 60 mL |
| Chopped fresh cilantro or parsley | 2 tbsp. | 30 mL |

### serving suggestion

Serve with heat-and-serve spring rolls or egg rolls (available in your grocer's freezer) cooked according to package directions, with plum sauce for dipping.

Put first 6 ingredients into medium bowl. Stir gently until shrimp are coated. Heat wok or Dutch oven on medium-high. Add shrimp mixture. Stir-fry for 1 to 2 minutes until shrimp just start to turn pink. Transfer to medium bowl. Set aside.

Heat cooking oil in same wok. Add onion wedges. Stir-fry for about 2 minutes until starting to soften.

Add broth and pineapple with juice. Bring to a boil. Reduce heat to medium. Cover. Simmer for 5 minutes, stirring occasionally, to blend flavours.

Add remaining 4 ingredients. Heat and stir for about 5 minutes until heated through. Add shrimp mixture. Stir for about 1 minute until heated through. Makes about 8 cups (2 L).

*1 cup (250 mL): 129 Calories; 2.8 g Total Fat (1.2 g Mono, 0.9 g Poly, 0.5 g Sat); 65 mg Cholesterol; 14 g Carbohydrate; 1 g Fibre; 12 g Protein; 608 mg Sodium*

*An egg drop-style soup with sophisticated flavours, this whips up quickly with easy-to-find ingredients.*

## about asparagus

Not only does asparagus have a great fresh flavour, but it's also very nutritious. It's high in vitamins A and C, protein, fibre, potassium and folate, low in calories and sodium and has no fat or cholesterol.

# Crab Asparagus Soup

| | | |
|---|---|---|
| Cooking oil | 1 tsp. | 5 mL |
| Sliced fresh white mushrooms | 1/2 cup | 125 mL |
| Chopped green onion | 1/4 cup | 60 mL |
| Garlic clove, minced (or 1/4 tsp., 1 mL, powder) | 1 | 1 |
| Finely grated, peeled ginger root | 1/4 tsp. | 1 mL |
| Pepper | 1/4 tsp. | 1 mL |
| Prepared chicken broth | 3 cups | 750 mL |
| Fresh asparagus, trimmed of tough ends, cut into 1 inch (2.5 cm) pieces | 1/2 lb. | 225 g |
| Can of crabmeat, drained, cartilage removed, flaked | 6 oz. | 170 g |
| Cornstarch | 2 tsp. | 10 mL |
| Soy sauce | 2 tsp. | 10 mL |
| Hoisin sauce | 2 tsp. | 10 mL |
| Large egg | 1 | 1 |
| Water | 1 tbsp. | 15 mL |

Heat cooking oil in medium saucepan on medium. Add next 5 ingredients. Cook for 5 to 10 minutes, stirring often, until onion is softened.

Add broth. Stir. Bring to a boil on medium-high.

Add asparagus and crabmeat. Cover. Reduce heat to medium. Boil gently for about 5 minutes until asparagus is tender-crisp.

Combine next 3 ingredients in small cup. Add to soup. Heat and stir for about 1 minute until boiling and slightly thickened.

Beat egg and water with fork in same small cup. Add to soup in thin stream, stirring constantly. Makes about 4 1/2 cups (1.1 L).

*1 cup (250 mL): 119 Calories; 3.7 g Total Fat (1.5 g Mono, 0.9 g Poly, 0.8 g Sat); 79 mg Cholesterol; 8 g Carbohydrate; 1 g Fibre; 14 g Protein; 900 mg Sodium*

Pictured at right.

*This hot and spicy Thai specialty features ginger, lemon grass and lime. Reduce the amount of red chilies if you like it milder.*

## dinner themes

Tom Yum Soup features a classic Thai combination of robust salty, sour and hot flavours. For this reason, this soup would make a great starter for any Asian-themed dinner that features sweet or spicy curries.

# Tom Yum Soup

| | | |
|---|---|---|
| Prepared chicken broth | 4 cups | 1 L |
| Thinly sliced fresh shiitake mushrooms | 1 cup | 250 mL |
| Ginger root slices (1/4 inch, 6 mm, thick) | 3 | 3 |
| Lemon grass, bulbs only (roots and stalks removed) | 3 | 3 |
| Uncooked medium shrimp (peeled and deveined) | 3/4 lb. | 340 g |
| Can of shoestring-style bamboo shoots, drained | 8 oz. | 227 mL |
| Thai hot chili peppers, chopped (see Tip, page 15) | 3 | 3 |
| Lime juice | 3 tbsp. | 50 mL |
| Fish sauce | 2 tbsp. | 30 mL |
| Chopped fresh cilantro (or parsley) | 2 tsp. | 10 mL |

Measure broth into large saucepan. Bring to a boil. Reduce heat to medium. Add mushrooms and ginger root. Simmer, uncovered, for about 5 minutes until mushrooms are tender.

Pound lemon grass bulbs with mallet or rolling pin until partially crushed. Add to broth mixture. Add next 3 ingredients. Stir. Simmer, uncovered, for about 2 minutes until shrimp turn pink. Remove from heat. Remove and discard ginger root and lemon grass.

Add remaining 3 ingredients. Stir. Makes about 5 cups (1.25 L). Serves 4.

*1 serving: 151 Calories; 2.9 g Total Fat (0.6 g Mono, 1.1 g Poly, 0.6 g Sat); 129 mg Cholesterol; 10 g Carbohydrate; 2 g Fibre; 21 g Protein; 2302 mg Sodium*

Pictured at right.

*A satisfying soup filled with delicate wontons, tasty shrimp and fresh vegetables. This soup is best served immediately, before the wontons become too soft.*

## basic pork wontons

| | | |
|---|---|---|
| Lean ground pork | 4 oz. | 113 g |
| Cold water | 1 tbsp. | 15 mL |
| Finely chopped green onion | 1 tbsp. | 15 mL |
| Dry sherry | 1 1/2 tsp. | 7 mL |
| Cornstarch | 3/4 tsp. | 4 mL |
| Ground ginger | 1/4 tsp. | 1 mL |
| Salt | 1/4 tsp. | 1 mL |
| Pepper, sprinkle | | |
| Wonton wrappers (keep covered with damp cloth) | 20 | 20 |

Combine first 8 ingredients in medium bowl until well mixed.

Place about 1 tsp. (5 mL) filling in centre of wonton wrapper. Brush wrapper around filling with water. Fold wrapper over filling. Pinch and pleat wrapper together around filling to seal. Repeat with remaining filling and wrappers. Makes 20 wontons.

# Wor Wonton Soup

| | | |
|---|---|---|
| Chinese dried mushrooms | 2 | 2 |
| Boiling water | 1 cup | 250 mL |
| Cans of condensed chicken broth (10 oz., 284 mL, each) | 3 | 3 |
| Water | 3 cups | 750 mL |
| Coarsely grated carrot | 2 tbsp. | 30 mL |
| Boneless pork loin, cut julienne into 1 1/2 inch (3.8 cm) lengths (see Tip, page 60) | 4 oz. | 113 g |
| Raw medium shrimp, peeled and deveined | 12 | 12 |
| Fresh pea pods, cut in half | 12 | 12 |
| Shredded spinach, lightly packed | 1/2 cup | 125 mL |
| Green onions, sliced | 2 | 2 |
| Wontons | 20 | 20 |
| Boiling water | 12 cups | 3 L |

Put mushrooms into small bowl. Add first amount of boiling water. Let stand for 20 minutes until softened. Strain through fine cloth or several layers of cheesecloth, reserving liquid. Remove and discard stems. Slice caps thinly.

Combine reserved liquid, mushrooms and next 4 ingredients in large pot or Dutch oven. Bring to a boil. Reduce heat. Cover. Boil gently for about 5 minutes until pork is tender.

Add shrimp, pea pods, spinach and green onion. Cover. Boil gently for about 4 minutes until shrimp are pink and pea pods are tender-crisp.

*(continued on next page)*

Add wontons to second amount of boiling water in large saucepan. Boil gently, uncovered, for about 3 minutes, stirring gently occasionally, until wrapper clings to filling and filling is fully cooked. Drain. Add wontons to hot broth. Serve immediately, ensuring each bowl gets 3 or 4 wontons and 2 shrimp. Makes about 9 cups (2.25 L). Serves 6.

*1 serving: 375 Calories; 2.7 g Total Fat (0.6 g Mono, 0.2 g Poly, 0.5 g Sat); 48 mg Cholesterol; 67 g Carbohydrate; 2 g Fibre; 18 g Protein; 1546 mg Sodium*

Pictured below.

**tip**

You can often find uncooked frozen wontons in the freezer section of your grocery store or in Asian markets. You may also try calling your favourite Chinese restaurant and ask to buy uncooked wontons.

# Hot and Sour Soup

*This simple soup makes a stimulating start to your meal. A gentle heat and a mild sour tang add to the complex flavours of the broth.*

## variation

Before dividing into individual servings, add 1/2 cup (125 mL) diced firm tofu and heat through.

## tip

To julienne, cut into very thin strips that resemble matchsticks.

## tip

For best results, beat the eggs in a small liquid measure. This way you can pour the eggs into the soup in a thin, even stream.

| | | |
|---|---|---|
| Prepared chicken broth | 6 cups | 1.5 L |
| Boneless pork loin, cut julienne into 1 1/2 inch (3.8 cm) lengths (see Tip, left) | 7 oz. | 200 g |
| Sliced fresh white mushrooms | 1 cup | 250 mL |
| Water | 1/2 cup | 125 mL |
| Cornstarch | 2 tbsp. | 30 mL |
| White vinegar | 3 tbsp. | 50 mL |
| Soy sauce | 2 tbsp. | 30 mL |
| Chili paste (sambal oelek) | 2 tsp. | 10 mL |
| Pepper | 1/4 tsp. | 1 mL |
| Large egg | 1 | 1 |
| Green onions, sliced | 2 | 2 |

Bring broth to a boil in large saucepan. Add pork. Return to a boil. Reduce heat. Cover. Boil gently for about 5 minutes until pork is tender.

Add mushrooms. Cover. Simmer for 10 minutes.

Stir water into cornstarch in small bowl. Add next 4 ingredients. Stir into pork mixture until boiling and slightly thickened.

Beat egg with fork in small cup. Add egg to pork mixture in thin stream, constantly stirring in circular motion until fine egg threads form.

Sprinkle individual servings with green onion. Makes about 7 cups (1.75 L). Serves 6.

*1 serving: 120 Calories; 4.5 g Total Fat (1.9 g Mono, 0.6 g Poly, 1.5 g Sat); 54 mg Cholesterol; 5 g Carbohydrate; trace Fibre; 13 g Protein; 1277 mg Sodium*

Pictured at right.

*A delicious reincarnation for leftover pork—just toss it into this hearty soup for a warm, filling meal.*

### variation

In place of navy beans you can use white kidney beans, mixed beans, black-eyed peas or another bean of your choice.

## Quick Leftover Pork Soup

|  | | |
|---|---|---|
| Cooking oil | 2 tsp. | 10 mL |
| Chopped onion | 1 1/2 cups | 375 mL |
| Dry white (or alcohol-free) wine (optional) | 1/4 cup | 60 mL |
| Water | 4 cups | 1 L |
| Can of navy beans (with liquid) | 19 oz. | 540 mL |
| Can of Italian-style diced tomatoes (with juice) | 14 oz. | 398 mL |
| Diced leftover roast pork | 2 cups | 500 mL |
| Diced potato | 2 cups | 500 mL |
| Grated carrot | 1/2 cup | 125 mL |
| Vegetable bouillon powder | 2 tbsp. | 30 mL |
| Pepper | 1/2 tsp. | 2 mL |
| Chopped fresh basil (or 1 1/2 tsp., 7 mL, dried) | 2 tbsp. | 30 mL |

Heat cooking oil in large pot or Dutch oven on medium. Add onion. Cook for 5 to 10 minutes, stirring often, until softened.

Add wine. Bring to a boil. Boil for 1 minute.

Add next 8 ingredients. Stir. Bring to a boil. Reduce heat to medium-low. Cover. Simmer for about 45 minutes until potato is soft.

Stir in basil. Makes 9 cups (2.25 L).

*1 cup (250 mL): 329 Calories; 5.0 g Total Fat (2.0 g Mono, 1.2 g Poly, 1.2 g Sat); 27 mg Cholesterol; 48 g Carbohydrate; 16 g Fibre; 24 g Protein; 888 mg Sodium*

# Pizza Topping Soup

| | | |
|---|---|---|
| Cooking oil | 1 tsp. | 5 mL |
| Hot Italian sausages, casings removed, chopped | 1 lb. | 454 g |
| Cans of diced tomatoes (with juice), 14 oz. (398 mL) each | 2 | 2 |
| Sliced fresh white mushrooms | 2 cups | 500 mL |
| Sliced green pepper | 1 3/4 cups | 425 mL |
| Can of condensed beef broth | 10 oz. | 284 mL |
| Chopped onion | 1 cup | 250 mL |
| Water | 1 cup | 250 mL |
| Can of tomato sauce | 7 1/2 oz. | 213 mL |
| Dried oregano | 1/2 tsp. | 2 mL |
| Dried basil | 1/2 tsp. | 2 mL |
| Cayenne pepper | 1/8 tsp. | 0.5 mL |
| Grated part-skim mozzarella cheese | 1 cup | 250 mL |

Heat cooking oil in medium frying pan on medium. Add sausage. Scramble-fry for 8 to 10 minutes until no longer pink. Drain. Transfer to 4 to 5 quart (4 to 5 L) slow cooker.

Add next 10 ingredients. Stir well. Cover. Cook on Low for 8 to 9 hours or on High for 4 to 4 1/2 hours. Makes about 9 1/3 cups (2.3 L) soup.

Ladle soup into 6 individual bowls. Sprinkle each with cheese. Serves 6.

*1 serving: 242 Calories; 13.3 g Total Fat (5.3 g Mono, 1.6 g Poly, 5.5 g Sat); 40 mg Cholesterol; 16 g Carbohydrate; 3 g Fibre; 16 g Protein; 1182 mg Sodium*

*Enjoy all the pizza toppings you love in a soup, all topped with melted mozzarella—just like a slice of your favourite pizza.*

## make ahead

The night before, prepare the tomato mixture. Chill overnight in a covered bowl. Assemble and cook as directed the next day.

## serving suggestion

Serve with focaccia or crusty bread for dipping.

*Hot sausage and vegetables in a rich, red broth with robust flavour—this soup can be served with bread or buns to make a complete meal. Ham replaces the more traditional salt cod in this recipe.*

## explore chorizo

Chorizo is a sausage popular in many countries, including Spain, Portugal, Mexico, Argentina, Brazil and Puerto Rico. It is usually made of pork, garlic, herbs and dried smoked red peppers (paprika); it can also be made with beef. Raw chorizo must be cooked before being eaten, while cured or smoked chorizo can be eaten as is. Lean chorizo sausages are often used on pizzas or in appetizers or tapas while fattier varieties work well in cooked dishes, and can also be used in place of ground meats.

# Portuguese Chowder

|  | | |
|---|---|---|
| Hot sausage (such as chorizo or hot Italian) | 1/2 lb. | 225 g |
| Chopped onion | 1 cup | 250 mL |
| Garlic cloves, minced (or 1/2 tsp., 2 mL, powder) | 2 | 2 |
| Olive (or cooking) oil | 1 tbsp. | 15 mL |
| Can of diced tomatoes, with juice | 28 oz. | 796 mL |
| Water | 3 cups | 750 mL |
| Diced potato | 2 cups | 500 mL |
| Diced celery | 1 cup | 250 mL |
| Diced carrot | 1 cup | 250 mL |
| Beef bouillon powder | 1 tbsp. | 15 mL |
| Finely chopped cabbage | 2 cups | 500 mL |
| Diced cooked ham | 1 cup | 250 mL |
| Can of kidney beans, with liquid | 14 oz. | 398 mL |
| Dry red (or alcohol-free) wine (optional) | 1/2 cup | 125 mL |

Remove sausage meat from casing. Scramble-fry sausage, onion and garlic in olive oil in large pot or Dutch oven until sausage is no longer pink and onion is soft.

Add next 6 ingredients. Bring to a boil. Reduce heat. Simmer, covered, for 20 minutes until vegetables are cooked.

Add cabbage, ham and kidney beans. Simmer, covered, for 15 minutes until cabbage is tender.

Stir in red wine. Makes 12 cups (3 L).

*1 cup (250 mL): 155 Calories; 6.0 g Total Fat (1.2 g Mono, 0.2 g Poly, 1.8 g Sat); 17 mg Cholesterol; 16 g Carbohydrate; 3 g Fibre; 7 g Protein; 813 mg Sodium*

Pictured at right.

*The favourite flavour combination of ham and cheese in a soup! This kid-friendly chowder is simple to prepare and has a quick cooking time—perfect for lunch.*

# Ham and Cheese Chowder

| | | |
|---|---|---|
| Butter (or hard margarine) | 2 tbsp. | 30 mL |
| Chopped onion | 1 cup | 250 mL |
| All-purpose flour | 2 tbsp. | 30 mL |
| Dill weed | 1/2 tsp. | 2 mL |
| Pepper | 1/4 tsp. | 1 mL |
| Chicken Stock (page 26), or prepared chicken broth | 2 cups | 500 mL |
| Diced peeled potato | 2 cups | 500 mL |
| Grated medium Cheddar cheese | 2 cups | 500 mL |
| Milk | 1 cup | 250 mL |
| Diced cooked ham | 1 cup | 250 mL |

Melt butter in large saucepan on medium. Add onion. Cook for 5 to 10 minutes, stirring often, until softened.

Add next 3 ingredients. Heat and stir for 1 minute.

Slowly stir in stock until combined. Heat and stir until boiling and thickened.

Add potato. Stir. Bring to a boil. Reduce heat to medium-low. Simmer, partially covered, for 15 to 20 minutes, stirring occasionally, until potato is tender.

Add remaining 3 ingredients. Heat and stir for about 5 minutes until heated through. Makes about 5 cups (1.25 L).

*1 cup (250 mL): 390 Calories; 24.1 g Total Fat (7.3 g Mono, 1.1 g Poly, 14.5 g Sat); 82 mg Cholesterol; 21 g Carbohydrate; 2 g Fibre; 23 g Protein; 1165 mg Sodium*

# Polish Sauerkraut Soup

| | | |
|---|---|---|
| Bacon slices, diced | 4 | 4 |
| Sweet and sour cut pork ribs, trimmed of fat and cut into 1-bone portions | 1 1/2 lbs. | 680 g |
| Garlic clove, minced (or 1/4 tsp., 1 mL, powder) | 1 | 1 |
| Seasoned salt | 1/2 tsp. | 2 mL |
| Paprika | 1/2 tsp. | 2 mL |
| Pepper | 1/4 tsp. | 1 mL |
| Water | 6 cups | 1.5 L |
| Cans of stewed tomatoes (with juice), 14 oz. (398 mL) each, slightly mashed | 2 | 2 |
| Jar of sauerkraut, rinsed and drained well | 17 1/2 oz. | 500 mL |
| Large onion, chopped | 1 | 1 |
| Sliced carrot | 1 cup | 250 mL |
| Bay leaf | 1 | 1 |
| Can of small white beans, rinsed and drained | 19 oz. | 540 mL |
| Medium potato, diced | 1 | 1 |

Cook bacon in large pot or Dutch oven on medium-high for about 5 minutes until starting to brown.

Add next 5 ingredients. Heat and stir for about 6 minutes until ribs are browned.

Add next 6 ingredients. Bring to a boil. Reduce heat to medium-low. Cover. Simmer for about 1 hour until ribs are tender. Remove and discard bay leaf.

Add beans and potato. Bring to a boil. Reduce heat to medium. Cover. Simmer for about 30 minutes until potato is tender but still holds its shape. Chill, covered, overnight if desired. Skim off and discard fat from surface before reheating. Makes about 14 cups (3.5 L).

*1 cup (250 mL): 332 Calories; 6.1 g Total Fat (2.6 g Mono, 0.8 g Poly, 2.1 g Sat); 14 mg Cholesterol; 31 g Carbohydrate; 8 g Fibre; 19 g Protein; 495 mg Sodium*

*This mildly flavoured soup is thick with chunky vegetables, beans and ribs. Smoky bacon and tomato go well with the hearty ingredients.*

## food fun

Sauerkraut is regarded as a speciality of Germany, but did you know that soured cabbage and other soured vegetable dishes are also enjoyed in Eastern Europe, Russia, the Balkans, Hungary, Italy, Northern China, Chile, Turkey, Korea, Japan, the Philippines and Indonesia? In the 18th century, sauerkraut even became a staple of British and German sailors' diets because its high vitamin C content and long shelf life helped prevent scurvy.

*Put those harvest veggies to good use and warm up with this chunky tomato soup, thick with beans and bacon.*

## make ahead

The night before, combine first 10 ingredients in slow cooker liner. Cover, chill overnight and then cook as directed.

## variation

Omit rosemary sprigs. Add 1/2 tsp. (2 mL) dried crushed rosemary to first 10 ingredients.

# Hearty Winter Soup

| | | |
|---|---|---|
| Bacon slices, cooked crisp and crumbled | 8 | 8 |
| Prepared chicken broth | 6 cups | 1.5 L |
| Chopped yellow turnip | 3 cups | 750 mL |
| Can of white kidney beans, rinsed and drained | 19 oz. | 540 mL |
| Chopped onion | 1 cup | 250 mL |
| Chopped carrot | 1 cup | 250 mL |
| Chopped celery | 1/2 cup | 125 mL |
| Tomato paste (see Tip, page 22) | 1/4 cup | 60 mL |
| Salt | 1/4 tsp. | 1 mL |
| Pepper | 1/4 tsp. | 1 mL |
| Frozen peas | 1 cup | 250 mL |
| Sprigs of fresh rosemary | 2 | 2 |
| Chopped fresh parsley (or 1 1/2 tsp., 7 mL, flakes) | 2 tbsp. | 30 mL |
| Lemon juice | 1 tbsp. | 15 mL |

Combine first 10 ingredients in 5 to 7 quart (5 to 7 L) slow cooker. Cover. Cook on Low for 9 to 10 hours or on High for 4 1/2 to 5 hours.

Add remaining 4 ingredients. Stir well. Cover. Cook on High for about 10 minutes until peas are heated through. Remove and discard rosemary sprigs. Makes about 11 cups (2.75 L).

*1 cup (250 mL): 119 Calories; 3.4 g Total Fat (1.5 g Mono, 0.6 g Poly, 1.1 g Sat); 4 mg Cholesterol; 15 g Carbohydrate; 4 g Fibre; 8 g Protein; 690 mg Sodium*

Pictured at right.

*Not too thin, not too heavy, and loaded with flavour. Cream and potatoes mellow the spicy bite of Mexican sausage and chilies.*

## about kale

Kale might once have been considered a lowly vegetable, but not anymore. It's packed with nutrition and antioxidants, it's beautiful enough to plant just for its good looks, it grows superbly even in quite cold climates and it can be harvested early or later in the season—in fact it tastes sweeter after a light frost. You can use it as a substitute for other greens such as spinach and chard as well. It's hard not to love a vegetable with this many virtues.

## storing kale tip

If you're not sure what to do with leftover kale, try cutting out the ribs and freezing the leaves. Once they're frozen, they can be broken up very easily and measured out for use in soups and sauces.

# Creamy Kale Soup

| | | |
|---|---|---|
| Bacon slices, diced | 2 | 2 |
| Chorizo sausage, casing removed, chopped | 8 oz. | 225 g |
| Diced onion | 1 cup | 250 mL |
| Garlic cloves, minced (or 1/2 tsp., 2 mL, powder) | 2 | 2 |
| All-purpose flour | 2 tsp. | 10 mL |
| Chicken Stock (page 26), or prepared chicken broth | 6 cups | 1.5 L |
| Dried crushed chilies | 1/4 tsp. | 1 mL |
| Medium unpeeled baking potatoes | 2 | 2 |
| Shredded kale leaves, lightly packed | 1 cup | 250 mL |
| Half-and-half cream | 1 cup | 250 mL |
| Grated Parmesan cheese, for garnish | | |

Cook bacon in large saucepan on medium until almost crisp. Add sausage. Scramble-fry for about 5 minutes until sausage is browned. Transfer sausage and bacon with slotted spoon to paper towel-lined plate to drain. Set aside.

Heat 2 tsp. (10 mL) drippings in same saucepan on medium. Add onion and garlic. Cook for 5 to 10 minutes, stirring often, until onion is softened.

Sprinkle with flour. Heat and stir for 1 minute. Add stock and chilies. Stir. Bring to a boil.

Cut potatoes in half lengthwise. Cut crosswise into 1/4 inch (6 mm) slices, making half moons. Add to stock. Boil gently, partially covered, for 10 minutes until potato is almost tender.

Add kale and sausage mixture. Boil gently, partially covered, for 5 minutes. Remove from heat.

Add cream. Stir. Garnish individual servings with Parmesan cheese. Makes about 9 cups (2.25 L).

*1 cup (250 mL): 289 Calories; 14.6 g Total Fat (6.2 g Mono, 1.2 g Poly, 6.4 g Sat); 3 mg Cholesterol; 15 g Carbohydrate; 1 g Fibre; 10 g Protein; 924 mg Sodium*

Pictured at right.

*A warm, hearty soup filled with lots of beans, deep green spinach and colourful vegetables.*

## variation

In place of navy beans you can use white kidney beans, mixed beans, black-eyed peas or another bean of your choice.

# Hearty Ham Bone Soup *A Classic!*

| | | |
|---|---|---|
| Water | 10 cups | 2.5 L |
| Leftover meaty ham bone | 1 | 1 |
| Celery ribs, diced | 4 | 4 |
| Medium carrots, sliced | 3 | 3 |
| Medium onions, chopped | 2 | 2 |
| Bay leaf | 1 | 1 |
| Parsley flakes | 1 tbsp. | 15 mL |
| Salt | 2 tsp. | 10 mL |
| Coarse ground pepper | 1/4 tsp. | 1 mL |
| Medium potatoes, peeled and diced | 2 | 2 |
| Can of mixed beans, rinsed and drained | 19 oz. | 540 mL |
| Can of navy beans, rinsed, drained and slightly mashed with fork | 14 oz. | 398 mL |
| Chopped fresh spinach, stems removed, lightly packed (optional) | 1 cup | 250 mL |

Put water and ham bone into large pot or Dutch oven. Bring to a boil. Boil, uncovered, for 5 minutes. Carefully skim off and discard foam from surface. Return to a boil.

Add next 7 ingredients. Reduce heat to medium-low. Cover. Simmer for about 2 hours until ham is falling off bone. Remove all meat from bone. Discard bone. Chop meat. Return to soup. Remove and discard bay leaf.

Add potato, mixed beans and navy beans. Bring to a boil. Reduce heat to medium-low. Cover. Simmer for about 20 minutes until potatoes are tender.

Add spinach. Cook for 5 minutes. Makes 12 cups (3 L). Serves 8.

*1 serving: 335 Calories; 3.5 g Total Fat (1.2 g Mono, 0.8 g Poly, 0.9 g Sat); 23 mg Cholesterol; 52 g Carbohydrate; 17 g Fibre; 27 g Protein; 1259 mg Sodium*

Pictured at right.

*This delicious lamb and bean soup has a savoury, complex broth. Made in the slow cooker, it is a meal in itself.*

## about bouquet garni

A traditional bouquet garni is a bunch of herbs tied together to make them easy to remove before you serve the dish, so you get all the flavour without the fuss. We've used a combination of dried herbs and spices, so we've wrapped them in cheesecloth to keep them in a tidy bundle.

## variation

In place of navy beans you can use white kidney beans, mixed beans, black-eyed peas or another bean of your choice.

# Lamb Bouquet Soup

| | | |
|---|---|---|
| Dried navy beans | 1 cup | 250 mL |
| Beef Stock (page 6), or prepared beef broth | 7 cups | 1.75 L |
| Lamb shanks (about 1 1/2 lbs., 680 g) | 2 | 2 |
| Chopped onion | 1 cup | 250 mL |
| Chopped celery | 1 cup | 250 mL |
| Pot barley | 1/2 cup | 125 mL |
| Sliced carrot | 1/2 cup | 125 mL |
| Chopped fresh rosemary (or 1/2 tsp., 2 mL, dried, crushed) | 2 tsp. | 10 mL |
| Paprika | 1/2 tsp. | 2 mL |
| ALLSPICE BOUQUET GARNI | | |
| Bay leaves | 2 | 2 |
| Whole allspice | 2 | 2 |
| Fresh parsley sprigs | 2 | 2 |
| Whole black peppercorns | 8 | 8 |
| Garlic clove | 1 | 1 |
| Diced fresh tomato | 1 1/2 cups | 375 mL |
| Brown sugar, packed | 2 tbsp. | 30 mL |
| Grated lemon zest | 1 tsp. | 5 mL |
| Salt | 1/2 tsp. | 2 mL |

Measure beans into small heatproof bowl. Add boiling water until 2 inches (5 cm) above beans. Let stand for at least 1 hour until cool. Drain. Rinse beans. Drain. Transfer to 5 to 7 quart (5 to 7 L) slow cooker.

Add next 8 ingredients. Stir.

**Allspice Bouquet Garni:** Place first 5 ingredients on 10 inch (25 cm) square piece of cheesecloth. Draw up corners and tie with butcher's string. Submerge in liquid in slow cooker. Cook, covered, on Low for about 10 hours or on High for about 5 hours until beans are tender and lamb is falling off bones. Remove and discard bouquet garni. Remove shanks to cutting board using slotted spoon. Keep bean mixture covered. Remove lamb from bones. Discard bones. Chop lamb coarsely. Return to slow cooker.

Add remaining 4 ingredients. Stir. Cook, covered, on High for about 15 minutes until heated through. Makes about 12 cups (3 L).

*1 cup (250 mL): 247 Calories; 10.4 g Total Fat (4.1 g Mono, 1.0 g Poly, 4.4 g Sat); 33 mg Cholesterol; 23 g Carbohydrate; 5 g Fibre; 15 g Protein; 639 mg Sodium*

## Scotch Broth

| | | |
|---|---|---|
| Water | 8 cups | 2 L |
| Lamb stew meat, cut into small pieces | 1 lb. | 454 g |
| Pearl or pot barley | 1/2 cup | 125 mL |
| Diced yellow turnip | 1 cup | 250 mL |
| Diced carrot | 2 cups | 500 mL |
| Medium onions, chopped | 2 | 2 |
| Leeks, white part only, sliced (optional) | 2 | 2 |
| Shredded cabbage, packed | 2 cups | 500 mL |
| Chopped celery | 1/2 cup | 125 mL |
| Salt | 2 tsp. | 10 mL |
| Pepper | 1/2 tsp. | 2 mL |
| Thyme | 1/4 tsp. | 1 mL |

Put water, lamb and barley into large saucepan. Bring to a boil. Cover and simmer 1 hour.

Add remaining 9 ingredients. Stir. Bring to a boil again. Cover and simmer about 30 minutes. Makes about 12 cups (3 L).

*1 cup (250 mL): 105 Calories; 2.3 g Total Fat (0.8 g Mono, 0.2 g Poly, 0.7 g Sat); 25 mg Cholesterol; 12 g Carbohydrate; 3 g Fibre; 9 g Protein; 442 mg Sodium*

Pictured below.

*This Scottish soup is made with lots of vegetables and thickened with barley. It is traditionally made with lamb, but beef may also be used. This thick soup may be thinned with water if you prefer, but be sure to adjust the seasonings.*

### about barley

A grain cultivated since ancient times, barley is low in gluten and has many culinary uses. Pearl barley has had the husk, bran and germ removed, making it faster-cooking with a smoother texture, but also making it less nutritious than whole barley. Pot or Scotch barley has had only the husk removed, so it's coarser and chewier than pearl barley, but it also retains some bran, B vitamins and potassium. Either one works well in Scotch Broth.

*This classic beet soup has the gorgeous colour you've come to expect, and is especially thrifty if you make it with vegetables from your own garden. Garnish with a sprinkle of fresh dill.*

## serving suggestion

Highlight the beautiful colour of beet soup by serving it in plain white bowls or in a simple soup tureen in a contrasting colour.

## tip

Don't get caught red-handed! Wear rubber gloves when handling beets.

# Borscht  *A Classic!*

| | | |
|---|---|---|
| Grated beets (about 1 1/2 lbs., 680 g), see Tip, left | 5 cups | 1.25 L |
| Chopped onion | 1 1/2 cups | 375 mL |
| Hot water | 10 cups | 2.5 L |
| Vegetable bouillon powder | 2 tbsp. | 30 mL |
| Coarsely grated cabbage | 2 cups | 500 mL |
| Celery rib, diced | 1 | 1 |
| Medium carrot, grated | 1 | 1 |
| Medium potato, grated | 1 | 1 |
| Granulated sugar | 1 tsp. | 5 mL |
| Salt | 1 tsp. | 5 mL |
| Pepper | 1/4 tsp. | 1 mL |
| Bay leaf | 1 | 1 |
| Dill weed | 1 1/2 tsp. | 7 mL |
| Garlic powder | 1/4 tsp. | 1 mL |
| Apple cider vinegar | 1/4 cup | 60 mL |
| Sour cream, for garnish | 3/4 cup | 175 mL |

Combine first 15 ingredients in large heavy pot or Dutch oven. Bring to a boil, stirring often. Reduce heat. Cover. Boil gently for about 1 hour, stirring occasionally, until slightly reduced. Remove and discard bay leaf.

Top individual servings with dollop of sour cream. Makes about 15 cups (3.75 L).

*1 cup (250 mL): 41 Calories; 0.1 g Total Fat (trace Mono, 0.1 g Poly, trace Sat); 0 mg Cholesterol; 10 g Carbohydrate; 2 g Fibre; 1 g Protein; 653 mg Sodium*

Pictured below.

# Garden Fresh Tomato Soup

| | | |
|---|---|---|
| Medium tomatoes (about 3 lbs., 1.4 kg) | 8 | 8 |
| Cooking oil | 2 tsp. | 10 mL |
| Chopped onion | 1 cup | 250 mL |
| Chopped carrot | 1/2 cup | 125 mL |
| Chopped celery | 1/2 cup | 125 mL |
| Garlic cloves, minced (or 1/2 tsp., 2 mL, powder) | 2 | 2 |
| Chicken Stock (page 26), or prepared chicken broth | 1 cup | 250 mL |
| Tomato paste (see Tip, page 22) | 2 tbsp. | 30 mL |
| Granulated sugar | 2 tsp. | 10 mL |
| Dried basil | 1/2 tsp. | 2 mL |
| Dried oregano | 1/2 tsp. | 2 mL |
| Dried thyme | 1/2 tsp. | 2 mL |
| Bay leaf | 1 | 1 |
| Salt | 1/2 tsp. | 2 mL |
| Pepper | 1/2 tsp. | 2 mL |

*Forget the canned tomatoes—this soup is a tangy treat full of fresh veggies. Perfect for when your kitchen is overflowing with harvested garden tomatoes.*

## cream of tomato soup

Add 1/2 cup (125 mL) whipping cream after processing. Heat and stir until heated through.

Cut 'X' through skin on bottom of tomatoes. Place tomatoes in boiling water in large saucepan for 30 seconds. Transfer to ice water in large bowl using slotted spoon. Let stand until cool enough to handle. Peel and discard skins. Cut each tomato into quarters. Remove seeds. Chop tomato. Set aside. Discard cooking water.

Heat cooking oil in same saucepan on medium. Add next 4 ingredients. Cook for 5 to 10 minutes, stirring occasionally, until vegetables are softened.

Add tomato and remaining 9 ingredients. Stir. Bring to a boil. Reduce heat to medium-low. Simmer, covered, for about 30 minutes, stirring occasionally, until vegetables are very soft. Discard bay leaf. Carefully process with hand blender or in blender until smooth (see Safety Tip). Makes about 5 cups (1.25 L).

*1 cup (250 mL): 114 Calories; 3.0 g Total Fat (1.3 g Mono, 1.0 g Poly, 0.4 g Sat); 0 mg Cholesterol; 22 g Carbohydrate; 5 g Fibre; 4 g Protein; 461 mg Sodium*

**Safety Tip:** Follow manufacturer's instructions for processing hot liquids.

*A nice and thick tomato soup that warms the body and the soul! Creamy tomato and vegetable flavours blend to create a delectable version of this favourite.*

# Mom's Creamed Tomato Soup     *A Classic!*

| | | |
|---|---|---|
| Chopped onion | 1/2 cup | 125 mL |
| Chopped celery | 1/2 cup | 125 mL |
| Hard margarine (or butter) | 1 tbsp. | 15 mL |
| Water | 1 cup | 250 mL |
| Cans of stewed tomatoes (14 oz., 398 mL, each) | 2 | 2 |
| Chicken (or vegetable) bouillon powder | 1 tbsp. | 15 mL |
| Granulated sugar | 1/2 tsp. | 2 mL |
| Pepper | 1/8 tsp. | 0.5 mL |
| Homogenized milk | 1 cup | 250 mL |
| All-purpose flour | 2 tbsp. | 30 mL |

Cheddar cheese fish crackers (optional)

Sauté onion and celery in margarine in medium saucepan for about 4 minutes until onion is soft and clear.

Add water, tomatoes, bouillon powder, sugar and pepper. Bring to a boil. Reduce heat. Simmer, partially covered, for 30 minutes. Purée in blender or with hand blender until smooth (see Safety Tip). Return to saucepan.

Gradually whisk milk into flour in small bowl until smooth. Add to tomato mixture. Heat and stir on medium until boiling and slightly thickened. Ladle into individual soup bowls.

Top with crackers. Makes 5 cups (1.25 L).

*1 cup (250 mL): 112 Calories; 4.1 g Total Fat (1.2 g Mono, 0.2 g Poly, 2.5 g Sat); 14 mg Cholesterol; 16 g Carbohydrate; trace Fibre; 4 g Protein; 1070 mg Sodium*

**Safety Tip:** Follow manufacturer's instructions for processing hot liquids.

# Tomato Gin Soup

| | | |
|---|---|---|
| Cooking oil | 1 tsp. | 5 mL |
| Chopped onion | 1 cup | 250 mL |
| Chopped celery | 1/2 cup | 125 mL |
| Garlic clove, minced | 1 | 1 |
|    (or 1/4 tsp., 1 mL, powder) | | |
| Jalapeño pepper, finely diced | 1 | 1 |
|    (see Tip, page 15) | | |
| Tomato juice | 4 cups | 1 L |
| Can of diced tomatoes (with juice) | 14 oz. | 398 mL |
| Water | 1 1/2 cups | 375 mL |
| Worcestershire sauce | 1 tbsp. | 15 mL |
| Grated lime zest (see Tip, page 104) | 1 tsp. | 5 mL |
| Gin | 1/3 cup | 75 mL |
| Lime juice | 1/4 cup | 60 mL |
| Liquid honey | 1 tbsp. | 15 mL |

Heat cooking oil in large saucepan on medium. Add next 4 ingredients. Cook for 5 to 10 minutes, stirring often, until onion and celery are softened.

Add next 5 ingredients. Bring to a boil. Reduce heat to medium-low. Simmer, partially covered, for about 15 minutes, stirring occasionally, until vegetables are tender. Carefully process with hand blender or in blender until smooth (see Safety Tip).

Add remaining 3 ingredients. Stir. Makes about 8 cups (2 L).

*1 cup (250 mL): 83 Calories; 0.8 g Total Fat (0.4 g Mono, 0.3 g Poly, 0.1 g Sat); 0 mg Cholesterol; 14 g Carbohydrate; 2 g Fibre; 2 g Protein; 579 mg Sodium*

**Safety Tip:** Follow manufacturer's instructions for processing hot liquids.

*A tipple of gin adds a cheeky flair to this fun, fresh and inviting lime and tomato soup.*

## about gin

Gin is an alcoholic spirit distilled from grains. It is closely associated with juniper, as it is infused with the essence of the bitter berries of this plant. In France, gin is known as *genièvre,* which is also French for "juniper berry."

*That's "garlic soup" to you! The mellow, roasted garlic flavour is subtly sweet in this rich yet light soup.*

# Zuppa d'Aglio

| | | |
|---|---|---|
| Large garlic bulb | 1 | 1 |
| Olive (or cooking) oil | 2 tbsp. | 30 mL |
| Small onion, chopped | 1 | 1 |
| Large celery rib, chopped | 1 | 1 |
| Dry (or alcohol-free) white wine | 1/2 cup | 125 mL |
| Chicken Stock (page 26), or prepared chicken broth | 8 cups | 2 L |
| All-purpose flour | 2 tbsp. | 30 mL |
| Water | 2 cups | 500 mL |
| Small potato, peeled and cut into 6 pieces | 1 | 1 |
| Whipping cream (or homogenized milk) | 1/2 cup | 125 mL |
| Chopped fresh basil (or 3/4 tsp., 4 mL, dried) | 1 tbsp. | 15 mL |
| Chopped fresh thyme leaves (or 1/4 tsp., 1 mL, dried) | 1 tsp. | 5 mL |
| Salt | 1 tsp. | 5 mL |
| Hot pepper sauce | 1/2 tsp. | 2 mL |

**Chopped fresh parsley, for garnish**
**Coarsely ground pepper, for garnish**

Cut garlic bulb in half horizontally. Remove any loose, papery outer skins. Preheat gas barbecue or frying pan to medium. Cook bulb halves, cut sides down, on greased grill or in small greased frying pan until exposed garlic is very brown. Cool until able to handle. Peel and separate garlic cloves.

Heat olive oil in large pot or Dutch oven on medium-high. Cook onion, celery and garlic cloves, stirring constantly, until all are golden.

Add wine. Boil, uncovered, for 2 minutes.

Stir 1/3 cup (75 mL) stock into flour in small cup until smooth. Add to onion mixture. Add remaining stock and water. Stir. Add potato. Bring to a boil, stirring constantly. Reduce heat to medium. Cover. Boil gently for 1 hour. Strain solids from liquid, returning liquid to pot. Purée solids in blender or food processor (see Safety Tip). Add purée to liquid. Bring to a boil.

*(continued on next page)*

Add whipping cream, basil, thyme, salt and hot pepper sauce. Stir until heated through. Do not boil. Remove from heat.

Sprinkle individual servings with parsley and pepper. Makes 8 cups (2 L). Serves 6.

*1 serving: 224 Calories; 13.9 g Total Fat (6.5 g Mono, 1.1 g Poly, 5.8 g Sat); 27 mg Cholesterol; 13 g Carbohydrate; 1 g Fibre; 8 g Protein; 1449 mg Sodium*

Pictured below.

**Safety Tip:** Follow manufacturer's instructions for processing hot liquids.

*Muhl-ih-guh-TAW-nee, which means "pepper water," is a traditional soup from India—a creamy, warmly spiced medley of potatoes, apples, lentils and onions. Garnish with yogurt and sprigs of fresh cilantro.*

## time-saving tip

If you've no time to make stock from scratch, make a quick substitute by using 8 cups (2 L) water plus 3 tbsp. (50 mL) chicken bouillon powder.

## tip

To bruise cardamom, pound pods with mallet or press with flat side of wide knife to "bruise," or crack them open slightly.

# Mulligatawny Soup

| | | |
|---|---|---|
| Chopped onion | 1 1/2 cups | 375 mL |
| Garlic cloves, minced (or 1/2 tsp., 2 mL, powder) | 2 | 2 |
| Finely grated ginger root (or 1/2 tsp., 2 mL, ground ginger) | 2 tsp. | 10 mL |
| Fresh small chilies, chopped (see Tip, page 15) | 2 | 2 |
| Curry powder | 1 tbsp. | 15 mL |
| Ground cumin | 1/4 – 2 tsp. | 1 – 10 mL |
| Ground coriander | 1/4 – 2 tsp. | 1 – 10 mL |
| Canola oil | 2 tsp. | 10 mL |
| Cinnamon stick (4 inch, 10 cm, length) | 1 | 1 |
| Whole green cardamom, bruised (see Tip, left) | 6 – 8 | 6 – 8 |
| Red lentils | 1 1/4 cups | 300 mL |
| Chicken Stock (page 26), or prepared chicken broth | 8 cups | 2 L |
| Medium potatoes, peeled and chopped | 2 | 2 |
| Medium cooking apples (such as McIntosh), peeled, cored and chopped | 2 | 2 |
| Buttermilk | 1 1/2 cups | 375 mL |
| Fresh cilantro leaves | 3 tbsp. | 50 mL |

Sauté first 7 ingredients in canola oil in large pot or Dutch oven for about 5 minutes until onion is soft.

Add next 6 ingredients. Stir. Bring to a boil. Reduce heat to medium-low. Cover. Simmer for about 25 minutes, stirring occasionally, until lentils and potato are soft. Cool slightly. Remove and discard cinnamon stick and cardamom. Process in blender, in 2 to 3 batches, until smooth (see Safety Tip). Return to pot.

Add buttermilk and cilantro. Heat and stir on medium for 5 to 7 minutes until heated through. Makes about 12 cups (3 L).

*1 cup (250 mL): 162 Calories; 2.9 g Total Fat (1.1 g Mono, 0.5 g Poly, 0.7 g Sat); 2 mg Cholesterol; 24 g Carbohydrate; 5 g Fibre; 11 g Protein; 548 mg Sodium*

Pictured at right.

**Safety Tip:** Follow manufacturer's instructions for processing hot liquids.

A classic, warming soup with delicious caramelized onions and a savoury herb undertone. Be sure to remind everyone—the bowls will be very hot!

## about french onion soup bowls

While French onion soup can be served in any broiler-proof serving bowls, this soup has become associated with distinctive oven-to-table dishes. The most familiar design has a single handle to help transport the hot bowls, but another variation, called a lion's head, has small handles on each side. French onion soup bowls were traditionally made of brown ceramic, but they now come in a variety of colours and can be made from porcelain, stoneware and earthenware.

# French Onion Soup

| | | |
|---|---|---|
| Onions, peeled (about 8 medium) | 2 lbs. | 900 g |
| Hard margarine (or butter) | 2 tbsp. | 30 mL |
| Salt | 1 tsp. | 5 mL |
| Garlic cloves, minced (or 1 tsp., 5 mL, powder) | 4 | 4 |
| Coarsely ground pepper (or 1/4 tsp., 1 mL, pepper) | 1/2 tsp. | 2 mL |
| Dry sherry | 1/2 cup | 125 mL |
| Bay leaves | 3 | 3 |
| Fresh thyme sprigs | 3 | 3 |
| Prepared beef broth | 4 cups | 1 L |
| Multi-grain rye bread slices, cut about 1/3 inch (1 cm) thick and lightly toasted or air-dried | 8 | 8 |
| Grated Gruyère cheese | 1 1/3 cups | 325 mL |

Cut each onion in half lengthwise. Lay flat side on cutting board. Cut crosswise into 1/8 inch (3 mm) slices.

Melt margarine in large pot or Dutch oven on medium-low. Add onion and salt. Stir. Cover. Cook for about 45 minutes, stirring occasionally, until onion is soft, but not browned.

Add garlic and pepper. Stir. Cook, uncovered, on medium-high, stirring frequently and scraping bottom of pot, until onion is deep caramel brown.

Add sherry. Stir well, scraping any browning from pot and blending with liquid.

Add bay leaves, thyme sprigs and broth. Bring to a boil. Reduce heat to medium-low. Cover. Simmer for 30 minutes, without stirring. Remove and discard bay leaves and thyme sprigs. Makes about 5 cups (1.25 L) soup.

Arrange 4 ovenproof serving bowls on baking sheet with sides. Place 2 slices of bread in each. Ladle soup over bread, allowing 1 to 2 minutes for bread to soak up liquid.

Sprinkle each with cheese. Broil until cheese is browned and bubbly. Let stand for 5 minutes. Carefully transfer hot soup bowls to plates. Serves 4.

*1 serving: 532 Calories; 19.7 g Total Fat (5.2 g Mono, 1.0 g Poly, 10.6 g Sat); 55 mg Cholesterol; 67 g Carbohydrate; 7 g Fibre; 22 g Protein; 2448 mg Sodium*

Pictured at right.

*A light starter soup with earthy mushrooms and fresh chives— perfect for priming the appetite for a main course.*

# Mushroom Consommé

| | | |
|---|---|---|
| Package of dried porcini mushrooms | 3/4 oz. | 22 g |
| Boiling water | 1 cup | 250 mL |
| Prepared beef broth | 4 cups | 1 L |
| Bay leaf | 1 | 1 |
| Whole clove | 1 | 1 |
| Butter (or hard margarine) | 2 tsp. | 10 mL |
| Sliced fresh brown (or white) mushrooms | 2 cups | 500 mL |
| Chopped fresh chives | 2 tbsp. | 30 mL |
| (or 1 1/2 tsp., 7 mL, dried) | | |
| Dry sherry | 1 tbsp. | 15 mL |
| Lemon juice | 1 tsp. | 5 mL |

Put dried mushrooms into small heatproof bowl. Add boiling water. Stir. Let stand for about 15 minutes until softened. Remove mushrooms. Strain liquid through triple layer of cheesecloth into large saucepan. Finely chop mushrooms and stems. Set aside.

Add next 3 ingredients to saucepan. Bring to a boil. Reduce heat to medium-low. Simmer, covered, for 15 minutes to blend flavours.

Melt butter in large frying pan on medium. Add brown and porcini mushrooms. Cook for about 10 minutes, stirring often, until mushrooms are browned and liquid is evaporated. Add to broth mixture.

Add remaining 3 ingredients. Stir. Discard bay leaf and clove. Makes about 5 cups (1.25 L). Serves 6.

*1 serving: 36 Calories; 1.6 g Total Fat (0.4 g Mono, 0.1 g Poly, 0.9 g Sat); 3 mg Cholesterol; 3 g Carbohydrate; 1 g Fibre; 2 g Protein; 784 mg Sodium*

# Creamy Mushroom Soup  *A Classic!*

| | | |
|---|---|---|
| Sliced fresh mushrooms (your favourite) | 6 cups | 1.5 L |
| Cooking oil | 2 tsp. | 10 mL |
| Pepper, sprinkle | | |
| | | |
| Cooking oil | 2 tsp. | 10 mL |
| Chopped green onion | 1/2 cup | 125 mL |
| Garlic cloves, minced | 2 | 2 |
| | | |
| All-purpose flour | 3 tbsp. | 50 mL |
| Low-sodium prepared chicken broth | 2 cups | 500 mL |
| Milk | 2 cups | 500 mL |
| Dry (or alcohol-free) white wine | 1/4 cup | 60 mL |
| | | |
| Reduced-sodium chicken bouillon powder | 2 tsp. | 10 mL |
| Pepper | 1/4 tsp. | 1 mL |
| Ground thyme (optional) | 1/8 tsp. | 0.5 mL |

*A long-time favourite you'll make again and again. Make it chunky or smooth to suit your preference—it's delicious either way.*

Put mushrooms into medium bowl. Add first amount of cooking oil. Stir until coated. Spread in single layer in greased baking sheet with sides. Sprinkle with first amount of pepper. Bake in 400°F (205°C) oven for about 10 minutes until mushrooms are softened. Do not drain.

Heat second amount of cooking oil in large pot or Dutch oven on medium. Add green onion and garlic. Cook for about 5 minutes, stirring often, until green onion is softened.

Add flour. Heat and stir for 1 minute. Slowly add next 3 ingredients, stirring constantly until boiling and thickened.

Add mushrooms with liquid and remaining 3 ingredients. Heat and stir for 3 to 4 minutes. Reduce heat to medium-low. Cover. Simmer for 5 minutes. Remove from heat. Cool slightly. Carefully process in blender or food processor until mushrooms are finely chopped (see Safety Tip). Return to same large pot. Heat and stir on medium for about 5 minutes until heated through. Makes 6 cups (1.5 L). Serves 6.

*1 serving: 116 Calories; 4.5 g Total Fat (2.2 g Mono, 1.1 g Poly, 0.9 g Sat); 4 mg Cholesterol; 12 g Carbohydrate; 1 g Fibre; 6 g Protein; 392 mg Sodium*

**Safety Tip:** Follow manufacturer's instructions for processing hot liquids.

*An excellent soup that can be blended to whatever texture you like. Raid the garden and try it with homegrown carrots!*

## carrot chowder

Cook 1 1/3 cups (325 mL) diced potato along with the carrot and onion. Has a similar flavour but is a touch mellower.

## curried carrot soup

Add 1/2 tsp. (2 mL) curry powder with flour. Has quite a mild flavour.

## Cream of Carrot Soup

| | | |
|---|---|---|
| Peeled and cut up carrot | 4 cups | 1 L |
| Chicken Stock (page 26), or prepared broth | 2 cups | 500 mL |
| Chopped onion | 1 cup | 250 mL |
| Butter (or hard margarine) | 3 tbsp. | 50 mL |
| All-purpose flour | 3 tbsp. | 50 mL |
| Salt | 1 tsp. | 5 mL |
| Pepper | 1/8 tsp. | 0.5 mL |
| Seasoned salt | 1/4 tsp. | 1 mL |
| Milk | 4 cups | 1 L |

Combine carrot, stock and onion in saucepan. Cook until vegetables are tender. Do not drain. Cool a bit. Run through blender (see Safety Tip). Set aside.

Melt butter in saucepan over medium heat. Stir in flour, salt, pepper and seasoned salt. Add milk. Heat and stir until it boils and thickens. Add carrot mixture. Reheat and serve. Makes 7 cups (1.75 L).

*1 cup (250 mL): 167 Calories; 6.9 g Total Fat (2.0 g Mono, 0.4 g Poly, 4.1 g Sat); 21 mg Cholesterol; 19 g Carbohydrate; 2 g Fibre; 8 g Protein; 764 mg Sodium*

Pictured on divider.

**Safety Tip:** Follow manufacturer's instructions for processing hot liquids.

*This thick and creamy soup has a distinctive pale green colour and the delicious fresh taste of asparagus.*

## Cream of Asparagus Soup

| | | |
|---|---|---|
| Fresh asparagus, trimmed of tough ends | 1 1/2 lbs. | 680 g |
| Water | | |
| Chopped onion | 3/4 cup | 175 mL |
| Cooking oil | 1 tbsp. | 15 mL |
| Chicken bouillon powder | 2 tsp. | 10 mL |
| All-purpose flour | 2 tbsp. | 30 mL |
| Salt | 3/4 tsp. | 4 mL |
| Pepper (white is best) | 1/4 tsp. | 1 mL |
| Milk | 2 cups | 500 mL |
| Ground nutmeg, sprinkle (optional) | | |

*(continued on next page)*

Cook asparagus in water in large saucepan until tender. Drain. Reserve 4 spears for garnish. Cut remaining spears into 2 inch (5 cm) pieces. Return to saucepan.

Sauté onion in cooking oil in small frying pan until soft. Add to asparagus.

Combine bouillon powder, flour, salt and pepper in medium bowl. Stir in milk until smooth. Gradually stir into asparagus mixture. Heat and stir until boiling and thickened. Cool slightly. Put into blender. Process, in batches, until smooth (see Safety Tip). Return to saucepan. Heat through.

Garnish individual servings with reserved asparagus spears. Sprinkle with nutmeg. Makes 4 cups (1 L).

*1 cup (250 mL): 150 Calories; 5.1 g Total Fat (2.6 g Mono, 1.2 g Poly, 1.1 g Sat); 8 mg Cholesterol; 20 g Carbohydrate; 4 g Fibre; 9 g Protein; 1062 mg Sodium*

Pictured below.

**Safety Tip:** Follow manufacturer's instructions for processing hot liquids.

Cream of Asparagus Soup, left

## about growing asparagus

Crazy about asparagus? Why not grow your own and enjoy tender spears every spring? Asparagus is a perennial plant in the lily family that can be grown relatively easily, with a bit of patience. Started from seed or planted as roots, called "crowns," asparagus will begin producing spears by the second or third spring. A properly cared for asparagus patch will be fruitful for many years.

*Not to worry, we don't expect you to dine on your garden flora—it's simple green peas that impart a nice, sweet flavour to this soup. The tangy Minted Yogurt topping bumps it up to sensational.*

## minted yogurt

| | | |
|---|---|---|
| Plain yogurt | 1/3 cup | 75 mL |
| Chopped fresh mint | 2 tbsp. | 30 mL |

Combine yogurt and mint in small bowl. Spoon onto individual servings of soup. Makes about 6 tbsp. (100 mL) yogurt.

# Sweet Pea Soup

| | | |
|---|---|---|
| Olive (or canola) oil | 2 tsp. | 10 mL |
| Finely chopped green onion | 1/2 cup | 125 mL |
| Garlic clove, minced (or 1/4 tsp., 1 mL, powder) | 1 | 1 |
| Frozen peas | 2 cups | 500 mL |
| Chopped or torn green leaf lettuce, lightly packed | 1 1/2 cups | 375 mL |
| Low-sodium prepared chicken (or vegetable) broth | 3 cups | 750 mL |
| Pepper | 1/4 tsp. | 1 mL |
| Frozen peas | 1/2 cup | 125 mL |

Heat olive oil in medium saucepan on medium. Add green onion and garlic. Cook for about 5 minutes, stirring occasionally, until green onion is softened.

Add first amount of peas and lettuce. Heat and stir for 1 minute.

Add broth and pepper. Bring to a boil. Reduce heat to medium-low. Simmer for 3 to 5 minutes, stirring occasionally, until peas are tender. Carefully process with hand blender or in blender until smooth (see Safety Tip).

Add second amount of peas. Heat and stir on medium for about 2 minutes until peas are tender. Makes about 4 1/2 cups (1.1 L) soup. Serves 4.

*1 serving with 1 1/2 tbsp. (25 mL) Minted Yogurt: 126 Calories; 3.8 g Total Fat (2.1 g Mono, 0.5 g Poly, 0.9 g Sat); 3 mg Cholesterol; 16 g Carbohydrate; 5 g Fibre; 8 g Protein; 144 mg Sodium*

**Safety Tip:** Follow manufacturer's instructions for processing hot liquids.

# Dill Pickle Soup

| | | |
|---|---|---|
| Butter (or hard margarine) | 2 tbsp. | 30 mL |
| Chopped peeled potato | 2 cups | 500 mL |
| Chopped onion | 1 cup | 250 mL |
| Chopped carrot | 1 cup | 250 mL |
| Pepper | 1/4 tsp. | 1 mL |
| All-purpose flour | 2 tbsp. | 30 mL |
| Chicken Stock (page 26), or prepared chicken broth | 4 cups | 1 L |
| Dill pickle juice | 1/4 cup | 60 mL |
| Half-and-half cream | 1 cup | 250 mL |
| Chopped dill pickles | 2/3 cup | 150 mL |
| Chopped fresh dill (or 1 tbsp., 15 mL, dill weed) | 1/4 cup | 60 mL |
| Sour cream | 1/2 cup | 125 mL |

*You're never in a pickle when you serve this fun and festive soup. Try adding cooked diced chicken, ham or sausage for extra protein.*

### serving suggestion

Dill Pickle Soup goes well with cheese sandwiches. Vary the cheese for different flavour combinations.

Melt butter in large saucepan on medium. Add next 4 ingredients. Stir. Cook, partially covered, for 8 to 10 minutes, stirring occasionally, until vegetables start to soften.

Sprinkle with flour. Heat and stir for 1 minute.

Slowly add 1 cup (250 mL) stock. Heat and stir until boiling and thickened. Add pickle juice and remaining stock. Cook, stirring often, until boiling. Reduce heat to medium-low. Simmer, covered, for about 15 minutes, stirring occasionally, until potato is tender.

Add cream and pickles. Stir. Cook for about 2 minutes until hot but not boiling.

Add dill. Carefully process with hand blender or in blender until smooth (see Safety Tip).

Spoon sour cream onto individual servings. Makes about 8 cups (2 L).

*1 cup (250 mL): 152 Calories; 8.6 g Total Fat (2.4 g Mono, 0.4 g Poly, 5.4 g Sat); 24 mg Cholesterol; 16 g Carbohydrate; 2 g Fibre; 4 g Protein; 623 mg Sodium*

**Safety Tip:** Follow manufacturer's instructions for processing hot liquids.

*This wonderful soup has been a family favourite forever. Get it on the stove when you walk in the door and it'll be ready in a jiffy!*

# Corn Soup

| | | |
|---|---|---|
| Milk | 3 1/2 cups | 875 mL |
| Finely chopped onion | 2 tbsp. | 30 mL |
| Butter (or hard margarine) | 1 tsp. | 5 mL |
| Cans of cream-style corn (10 oz., 284 mL, each) | 2 | 2 |
| Milk | 1/2 cup | 125 mL |
| All-purpose flour | 2 tbsp. | 30 mL |
| Salt | 1 tsp. | 5 mL |
| Pepper | 1/8 tsp. | 0.5 mL |

Butter, chives or parsley for garnish

Heat first amount of milk in large heavy saucepan.

Sauté onion in butter until clear and soft. Put into cone-shaped ricer.

Add corn to onion. Press through cone ricer. If you don't have a cone-shaped ricer, onion and corn may be puréed in blender. Rub through strainer if it isn't smooth enough.

Mix second amount of milk with flour, salt and pepper until no lumps remain. Stir into hot milk until it boils and thickens. Add corn and onion mixture. Heat through.

Serve with a dab of butter, chopped chives or parsley. Makes about 7 1/2 cups (1.9 L).

*1 cup (250 mL): 129 Calories; 2.1 g Total Fat (0.7 g Mono, trace Poly, 1.1 g Sat); 9 mg Cholesterol; 22 g Carbohydrate; 1 g Fibre; 6 g Protein; 639 mg Sodium*

# Quick Broccoli Soup

| | | |
|---|---|---|
| Can of condensed cream of mushroom soup | 10 oz. | 284 mL |
| Milk (1 soup can) | 10 oz. | 284 mL |
| Grated sharp Cheddar cheese | 1 cup | 250 mL |
| Frozen chopped broccoli, thawed, chopped into tiny bits | 1 cup | 250 mL |
| Worcestershire sauce | 1/4 tsp. | 1 mL |

Stir soup and milk vigorously in large saucepan. Heat on medium for about 8 minutes, stirring often, until heated through.

Add cheese, broccoli and Worcestershire sauce. Heat for about 5 minutes, stirring often, until simmering. Reduce heat to medium-low. Simmer, uncovered, for about 5 minutes until broccoli is tender. Makes 4 1/2 cups (1.1 L).

*1 cup (250 mL): 197 Calories; 12.7 g Total Fat (2.6 g Mono, 0.2 g Poly, 6.5 Sat); 33 mg Cholesterol; 11 g Carbohydrate; 2 g Fibre; 11 g Protein; 651 mg Sodium*

Pictured below.

*A cheese and broccoli soup that is easy to prepare, and thick and satisfying to eat.*

## serving suggestion

Serve this soup up in big mugs with warm biscuits on the side. Garnish with some grated Cheddar cheese.

*Roasting the cauliflower adds a rich dimension to this creamy-textured soup, every bowl accented with a tangy red pepper drizzle.*

# Roasted Cauliflower Soup

| | | |
|---|---|---|
| Cauliflower florets | 8 cups | 2 L |
| Olive oil | 2 tbsp. | 30 mL |
| Dried thyme | 1/4 tsp. | 1 mL |
| Salt | 1/2 tsp. | 2 mL |
| Pepper | 1/4 tsp. | 1 mL |
| Prepared vegetable broth | 3 cups | 750 mL |
| Roasted red peppers | 1/2 cup | 125 mL |
| Prepared vegetable broth | 1 tbsp. | 15 mL |
| Dried basil | 1/4 tsp. | 1 mL |

Preheat oven to 450°F (230°C). Put cauliflower into large bowl. Drizzle with olive oil. Sprinkle with next 3 ingredients. Toss until coated. Transfer to large ungreased baking sheet with sides. Spread evenly. Bake for about 15 minutes, stirring at halftime, until tender and starting to brown.

Meanwhile, measure first amount of broth into medium saucepan. Bring to a boil. Reduce heat to low. Cover to keep hot.

Put remaining 3 ingredients into blender or food processor. Process until smooth. Transfer to small cup. Rinse blender. Put cauliflower into blender. Add 2 cups (500 mL) hot broth. Process until smooth (see Safety Tip). Add to remaining hot broth. Stir. Makes about 5 1/2 cups (1.4 L) soup. Ladle into 4 soup bowls. Drizzle with red pepper mixture. Serves 4.

*1 serving: 214 Calories; 8.0 g Total Fat (5.0 g Mono, 0.9 g Poly, 1.0 g Sat); trace Cholesterol; 31 g Carbohydrate; 13 g Fibre; 10 g Protein; 896 mg Sodium*

Pictured at right.

**Safety Tip:** Follow manufacturer's instructions for processing hot liquids.

*This sweet, velvety soup is simple to prepare but has such sophisticated flavours. Your guests will never guess how easy it is to make.*

## about caramelizing onions

Caramelizing essentially turns the natural sugars in onions into caramel. The ingredients used can be as simple as onions with oil or butter, but the pan can also be deglazed with a little water or wine during cooking. Sometimes, as in this recipe, a small amount of sugar is added to the onions for extra sweetness.

# Caramelized Onion Sweet Potato Soup

| | | |
|---|---|---|
| Butter (or hard margarine) | 1/4 cup | 60 mL |
| Coarsely chopped onion | 4 cups | 1 L |
| Brown sugar, packed | 1 tbsp. | 15 mL |
| Coarsely chopped fresh peeled orange-fleshed sweet potato (about 1 lb., 454 g) | 3 cups | 750 mL |
| Prepared chicken broth | 3 cups | 750 mL |
| Dry sherry | 2 tbsp. | 30 mL |
| Dried thyme | 1/4 tsp. | 1 mL |
| Ground allspice | 1/4 tsp. | 1 mL |
| Salt | 1/8 tsp. | 0.5 mL |
| Pepper | 1/4 tsp. | 1 mL |

Melt butter in large saucepan on medium. Add onion and brown sugar. Cook, uncovered, for about 30 minutes, stirring occasionally, until onion is caramelized.

Add remaining 7 ingredients. Stir. Bring to a boil. Reduce heat to medium-low. Simmer, covered, for about 20 minutes, stirring occasionally, until sweet potato is tender. Carefully process with hand blender or in blender until smooth (see Safety Tip). Makes about 5 cups (1.25 L). Serves 4.

*1 serving: 270 Calories; 12.5 g Total Fat (3.3 g Mono, 0.9 g Poly, 7.5 g Sat); 30 mg Cholesterol; 37 g Carbohydrate; 5 g Fibre; 4 g Protein; 1301 mg Sodium*

Pictured at right.

**Safety Tip:** Follow manufacturer's instructions for processing hot liquids.

*Butternut squash is perfectly partnered with leek and potatoes in this rich, velvety-textured soup.*

## make ahead

Store in an airtight container in the freezer for up to 1 month. Thaw overnight in the refrigerator. Reheat the soup in a large pot or Dutch oven on medium heat for about 30 minutes, stirring occasionally, until heated through.

## tip

Some people have an allergic reaction to raw squash flesh, so wear rubber gloves when cutting or handling raw butternut squash or acorn squash.

# Silky Butternut Squash Soup

| | | |
|---|---|---|
| Cooking oil | 1 tbsp. | 15 mL |
| Thinly sliced leek (white part only) | 1 1/2 cups | 375 mL |
| Ground ginger | 1 tbsp. | 15 mL |
| Garlic cloves, minced (or 3/4 tsp., 4 mL, powder) | 3 | 3 |
| Chopped peeled butternut squash (see Tip, left) | 10 cups | 2.5 L |
| Chopped peeled potato | 4 1/2 cups | 1.1 L |
| Prepared chicken broth | 8 cups | 2 L |
| Pepper | 1/2 tsp. | 2 mL |

Heat cooking oil in large pot or Dutch oven on medium. Add next 3 ingredients. Stir. Cook for about 5 minutes, stirring often, until leek is softened.

Add remaining 4 ingredients. Stir. Bring to a boil. Reduce heat to medium-low. Simmer, covered, for about 20 minutes, stirring occasionally, until squash and potato are softened. Remove from heat. Let stand for about 10 minutes until slightly cooled. Process squash mixture with hand blender (or in blender or food processor in small batches) until smooth (see Safety Tip). Heat and stir on medium for about 5 minutes until heated through. Makes about 16 cups (4 L). Serves 12.

*1 serving: 151 Calories; 2.4 g Total Fat (1.1 g Mono, 0.6 g Poly, 0.4 g Sat); 0 mg Cholesterol; 28 g Carbohydrate; 3 g Fibre; 6 g Protein; 558 mg Sodium*

Pictured at right.

**Safety Tip:** Follow manufacturer's instructions for processing hot liquids.

*The perfect blend of pumpkin and spices! This thick pumpkin and apple soup, served with slices of whole-wheat bread, is just what you need on a chilly fall day.*

## about canned pumpkin

Be careful to purchase the right type of canned pumpkin that your recipe calls for. Pure pumpkin is just that—pumpkin with nothing added. Pumpkin pie filling, on the other hand, is pumpkin that has been blended with sugar and spices.

# Autumn Pumpkin Soup

| | | |
|---|---|---|
| Olive (or canola) oil | 2 tsp. | 10 mL |
| Chopped onion | 1 1/2 cups | 375 mL |
| Low-sodium prepared chicken (or vegetable) broth | 4 cups | 1 L |
| Can of pure pumpkin (no spices) | 14 oz. | 398 mL |
| Unsweetened applesauce | 1 cup | 250 mL |
| Bay leaf | 1 | 1 |
| Chopped fresh thyme (or 1/2 tsp., 2 mL, dried) | 2 tsp. | 10 mL |
| Lemon pepper | 1 tsp. | 5 mL |
| Salt, sprinkle | | |

Heat olive oil in large saucepan on medium. Add onion. Cook for 5 to 10 minutes, stirring occasionally, until softened and starting to brown.

Add remaining 7 ingredients. Stir. Bring to a boil. Reduce heat to medium-low. Simmer, partially covered, for 10 minutes to blend flavours. Discard bay leaf. Makes about 7 cups (1.75 L).

*1 cup (250 mL): 72 Calories; 1.9 g Total Fat (1.2 g Mono, 0.2 g Poly, 0.4 g Sat); 0 mg Cholesterol; 13 g Carbohydrate; 3 g Fibre; 2 g Protein; 42 mg Sodium*

Pictured at right.

*Who wouldn't be mellow after supping on this sunny, golden split-pea soup? This sweet vegetable blend has a delicious hint of dill.*

## about sweet potatoes

Sweet potatoes are related to morning glories, which are native to Central America, but their name is misleading because they're not related to potatoes. The kind commonly found in North America has orange or yellow flesh and is soft and moist when cooked. Although they are sometimes called yams, sweet potatoes are not true yams, which are tubers native to Africa and east Asia and not often found in local supermarkets.

## about yellow zucchini

Yellow zucchini is essentially the same vegetable as green zucchini—it's simply a different variety, just as tomatoes come in many varieties that look different from each other. If yellow zucchini is not available, use peeled green zucchini.

# Mellow Yellow Soup

|  | | |
|---|---|---|
| Cooking oil | 2 tsp. | 10 mL |
| Chopped onion | 1 cup | 250 mL |
| Grated carrot | 1 cup | 250 mL |
| Vegetable (or chicken) broth | 6 cups | 1.5 L |
| Chopped yellow zucchini (with peel) | 1 1/2 cups | 375 mL |
| Chopped, peeled sweet potato (or yam) | 1 cup | 250 mL |
| Frozen kernel corn | 1 cup | 250 mL |
| Yellow split peas, rinsed and drained | 3/4 cup | 175 mL |
| Dill weed | 1/2 tsp. | 2 mL |
| Turmeric | 1/4 tsp. | 1 mL |
| Dried thyme | 1/4 tsp. | 1 mL |
| Bay leaf | 1 | 1 |

Heat cooking oil in large saucepan on medium. Add onion and carrot. Cook for 5 to 10 minutes, stirring often, until onion is softened.

Add remaining 9 ingredients. Stir. Bring to a boil. Reduce heat to medium-low. Simmer, covered, for about 1 hour, stirring occasionally, until sweet potato is tender and split peas are very soft. Discard bay leaf. Makes about 8 cups (2 L).

*1 cup (250 mL): 101 Calories; 1.9 g Total Fat (0.8 g Mono, 0.5 g Poly, 0.5 g Sat); 0 mg Cholesterol; 18 g Carbohydrate; 3 g Fibre; 5 g Protein; 700 mg Sodium*

# Lemon Lentil Soup

| | | |
|---|---|---|
| Olive (or cooking) oil | 1 tbsp. | 15 mL |
| Diced onion | 1 1/2 cups | 375 mL |
| | | |
| Diced carrot | 1 cup | 250 mL |
| Chopped fresh oregano | 1 1/2 tbsp. | 25 mL |
|    (or 1 1/4 tsp., 6 mL, dried) | | |
| Garlic cloves, minced | 3 | 3 |
| Chopped fresh rosemary (or 1/4 tsp., | 1 tsp. | 5 mL |
|    1 mL, dried, crushed) | | |
| Salt | 1/2 tsp. | 2 mL |
| Pepper | 1/2 tsp. | 2 mL |
| Dried crushed chilies | 1/4 tsp. | 1 mL |
| Bay leaf | 1 | 1 |
| | | |
| Chicken Stock (page 26), or prepared | 6 cups | 1.5 L |
|    chicken broth | | |
| Dried red split lentils | 1 1/2 cups | 375 mL |
| | | |
| Lemon juice | 6 tbsp. | 100 mL |
| Grated lemon zest (see Tip, page 104) | 1 tsp. | 5 mL |
| Pepper | 1/8 tsp. | 0.5 mL |
| | | |
| Crumbled feta cheese | 1/4 cup | 60 mL |
| Chopped fresh parsley | 1/4 cup | 60 mL |

*This vibrant Mediterranean-inspired soup offers a fresh lemon background for a delightful spectrum of flavours.*

## about lentils

Lentils are tiny legumes available in many varieties, including brown, green, red and yellow. Rich in protein and carbohydrates, lentils are an ideal substitute for meat and are therefore a staple in vegetarian diets. They are dried after ripening, and are always eaten cooked.

Heat olive oil in large saucepan on medium-high. Add onion. Cook for 5 to 10 minutes, stirring often, until onion starts to brown.

Add next 8 ingredients. Cook for about 3 minutes, stirring often, until carrot is tender-crisp.

Add chicken stock and lentils. Bring to a boil. Reduce heat to medium-low. Simmer, partially covered, for about 20 minutes, stirring occasionally, until lentils are very soft. Discard bay leaf.

Stir in next 3 ingredients.

Sprinkle feta cheese and parsley on individual servings. Makes about 7 cups (1.75 L).

*1 cup (250 mL): 228 Calories; 4.3 g Total Fat (1.8 g Mono, 0.5 g Poly, 1.7 g Sat); 5 mg Cholesterol; 35 g Carbohydrate; 6 g Fibre; 15 g Protein; 995 mg Sodium*

*Different and delicious—not your everyday potato soup! Leek and lemon enhance sweet pear to give this soup an intriguing elegance.*

## about cooking with pears

When cooking or baking with pears, it may be important to use firm, not-quite-ripe fruit that will hold its shape. Since this soup is puréed until smooth, feel free to use your favourite variety of this delectably juicy fruit—pears at their peak will offer all the more flavour.

## tip

When a recipe calls for grated zest and juice, it's easier to grate the fruit first, then juice it. Be careful not to grate down to the pith (white part of the peel), which is bitter and best avoided.

# Potato Pear Soup

| | | |
|---|---|---|
| Olive oil | 2 tsp. | 10 mL |
| Chopped peeled pear | 3 cups | 750 mL |
| Sliced leek (white part only) | 1 cup | 250 mL |
| Chopped peeled potato | 3 cups | 750 mL |
| Low-sodium prepared chicken broth | 3 cups | 750 mL |
| Pepper | 1/8 tsp. | 0.5 mL |
| Lemon juice | 1 tbsp. | 15 mL |
| Grated lemon zest (see Tip, left) | 1/2 tsp. | 2 mL |

Heat olive oil in large saucepan on medium. Add pear and leek. Cook for about 5 minutes, stirring often, until leek is softened.

Add next 3 ingredients. Stir. Bring to a boil. Reduce heat to medium-low. Simmer, covered, for about 10 minutes until potato is soft. Carefully process with hand blender or in blender until smooth (see Safety Tip).

Stir in lemon juice and lemon zest. Makes about 6 cups (1.5 L).

*1 cup (250 mL): 148 Calories; 2.1 g Total Fat (1.3 g Mono, 0.3 g Poly, 0.3 g Sat); 0 mg Cholesterol; 31 g Carbohydrate; 4 g Fibre; 3 g Protein; 26 mg Sodium*

**Safety Tip:** Follow manufacturer's instructions for processing hot liquids.

# Fennel and Grapefruit Soup

| | | |
|---|---|---|
| Canola oil | 2 tsp. | 10 mL |
| Chopped fennel bulb (white part only) | 2 cups | 500 mL |
| Chopped onion | 1/2 cup | 125 mL |
| Garlic clove, minced | 1 | 1 |
| (or 1/4 tsp., 1 mL, powder) | | |
| Fennel seeds | 1/2 tsp. | 2 mL |
| Ground ginger | 1/4 tsp. | 1 mL |
| Brown sugar, packed | 1 tsp. | 5 mL |
| Low-sodium prepared chicken broth | 2 cups | 500 mL |
| Red grapefruit juice | 1/4 cup | 60 mL |
| Instant potato flakes | 1/2 cup | 125 mL |
| 2% evaporated milk | 1/2 cup | 125 mL |

Sliced green onion, for garnish

Heat canola oil in large saucepan on medium. Add next 5 ingredients. Cook for about 10 minutes, stirring often, until fennel and onion start to brown.

Add sugar. Heat and stir for about 1 minute until fennel and onion are golden.

Add broth and juice. Stir. Bring to a boil. Add potato flakes. Heat and stir until boiling and thickened. Add evaporated milk. Cook and stir until heated through. Carefully process with hand blender or in blender until smooth (see Safety Tip).

Garnish with green onion. Makes about 4 cups (1 L). Serves 4.

*1 serving: 158 Calories; 3.4 g Total Fat (1.6 g Mono, 0.7 g Poly, 0.6 g Sat); 5 mg Cholesterol; 28 g Carbohydrate; 7 g Fibre; 7 g Protein; 441 mg Sodium*

**Safety Tip:** Follow manufacturer's instructions for processing hot liquids.

*Ready to try something completely new? Caramelizing onion and fennel brings out a natural sweetness that is brightened by tart grapefruit juice. These flavours go surprisingly well together!*

*This twist on traditional vichyssoise forgoes regular potatoes for sweet potatoes, giving it a unique flavour that's far from ordinary. The lime sour cream adds a delectable kick.*

## lime sour cream

| | | |
|---|---|---|
| Sour cream | 1/3 cup | 75 mL |
| Lime juice | 1 tbsp. | 15 mL |
| Grated lime zest | 1 tsp. | 5 mL |
| (see Tip, page 104) | | |

Stir all 3 ingredients in small bowl. Drizzle onto individual servings of soup. Makes about 1/3 cup (75 mL).

## about sweet potato

There is much confusion regarding sweet potatoes and yams. Some are orange-fleshed, while others are white-fleshed. For this recipe, we've used a white-fleshed sweet potato, but the orange-fleshed ones will work just as well!

# Sweet Potato Vichyssoise

| | | |
|---|---|---|
| Butter (or hard margarine) | 3 tbsp. | 50 mL |
| Chopped peeled sweet potato | 2 1/2 cups | 625 mL |
| Sliced leek (white part only) | 2 cups | 500 mL |
| Chicken Stock (page 26), or prepared chicken broth | 4 cups | 1 L |
| Chopped fresh thyme (or 1/2 tsp., 2 mL, dried) | 2 tsp. | 10 mL |
| Salt | 1/2 tsp. | 2 mL |
| Pepper | 1/2 tsp. | 2 mL |
| Whipping cream | 1/2 cup | 125 mL |

Heat butter in large saucepan on medium until melted. Add sweet potato and leek. Cook for about 5 minutes, stirring occasionally, until leek is softened.

Add next 4 ingredients. Stir. Bring to a boil. Reduce heat to medium-low. Simmer, partially covered, for about 20 minutes, stirring occasionally, until sweet potato is tender.

Add whipping cream. Carefully process with hand blender or in blender until smooth (see Safety Tip). Transfer to large bowl. Cool at room temperature before covering. Chill for at least 2 hours until cold. Makes 6 cups (1.5 L). Serves 6.

*1 serving with 2 1/2 tsp. (12 mL) Lime Sour Cream: 228 Calories; 15.1 g Total Fat (4.2 g Mono, 0.6 g Poly, 9.4 g Sat); 45 mg Cholesterol; 21 g Carbohydrate; 3 g Fibre; 4 g Protein; 857 mg Sodium*

Pictured at right.

**Safety Tip:** Follow manufacturer's instructions for processing hot liquids.

*The texture of puréed wild rice combines with the fresh flavours of avocado and cucumber. Sure to infuse some cool into the hottest summer day. Try garnishing with a spoon of salsa for a spicy twist.*

## Avocado Rice Soup

| | | |
|---|---|---|
| Chopped avocado | 1 1/2 cups | 375 mL |
| Lemon juice | 2 tbsp. | 30 mL |
| Prepared vegetable broth | 3 cups | 750 mL |
| Ground cumin | 1/4 tsp. | 1 mL |
| Wild rice | 1/3 cup | 75 mL |
| Chopped peeled English cucumber, seeds removed | 1 cup | 250 mL |
| Milk | 1/2 cup | 125 mL |
| Lemon juice | 1 tbsp. | 15 mL |
| Salt | 1/2 tsp. | 2 mL |
| Pepper | 1/4 tsp. | 1 mL |

Toss avocado and lemon juice in medium bowl. Set aside.

Combine broth and cumin in medium saucepan. Bring to a boil. Add wild rice. Stir. Reduce heat to medium-low. Simmer, covered, for about 75 minutes until wild rice is tender. Remove from heat.

Add remaining 5 ingredients and avocado mixture. Carefully process with hand blender or in blender until smooth (see Safety Tip). Pour into large bowl. Cool to room temperature. Chill, covered, for about 3 hours until cold. Makes about 5 cups (1.25 L).

*1 cup (250 mL): 134 Calories; 7.1 g Total Fat (4.5 g Mono, 0.9 g Poly, 1.1 g Sat); 1 mg Cholesterol; 16 g Carbohydrate; 4 g Fibre; 4 g Protein; 533 mg Sodium*

Pictured at right.

**Safety Tip:** Follow manufacturer's instructions for processing hot liquids.

*A creamy blend of potato and leek, Vichyssoise (vihsh-ee-SWAHZ) is best when served very cold.*

## Vichyssoise   *A Classic!*

| | | |
|---|---|---|
| Peeled, cubed potatoes | 4 cups | 1 L |
| Leeks (white part only), cut up | 3 | 3 |
| Medium onion, sliced | 1 | 1 |
| Parsley flakes | 1 tsp. | 5 mL |
| Salt | 1 tsp. | 5 mL |
| Pepper | 1/4 tsp. | 1 mL |
| Ground nutmeg, sprinkle | | |
| Can of condensed chicken broth | 10 oz. | 284 mL |
| Water | 1 3/4 cups | 425 mL |

*(continued on next page)*

| Skim evaporated milk (or light cream) | 2/3 cup | 150 mL |
| Milk | 1 cup | 250 mL |

**Chopped chives, for garnish**

Combine first 9 ingredients in large saucepan. Cook until vegetables are tender. Do not drain. Purée in blender (see Safety Tip). Pour into large bowl.

Stir in both milks. Cover. Chill for several hours.

Sprinkle chives on top. Makes 8 cups (2 L).

*1 cup (250 mL): 112 Calories; 0.7 g Total Fat (0.1 g Mono, trace Poly, 0.2 g Sat); 3 mg Cholesterol; 22 g Carbohydrate; 2 g Fibre; 4 g Protein; 567 mg Sodium*

**Safety Tip:** Follow manufacturer's instructions for processing hot liquids.

Avocado Rice Soup, left

## food fun

Although some argue that vichyssoise is a classic French soup invented in France in the 1800s and originally served hot, others believe that it was invented by French chef Louis Diat in New York in 1930 and named after his home town, Vichy. A third argument provides a compromise—claiming that Diat altered an old French recipe for hot soup so it could be served chilled.

*This sweet and refreshing soup is wonderfully balanced with tangy dill and buttermilk. Try serving it with Herbed Tortillas for dunking.*

## herbed tortillas

| | | |
|---|---|---|
| Flour tortillas (9 inch, 23 cm, diameter) | 2 | 2 |
| Olive (or cooking) oil | 1 tsp. | 5 mL |
| Italian seasoning | 1 tsp. | 5 mL |
| Dried crushed chilies | 1/2 tsp. | 2 mL |

Brush tortillas with olive oil. Combine Italian seasoning and chilies in small cup. Sprinkle over tortillas. Cut into 8 wedges each. Arrange wedges on greased baking sheet. Bake in 350°F (175°C) oven for about 10 minutes until crisp and lightly browned. Serve with soup. Makes 16 wedges.

Pictured at right.

# Chilled Pea Dill Soup

| | | |
|---|---|---|
| Cooking oil | 1 tsp. | 5 mL |
| Chopped celery | 1 cup | 250 mL |
| Chopped onion | 1 cup | 250 mL |
| Garlic clove, minced (or 1/4 tsp., 1 mL, powder) | 1 | 1 |
| Salt | 1/2 tsp. | 2 mL |
| Pepper | 1/4 tsp. | 1 mL |
| Prepared vegetable broth | 2 cups | 500 mL |
| Frozen peas | 2 cups | 500 mL |
| Dried dillweed | 2 tsp. | 10 mL |
| Buttermilk | 1 1/2 cups | 375 mL |

Heat cooking oil in large saucepan or Dutch oven on medium. Add next 5 ingredients. Cook, uncovered, for 5 to 10 minutes, stirring often, until onion is softened.

Add broth. Bring to a boil.

Add peas and dill. Bring to a boil. Reduce heat to medium. Boil gently, uncovered, for 3 to 5 minutes until peas are tender. Carefully process with hand blender or in blender until smooth (see Safety Tip). Pour into large bowl.

Add buttermilk. Stir. Chill for 2 hours. Makes about 5 cups (1.25 L) soup. Serves 4.

*1 serving with 4 Herbed Tortilla wedges: 217 Calories; 5.7 g Total Fat (1.8 g Mono, 0.7 g Poly, 1.3 g Sat); 3 mg Cholesterol; 33 g Carbohydrate; 5 g Fibre; 10 g Protein; 881 mg Sodium*

Pictured at right.

**Safety Tip:** Follow manufacturer's instructions for processing hot liquids.

Left: Chilled Pea Dill Soup, above
Right: Herbed Tortillas, left

*Borscht by any other name is still beet soup—but this chilled version delivers a whole new taste sensation.*

## Chilled Beet Soup

| | | |
|---|---|---|
| Cans of whole baby beets (14 oz., 398 mL, each), with liquid | 2 | 2 |
| Prepared vegetable broth, chilled | 1 1/2 cups | 375 mL |
| Light sour cream | 1/2 cup | 125 mL |
| Chopped green onion | 1/3 cup | 75 mL |
| Chopped fresh dill (or 1 tbsp., 15 mL, dried) | 1/4 cup | 60 mL |
| Dill pickle juice | 2 tbsp. | 30 mL |
| Granulated sugar | 1 tbsp. | 15 mL |
| Pepper | 1/4 tsp. | 1 mL |
| Chopped dill pickle | 2 tbsp. | 30 mL |

Put beets into large bowl. Mash until beets are crushed. Add next 7 ingredients. Stir well.

Stir in pickle. Makes about 6 cups (1.5 L). Serves 4.

*1 serving: 122 Calories; 2.9 g Total Fat (trace Mono, trace Poly, 1.5 g Sat); 10 mg Cholesterol; 21 g Carbohydrate; 3 g Fibre; 4 g Protein; 896 mg Sodium*

Pictured at right.

*You'll love the refreshing dill and cucumber flavours in this easy-to-make chilled soup. Serve with a dollop of sour cream for an attractive finish.*

## Gazpacho   *A Classic!*

| | | |
|---|---|---|
| Medium tomatoes, peeled and coarsely chopped | 6 | 6 |
| English cucumber (with peel), coarsely chopped | 1 | 1 |
| Coarsely chopped red onion | 3/4 cup | 175 mL |
| Garlic cloves, minced (or 1/2 tsp., 2 mL, powder) | 2 | 2 |
| Chopped fresh dill (or 1 1/2 tsp., 7 mL, dill weed) | 2 tbsp. | 30 mL |
| Balsamic vinegar | 2 tbsp. | 30 mL |
| Granulated sugar | 1 tsp. | 5 mL |
| Hot pepper sauce | 1 tsp. | 5 mL |
| Salt | 1/2 tsp. | 2 mL |
| Coarsely ground pepper (or sprinkle of pepper) | 1/4 tsp. | 1 mL |

*(continued on next page)*

| Tomato juice | 19 oz. | 540 mL |
|---|---|---|
| Large avocado, finely chopped | 1 | 1 |

Put first 10 ingredients into food processor. Pulse with on/off motion for about 20 seconds until finely chopped. Put into large bowl.

Add tomato juice. Stir. Cover. Chill for at least 3 hours or overnight.

Scatter avocado over individual servings. Makes about 7 1/2 cups (1.9 L).

*1 cup (250 mL):* 95 Calories; 4.3 g Total Fat (2.7 g Mono, 0.7 g Poly, 0.6 g Sat); 0 mg Cholesterol; 14 g Carbohydrate; 4 g Fibre; 3 g Protein; 375 mg Sodium

Pictured below.

Left: Gazpacho, left
Right: Chilled Beet Soup, left

*Put a tropical spin on gazpacho with mango, shrimp and lime. When tomatoes are in season, this recipe is a great way to use up the overripe ones—just replace the canned tomatoes in the recipe with fresh.*

## about gazpacho

This summertime refresher has very rustic origins in the Andalusia region of Spain. It began as labourers' food made of simple, portable ingredients—bread and vegetables. In Spain, it has several variations: topped with raw onion rings or grapes and almonds, made with a veal bouillon or mayonnaise base, thickened with cream and cornstarch or flavoured with cumin and basil. Modern gazpacho can include such a wide variety of ingredients that the word itself is often used as a generic term for chilled vegetable soup.

# South Seas Gazpacho

| | | |
|---|---|---|
| Can of diced tomatoes (with juice) | 28 oz. | 796 mL |
| Chopped English cucumber (with peel) | 1 cup | 250 mL |
| Chopped red pepper | 1/2 cup | 125 mL |
| Chopped onion | 1/4 cup | 60 mL |
| Chopped frozen mango pieces, thawed | 1 1/2 cups | 375 mL |
| Lime juice | 2 tbsp. | 30 mL |
| Chopped fresh dill (or 1 tsp., 5 mL, dried) | 4 tsp. | 20 mL |
| Olive oil | 1 tbsp. | 15 mL |
| Celery salt | 1/2 tsp. | 2 mL |
| Grated lime zest (see Tip, page 104) | 1/2 tsp. | 2 mL |
| Chopped cooked salad shrimp | 1 3/4 cups | 425 mL |
| Sour cream | 1/4 cup | 60 mL |
| Mayonnaise | 3 tbsp. | 50 mL |
| Chopped fresh cilantro (or parsley) | 1 tsp. | 5 mL |
| Grated lime zest | 1/4 tsp. | 1 mL |

Process first 4 ingredients in food processor with on/off motion until almost smooth. Transfer to large bowl.

Process next 6 ingredients until smooth. Add to tomato mixture. Stir. Chill, covered, for at least 2 hours to blend flavours.

Add shrimp. Stir. Ladle into 6 chilled serving bowls.

Combine remaining 4 ingredients in small bowl. Spoon about 1 tbsp. (15 mL) over each serving. Makes 6 cups (1.5 L). Serves 6.

*1 serving: 231 Calories; 14.6 g Total Fat (3.0 g Mono, 2.9 g Poly, 3.0 g Sat); 69 mg Cholesterol; 17 g Carbohydrate; 1 g Fibre; 10 g Protein; 601 mg Sodium*

Pictured at right.

*This chilled soup is Scandinavian in origin, made with simple ingredients that are easy to keep on hand. Serve as a starter soup or as a light dessert.*

## serving suggestion

Fruit Soup looks elegant served in martini glasses or small soup bowls in contrasting colours. Garnish with mint or a light sprinkling of cinnamon.

# Fruit Soup  *A Classic!*

| | | |
|---|---|---|
| Water | 4 cups | 1 L |
| Pineapple juice | 2 1/4 cups | 550 mL |
| Chopped mixed dried fruit (prunes, apricots, apples, peaches), lightly packed | 2 cups | 500 mL |
| Raisins or currants | 1/2 cup | 125 mL |
| Orange juice | 1/2 cup | 125 mL |
| Cinnamon | 1/4 tsp. | 1 mL |
| Granulated sugar | 1/3 cup | 75 mL |
| Minute tapioca | 2 tbsp. | 30 mL |

Put water and pineapple juice into large saucepan. Add remaining ingredients. Bring to a boil over medium heat. Cover. Simmer gently for 30 minutes. Cool. Serve chilled. Makes 4 cups (1 L).

*1 cup (250 mL): 406 Calories; 0.5 g Total Fat (0.2 g Mono, 0.1 g Poly, trace Sat); 0 mg Cholesterol; 105 g Carbohydrate; 7 g Fibre; 3 g Protein; 23 mg Sodium*

*A smooth and refreshing cantaloupe purée topped off with a fun sprinkle of blueberries—perfect for enjoying on the patio with a summertime brunch.*

## about dessert tofu

What's dessert tofu? Tofu comes in several varieties that differ in firmness, the softest of which is called silken tofu. This type has the highest moisture content and a fine, soft, custard-like texture. Dessert tofu is very much like silken tofu, but with different flavours and sweeteners added to it. You can add it to recipes or eat it as a snack on its own.

# Frosty Fruit Soup

| | | |
|---|---|---|
| Frozen chopped cantaloupe | 1 cup | 250 mL |
| Tropical fruit juice | 3/4 cup | 175 mL |
| Peach dessert tofu | 1/3 cup | 75 mL |
| Fresh (or frozen) blueberries | 1/4 cup | 60 mL |

Put the first 3 ingredients into the blender. Cover with the lid. Process until smooth. Pour into the bowl.

Scatter the blueberries over top. Serves 1.

*1 serving: 263 Calories; 4.9 g Total Fat (0.9 g Mono, 2.4 g Poly, 0.6 g Sat); 0 mg Cholesterol; 50 g Carbohydrate; 3 g Fibre; 9 g Protein; 26 mg Sodium*

Pictured at right.

Frosty Fruit Soup, above

*Serve up a taste of summer at your next outdoor party! Arrange the serving bowl on a bed of ice, surrounding it with fresh fruit slices for an inviting presentation.*

## potluck suggestion

This dessert soup serves up to 16, making it perfect for a large gathering.

*This sweet treat makes a perfect palate cleanser between courses, or a refreshing dessert. Serve it in punch cups for extra style points.*

## about mango

North Americans often think of the mango mainly as a sweet fruit, but in tropical cuisines it plays a more diverse role. The young leaves and shoots of the mango tree are eaten with spicy chili relishes; unripe and semi-ripe mangoes are pickled, made into relishes or eaten raw with salt and chillies; and ripe mangoes are eaten on their own, with or in curries, as a sun-dried snack or as a dessert purée.

# West Indies Summer Soup

| Diced cantaloupe | 4 cups | 1 L |
| Diced ripe mango | 2 cups | 500 mL |
| Orange juice | 2 cups | 500 mL |
| Plain yogurt | 1 cup | 250 mL |
| Lime juice | 2 tbsp. | 30 mL |
| Liquid honey | 2 tbsp. | 30 mL |
| Ground ginger | 1 tsp. | 5 mL |
| Ground cinnamon | 1/2 tsp. | 2 mL |

Process all 8 ingredients in blender, in batches, or food processor until smooth. Transfer to large serving bowl. Chill for at least 2 hours until cold. Makes about 8 cups (2 L).

*1 cup (250 mL): 126 Calories; 1 g Total Fat (0.2 g Mono, 0.1 g Poly, 0.4 g Sat); 2 mg Cholesterol; 29 g Carbohydrate; 2 g Fibre; 3 g Protein; 32 mg Sodium*

Pictured at right.

# Pineapple Mango Soup

| Cans of sliced mango (with syrup), (14 oz., 398 mL, each) | 2 | 2 |
| Chopped fresh pineapple | 6 cups | 1.5 L |
| Canned coconut milk | 1/2 cup | 125 mL |

Process all 3 ingredients in blender, in batches, or food processor until smooth. Press through sieve into large bowl. Discard solids. Stir. Chill, covered, for at least 2 hours until cold. Makes about 6 cups (1.5 L).

*1 cup (250 mL): 237 Calories; 5.2 g Total Fat (0.3 g Mono, 0.3 g Poly, 3.9 g Sat); 0 mg Cholesterol; 52 g Carbohydrate; 3 g Fibre; 1 g Protein; 34 mg Sodium*

Pictured at right.

Left: Pineapple Mango Soup, above
Right: West Indies Summer Soup, above

*Similar to a cheery apple cider, this is a clear, golden soup with a bit of apple texture.*

### serving suggestion

Apple Soup is attractive when garnished with a cinnamon stick over each bowl.

# Apple Soup

| | | |
|---|---|---|
| Apple juice | 4 cups | 1 L |
| Apples, peeled, cored and diced | 4 | 4 |
| Cinnamon | 1/2 tsp. | 2 mL |
| Lemon juice | 1 tsp. | 5 mL |
| Brown sugar, packed | 1/2 cup | 125 mL |
| Cinnamon sticks (optional) | | |

Simmer all together, covered, in large pot until apples are barely tender. Chill. Serve cold. Makes 5 1/2 cups (1.4 L).

*1 cup (250 mL): 191 Calories; 0.1 g Total Fat (trace Mono, trace Poly, trace Sat); 0 mg Cholesterol; 51 g Carbohydrate; 1 g Fibre; trace Protein; 7 mg Sodium*

Pictured at right.

*There is a pleasing tartness to this cool summer soup, which looks lovely served with a sour cream or whipped cream garnish. It's easily doubled or tripled.*

# Cherry Soup

| | | |
|---|---|---|
| Can of pitted Bing cherries in heavy syrup | 14 oz. | 398 mL |
| Red wine vinegar | 1 tbsp. | 15 mL |
| Granulated sugar | 2 tsp. | 10 mL |
| Ground cinnamon | 1/8 tsp. | 0.5 mL |
| Salt sprinkle (optional) | | |
| Sour cream, whipped cream or heavy cream (for garnish) | | |

Add cherries with syrup and next 4 ingredients to blender. Blend until smooth. Chill.

Serve with a dab of sour cream or plain whipped cream, or pour a bit of heavy cream in center of bowl. Swirl with spoon. Makes about 1 3/4 cups (425 mL).

*1/2 cup (125 mL): 100 Calories; 0.2 g Total Fat (0.1 g Mono, 0.1 g Poly, trace Sat); 0 mg Cholesterol; 26 g Carbohydrate; 2 g Fibre; 1 g Protein; 3 mg Sodium*

Pictured at right.

Left: Apple Soup, above
Right: Cherry Soup, above

*Indulge in the summer-fresh strawberry taste and hint of citrus in this vibrantly red, refreshing soup.*

## Strawberry Soup

| | | |
|---|---|---|
| Granulated sugar | 3/4 cup | 175 mL |
| Water | 1 1/2 cups | 375 mL |
| Fresh strawberries, halved (about 1 1/2 lbs., 680 g) | 4 cups | 1 L |
| Grated lemon zest | 1 1/2 tsp. | 7 mL |
| Grated orange zest | 2 tsp. | 10 mL |
| Sherry (or fresh orange juice) | 1/4 cup | 60 mL |
| Whipping cream (optional) | 4 tsp. | 20 mL |

Combine sugar and water in small saucepan. Bring to a boil on medium, stirring occasionally. Reduce heat to medium-low. Simmer for 10 minutes. Cool.

Combine next 4 ingredients in large bowl. Add sugar mixture. Stir. Process, in 2 batches, in blender until smooth. Strain juice into large bowl. Discard seeds. Pour into container. Chill.

Garnish individual servings with swirls of whipping cream. Serve chilled. Makes 3 1/2 cups (875 mL). Serves 4.

*1 serving: 154 Calories; 0.5 g Total Fat (0.1 g Mono, 0.2 g Poly, trace Sat); 0 mg Cholesterol; 41 g Carbohydrate; 3 g Fibre; 1 g Protein; 92 mg Sodium*

Pictured below.

# Strawberry Cucumber Soup

| | | |
|---|---|---|
| Coarsely chopped, peeled English cucumber, seeds removed | 3 cups | 750 mL |
| Frozen whole strawberries, partially thawed | 3 cups | 750 mL |
| White grape juice | 1 cup | 250 mL |
| Granulated sugar | 1/4 cup | 60 mL |
| Ground ginger | 1 tsp. | 5 mL |
| Ground cinnamon | 1/4 tsp. | 1 mL |
| Salt | 1/4 tsp. | 1 mL |
| Pepper | 1/4 tsp. | 1 mL |
| Half-and-half cream | 1/2 cup | 125 mL |

Put cucumber into blender or food processor. Process until smooth.

Add next 7 ingredients. Process until almost smooth. Transfer to medium bowl.

Add cream. Stir. Chill. Makes about 5 1/2 cups (1.4 L). Serves 12.

*1 serving: 58 Calories; 1.4 g Total Fat (0.4 g Mono, 0.1 g Poly, 0.8 g Sat); 4 mg Cholesterol; 11 g Carbohydrate; 1 g Fibre; 1 g Protein; 55 mg Sodium*

Pictured below.

*There's something so refined about a lovely chilled soup. This cool blend is mildly sweetened with cinnamon and ginger, and can be garnished with thin slices of cucumber or strawberries.*

## about fruit soups

Ever wonder where the idea to make a soup from fruit originated? It's not really clear who thought it up, but certain parts of the world do seem to be better known than others for their love of cold and warm fruit soups. The cuisines of Scandinavia, Russia, Eastern Europe, the Middle East, Baltic countries, central Asia and China all feature such soups, while those of Japan, South America, southeast Asia, the South Pacific, Africa and Western Europe generally don't.

## serving suggestion

Try serving this soup in small punch glasses as a starter before a holiday dinner.

Throughout this book measurements are given in Conventional and Metric measure. To compensate for differences between the two measurements due to rounding, a full metric measure is not always used. The cup used is the standard 8 fluid ounce. Temperature is given in degrees Fahrenheit and Celsius. Baking pan measurements are in inches and centimetres as well as quarts and litres. An exact metric conversion is given on this page as well as the working equivalent (Metric Standard Measure).

## Pans

| Conventional – Inches | Metric – Centimetres |
|---|---|
| 8 × 8 inch | 20 × 20 cm |
| 9 × 9 inch | 23 × 23 cm |
| 9 × 13 inch | 23 × 33 cm |
| 10 × 15 inch | 25 × 38 cm |
| 11 × 17 inch | 28 × 43 cm |
| 8 × 2 inch round | 20 × 5 cm |
| 9 × 2 inch round | 23 × 5 cm |
| 10 × 4 1/2 inch tube | 25 × 11 cm |
| 8 × 4 × 3 inch loaf | 20 × 10 × 7.5 cm |
| 9 × 5 × 3 inch loaf | 23 × 12.5 × 7.5 cm |

## Oven Temperatures

| Fahrenheit (°F) | Celsius (°C) | Fahrenheit (°F) | Celsius (°C) |
|---|---|---|---|
| 175° | 80° | 350° | 175° |
| 200° | 95° | 375° | 190° |
| 225° | 110° | 400° | 205° |
| 250° | 120° | 425° | 220° |
| 275° | 140° | 450° | 230° |
| 300° | 150° | 475° | 240° |
| 325° | 160° | 500° | 260° |

## Spoons

| Conventional Measure | Metric Exact Conversion Millilitre (mL) | Metric Standard Measure Millilitre (mL) |
|---|---|---|
| 1/8 teaspoon (tsp.) | 0.6 mL | 0.5 mL |
| 1/4 teaspoon (tsp.) | 1.2 mL | 1 mL |
| 1/2 teaspoon (tsp.) | 2.4 mL | 2 mL |
| 1 teaspoon (tsp.) | 4.7 mL | 5 mL |
| 2 teaspoons (tsp.) | 9.4 mL | 10 mL |
| 1 tablespoon (tbsp.) | 14.2 mL | 15 mL |

## Cups

| | | |
|---|---|---|
| 1/4 cup (4 tbsp.) | 56.8 mL | 60 mL |
| 1/3 cup (5 1/3 tbsp.) | 75.6 mL | 75 mL |
| 1/2 cup (8 tbsp.) | 113.7 mL | 125 mL |
| 2/3 cup (10 2/3 tbsp.) | 151.2 mL | 150 mL |
| 3/4 cup (12 tbsp.) | 170.5 mL | 175 mL |
| 1 cup (16 tbsp.) | 227.3 mL | 250 mL |
| 4 1/2 cups | 1022.9 mL | 1000 mL(1 L) |

## Dry Measurements

| Conventional Measure Ounces (oz.) | Metric Exact Conversion Grams (g) | Metric Standard Measure Grams (g) |
|---|---|---|
| 1 oz. | 28.3 g | 28 g |
| 2 oz. | 56.7 g | 57 g |
| 3 oz. | 85.0 g | 85 g |
| 4 oz. | 113.4 g | 125 g |
| 5 oz. | 141.7 g | 140 g |
| 6 oz. | 170.1 g | 170 g |
| 7 oz. | 198.4 g | 200 g |
| 8 oz. | 226.8 g | 250 g |
| 16 oz. | 453.6 g | 500 g |
| 32 oz. | 907.2 g | 1000 g (1 kg) |

## Casseroles

| Canada & Britain | | United States | |
|---|---|---|---|
| Standard Size Casserole | Exact Metric Measure | Standard Size Casserole | Exact Metric Measure |
| 1 qt. (5 cups) | 1.13 L | 1 qt. (4 cups) | 900 mL |
| 1 1/2 qts. (7 1/2 cups) | 1.69 L | 1 1/2 qts. (6 cups) | 1.35 L |
| 2 qts. (10 cups) | 2.25 L | 2 qts. (8 cups) | 1.8 L |
| 2 1/2 qts. (12 1/2 cups) | 2.81 L | 2 1/2 qts. (10 cups) | 2.25 L |
| 3 qts. (15 cups) | 3.38 L | 3 qts. (12 cups) | 2.7 L |
| 4 qts. (20 cups) | 4.5 L | 4 qts. (16 cups) | 3.6 L |
| 5 qts. (25 cups) | 5.63 L | 5 qts. (20 cups) | 4.5 L |

## Tip Index

## Recipe Index

*Paella (pah-EH-yuh) is a dish from the Valencia region of Spain. Saffron is a nice touch but can be a bit expensive; if you choose to go without, you can add 1 tsp. (5 mL) of turmeric along with the rice.*

## Slow Cooker Paella

| | | |
|---|---|---|
| Cooking oil | 1 tbsp. | 15 mL |
| Chopped onion | 1 cup | 250 mL |
| Garlic cloves, minced | 2 | 2 |
| Sliced Chorizo (or hot Italian) sausage | 1 cup | 250 mL |
| Boneless, skinless chicken breast halves (4 – 6 oz., 113 – 170 g, each) | 8 | 8 |
| Large tomatoes, seeded and chopped | 3 | 3 |
| Salt | 1 tsp. | 5 mL |
| Pepper | 1/2 tsp. | 2 mL |
| Prepared chicken broth | 4 cups | 1 L |
| Water | 1 cup | 250 mL |
| Saffron threads (optional) | 1/4 tsp. | 1 mL |
| Converted white rice | 2 1/2 cups | 625 mL |
| Chopped red pepper | 1 cup | 250 mL |
| Fresh peas | 1 cup | 250 mL |
| Clams, cleaned | 1 lb. | 454 g |
| Small bay scallops | 1 lb. | 454 g |
| Uncooked shrimp (peeled and deveined) | 1 lb. | 454 g |
| Chopped fresh thyme | 2 tbsp. | 30 mL |

Heat cooking oil in large saucepan on medium. Add onions and garlic. Cook for about 5 minutes, stirring often, until softened.

Add sausage and chicken. Cook for 5 to 7 minutes until browned on all sides. Add tomatoes, salt and pepper. Heat and stir for 1 minute. Remove from heat. Place in 5 quart (5 L) slow cooker.

*(continued on opposite page)*